CHRISTOPHER COLUMBUS

"A Man among the Gentiles"

CHRISTOPHER COLUMBUS
by William J. Parkinson, 1899–1993

No portrait of Columbus was painted during his lifetime. A few detailed descriptions of his appearance were left by those who knew him, and some of the portraits painted over the centuries are based on those descriptions; others are purely imaginative.

The painting above is the only portrait of the discoverer of America by an artist who claimed to have actually seen Columbus. Painted by Utah artist William Parkinson, the painting is owned by Edward and Janie Rogers of Salt Lake City, Utah. When Mr. Rogers asked the artist whom he had used as a model, Parkinson responded that he had used no one: Columbus had appeared to him during the night, and he painted the portrait immediately afterwards. Parkinson was reluctant to sell the painting because the inspiration meant so much to him, but he was near the end of his life and desired that the work be seen and shared. It is reproduced here by courtesy of the owners.

CHRISTOPHER COLUMBUS

"A Man among the Gentiles"

CLARK B. HINCKLEY

DESERET
BOOK

SALT LAKE CITY, UTAH

Visit us at DeseretBook.com

Library of Congress Cataloging-in-Publication Data

Hinckley, Clark B., author.
    Christopher Columbus : "a man among the gentiles" / Clark B. Hinckley.
        pages cm
    Includes bibliographical references and index.
    ISBN 978-1-60907-920-8 (hardbound : alk. paper)
1. Columbus, Christopher. 2. Explorers—America—Biography. 3. America—Discovery and exploration—Spanish. 4. The Church of Jesus Christ of Latter-day Saints—Doctrines. 5. Mormon Church—Doctrines. I. Title.
    E111.H623 2014
    970.01'5092—dc23
    [B]   2014012920

Printed in the United States of America
Publishers Printing, Salt Lake City, UT

10   9   8   7   6   5   4   3   2   1

To the 342 missionaries with whom I served in the Spain Barcelona Mission from 2009 to 2012. Like Columbus, many of them went to Spain as foreigners, learned Spanish as a second language, and bore a message that went against the accepted norm. Like Columbus, they often met with rejection, even ridicule, and suffered moments of great discouragement. But also, like Columbus, they were filled with the fire of the Holy Ghost, persisted against seemingly insurmountable odds, and ultimately changed the world.

*With a hand that could be felt, the Lord opened my mind
to the fact that it would be possible to sail and he opened my will
to desire to accomplish the project . . . This was the fire that burned
within me . . . Who can doubt that this fire was not merely mine,
but also of the Holy Spirit . . . urging me to press forward?*

CHRISTOPHER COLUMBUS

CONTENTS

CONTENTS

ACKNOWLEDGMENTS

It is one thing to conceive of a book, to nurture an idea, and to naïvely begin the project. Ideas and dreams are largely solo pursuits, undertaken in quiet—and quite often irrational—moments. It is another thing to actually produce a book. This book, like all others, is the product of the efforts of many people, only a few of whom I can mention here.

While I was living in Barcelona, Bob and Donna Smith, whom I had never met but were friends of a friend, paid me a short visit, and the conversation turned to Columbus. They mentioned a new book on Columbus written by Carol Delaney, and a few weeks later they graciously sent me a copy. It was the first book I read upon returning to the United States.

The idea of writing a book about Columbus formed gradually over many months and ultimately took shape in a few sample chapters. My sister, Virginia H. Pearce, a seasoned and successful author, patiently read those early chapters and gave me the encouragement to keep writing. As the manuscript grew, my wife Kathleen, always my greatest fan, read every chapter as it came out of the printer and gave both constructive suggestions and continuous encouragement.

This book owes its existence, in large measure, to Jana Erickson and her excellent team at Deseret Book who were willing to take a chance on publishing a book by an unknown author with what might be charitably described as unusual credentials. In particular, Suzanne Brady's painless (for me) and excellent editing has greatly enhanced the readers' experience.

It would be impossible to read in a lifetime all that has been written about Columbus, but this work would simply not have been possible without the excellent scholarship of many outstanding researchers and writers, some deceased and some living. I owe special thanks to De Lamar Jensen, emeritus professor of history at Brigham Young University, who not only shared with me much of his research (some of it unpublished) but generously read an early draft of the manuscript, made excellent suggestions, and provided encouragement. Carol Delaney, emerita professor at Stanford University and a research scholar at Brown University, whose book I received unexpectedly in the mail, was gracious in responding to my questions and kind enough to meet with me on a beautiful fall afternoon in Providence, Rhode Island. A cultural anthropologist, her work on Columbus and his world helped me see him through a fifteenth-century lens rather than a twenty-first-century lens.

Shortly after the manuscript was submitted for publication, I met Ben Rogers at a Christmas party, where he shared with me a family story about Columbus. That chance meeting led to the inclusion in this work of a copy of the only portrait of Columbus painted by an artist who claimed to have seen the famous mariner.

In spite of the valuable input and advice of others, this book, like both its protagonist and its author, is flawed and imperfect. Nevertheless, the entire project has been for me the source of much enjoyment and excitement. No author could wish for more.

INTRODUCTION

History has all the world's best stories, and the life of the weaver's son who discovered America could hardly be matched even by the most inventive imagination.[1]

FELIPE FERNANDEZ-ARMESTO

t noon on the Ides of March in 1493, a small wooden ship rode the rising tide up the Río Tinto and into the harbor of Palos, Spain, where she dropped anchor. She wasn't much of a ship—her deck was only about fifty-five feet long; she was weathered but solidly built and appeared to be newly caulked. The villagers onshore recognized her as a caravel owned by Juan Niño of Moguer, the neighboring town just upriver. Named the *Santa Clara* but usually called the *Niña* after her owner, she had last been seen in Palos on 3 August 1492, sailing down the ebb tide with two other ships, the *Santa María* and the *Pinta,* at the beginning of an attempt to reach the Orient by sailing west across the uncharted Ocean Sea. News of the appearance of the *Niña* back in the harbor spread through the town, and a crowd quickly gathered to meet the crew as they rowed to shore in a small boat. Later that afternoon the *Pinta* rode the same tide into the harbor. The *Santa María* had not survived the trip. She had run aground on a coral reef near a small island on the other side of the world and remained there, along with thirty-nine of the men who had left Palos the previous summer.

The most momentous sea voyage in history ended where it began, at a small village on the Atlantic coast of Spain. The town of Palos de la Frontera, as it is called today, remains relatively unknown, but the name of the Genoese sea captain who was rowed to shore just past noon on 15 March 1493 is one of the most widely recognized names in history: Christopher Columbus.

Columbus's return to Palos marked the fulfillment of a prophecy made more than two thousand years earlier by the prophet Nephi:

> And I looked and beheld a man among the Gentiles, who was separated from the seed of my brethren by the many waters; and I beheld the Spirit of God, that it came down and wrought upon the man; and he went forth upon the many waters, even unto the seed of my brethren, who were in the promised land.[2]

Over five hundred years have now passed since the fulfillment of that prophecy. Today the name of Christopher Columbus is known to schoolchildren on every continent and in virtually every corner of the globe. No explorer before or since has achieved anywhere near the degree of fame and recognition as that achieved by the Discoverer of America. He died in 1506, and the first history of his life and discoveries was published just five years later. Over the centuries, both the man and his works have been the subject of countless books and academic publications. For five centuries scholars have analyzed his life, his achievements, and his character. If all that has been written about Columbus were brought together in one place, the load would easily sink the small ship that carried him to America.

Yet most Americans know surprisingly little about this seemingly well-known man beyond the fact that he discovered America in 1492.

Many of those who claim to know more question whether Columbus actually "discovered" America and view him as a greedy gold-seeker, bent on enslaving the peaceful native people and despoiling the pristine environment.

Members of The Church of Jesus Christ of Latter-day Saints generally have a positive view of Columbus, and if asked, most would declare that he was inspired by God and played an important role in the Restoration. But if asked to name key historical figures who played a role in the Restoration, Latter-day Saints are more likely to name Martin Luther, George Washington, and even John Wycliffe than Christopher Columbus.

Yet Nephi suggests that Columbus stands out among historical figures as an instrument of Deity. In the forty-two verses of 1 Nephi 13, Nephi singles out only one individual: "a man among the Gentiles" who, wrought upon by the Holy Ghost, "went forth upon the many waters even unto . . . the promised land." In fact, Lehi and Nephi, in their extensive prophetic accounts of the latter-day Restoration, identify only two individuals: Christopher Columbus and Joseph Smith.

In many ways, Columbus is a type and shadow of Joseph Smith. Both Columbus and Joseph Smith began a course early in life that would bear great fruit. It could be said of both, as one contemporary said of Columbus, they were men "of great intellect but without much formal education."[3] Both suffered persecution and extreme discouragement, both received divine words of comfort when they thought all was lost,[4] and both left behind a world irreversibly changed.

The voyage of Columbus is the first event mentioned by Nephi that leads to the Restoration. A study of history makes it clear why the work of Columbus was so important—it was the great turning point of history and set in motion a series of events that would create the modern world and culminate with the work of Joseph Smith. In a sense, these two men stand as bookends to the Restoration—one at the beginning and one at the end. The life and accomplishments of Columbus are of particular interest to Latter-day Saints because they mark the beginning of the Restoration.

After his arrival at Palos in the spring of 1493, Columbus traveled to Barcelona, where King Ferdinand and Queen Isabella were holding court. There, in the old Palau del Rei, which still stands next to the Barcelona Cathedral, Columbus met with the monarchs and reported on his voyage. I spent three years in Barcelona and often visited the small plaza facing the old palace. There I imagined the silver-haired Columbus, regal as a Roman senator, ascending the steps to greet the monarchs, followed by a parade that included live parrots, strange Indians, and marvelous artifacts of gold.

It was in Barcelona that I first read a statement by Columbus in which he declared that he was inspired and motivated by the Holy Ghost to undertake his voyage across the sea. I was struck by his declaration of divine guidance, as he seemed to describe the literal fulfillment of Nephi's prophecy. I considered myself well read, but I had been unaware of Columbus's declaration that, just as Nephi had described, he had been "wrought upon"[5] by the Holy Ghost. I became intrigued by this man who is so widely recognized but so little known and began to read and research the life of this most famous of all discoverers.

I learned that many historians—and much of the general public—view Columbus as a man wrapped in mystery. At first this struck me as odd. The archives in Seville, Simancas, Madrid, and elsewhere contain more than eighty letters and miscellaneous documents, including those describing his Third and Fourth Voyages, an abstract of his journal of the First Voyage, a Will and Testament, a Book of Privileges, over twenty-five hundred postils (handwritten margin notes) in books he owned, and a lengthy collection of authoritative writings, prophetic statements, and scriptures to which historians have given the title *Libro de las profecías,* the "Book of Prophecies." "We are extremely well informed about

Columbus. No contemporary of humble origins or maritime vocation has left so many traces in the records, or so much writing of his own."[6] We know far more about Columbus than we do about his contemporaries Vasco da Gama, Magellan, Vespucci, or Cabot, yet none of them carry the air of mystery that seems to pervade so much of the popular literature about Columbus. Salvador de Madariaga, the Spanish diplomat and historian, wrote: "Mystery surrounds him. . . . No one knows who he is, where he comes from, what he actually wishes to do."[7]

The mystery surrounding Columbus stems, in part, from the lack of information we have about his youth and the years prior to the First Voyage. Historians want to know not just who he was and where he came from but where he got the idea to *buscar el Levante por el Poniente*—"find the East by sailing west"—how and when the plan developed, and how a weaver's son from a foreign country ultimately received the backing of the monarchs of Castile and Aragon. Yet, with the exception of some of the postils in his library, nearly everything that survives of Columbus's writings was written after he boarded the *Santa María* in 1492.

The first forty years of Columbus's life can be sketched only by relying on statements he and others made years after the events occurred and on such contemporary documents as records in Genoa that mention Columbus and his family and enable historians to verify his presence there. The documented facts create a few dots on a broad canvas but leave most of the picture blank. The result is that nearly every biographer of Columbus includes a substantial amount of creative nonfiction (with the emphasis on *creative*) when writing about Columbus's life prior to the First Voyage. Many of the episodes that are today widely considered factual events in the early life of Columbus are based on circumstantial evidence and lack documented verification—they *could* have happened, they *might* have happened, but we don't really know if they *actually* happened.

In addition, the popular story of Columbus has been so enshrouded by myth over the centuries that many of the facts known to scholars are unknown to the larger population. Contrary to popular notions, Queen Isabella did not pawn her jewels to finance the voyage, and no educated person in Columbus's age believed the world was flat. Most of the discussion and disagreement around Columbus's proposal regarded the width of the ocean, and in this, both Columbus and his critics were wrong—Columbus vastly underestimated the circumference of the earth while overestimating the land mass of Asia, and no one imagined there was a new continent between Europe and Asia. The fear of sailors was not that they would fall off the edge of the earth but that they would be unable to return safely if they sailed too far out to sea. That fear had prompted earlier attempts to cross the Atlantic to northern latitudes where the prevailing western winds gave some assurance that a return voyage would be possible. But sailing against those winds made progress difficult and doomed those earlier attempts to failure.

Latter-day Saints have adopted and also created a body of mythology around Columbus, much of which has little or no factual basis. I have heard presentations claiming that Columbus locked himself in his cabin during the final three days of the first Atlantic crossing with instructions that he not be disturbed, ostensibly to give him time to fast and pray. But Columbus's own journal makes it clear that he was actively engaged in captaining the ship and coordinating the movement of his fleet without interruption. Both the popular and the scholarly perception of Columbus has become so infused with speculation and myth that Foster Provost, writing in 1986, concluded "that in the absence of much more documentary evidence, a large proportion of what passes for Columbus biography is simply fiction."[8]

In recent decades there has been an effort by historians to cut through the myths that have built up around Columbus during half a millennium. Miles C. Davidson made a concerted effort to document what is known and what is not known with his very helpful *Columbus,*

Then and Now, published by the University of Oklahoma Press. He focuses particularly on some of the assumptions made by noted historian Samuel Eliot Morison in his 1942 biography and perpetuated in subsequent biographies. Felipe Fernandez-Armesto made a valuable contribution with the publication of *Columbus* in 1991, in which he attempted to include only information that could be corroborated by, or at least reasonably inferred from, reliable contemporary sources. Although there remains much disagreement surrounding various episodes of Columbus's life, both of these publications have helped scholars and readers separate fact from speculation. Additional research by a host of scholars over the past twenty-five years has done much to shed light on both what we know about Columbus and what we don't know. All of this work has helped, at least within the academic community, to reduce some of the mystery around Columbus.

But more challenging to scholars than what we don't know about Columbus's life is what we do know. Other contemporary explorers are not enveloped in mystery precisely because we have so little of their own writings. Columbus left us a wealth of material in which he discloses his thoughts, his reasoning, and his motivations. But because so much of this material is deeply religious in content, scholars struggle with how to interpret it. They often see Columbus as a mystic who seems to be out of touch with reality. They accuse him of being a "visionary man" in the way the prophet Lehi was accused (1 Nephi 2:11; 5:2, 4). Or they simply ignore much of what he wrote.[9]

This tendency to ignore or discount Columbus's most deeply religious and spiritual writings is evidenced in the history of the *Libro de las profecías.* It was written by Columbus during 1501 and 1502, with some additions as late as 1505. It is his most extensive work, comprising 84 folio sheets (168 pages), in which he summarizes the thoughts and beliefs that were the driving forces of his life and provides support for those beliefs with citations from the Bible and a variety of other sources. Yet it has been largely ignored by scholars. It remained bound in vellum and unpublished in the *Biblioteca Colombina* in Seville for nearly four hundred years, until a transcription was included in the 1892–94 edition of *Raccolta di documenti e studi pubblicati dalla R. Commissione Colombiana,* the collection of documents published by the Columbus Commission as part of the four hundredth anniversary of the First Voyage. Only 560 copies of *Raccolta* were printed. When Professor Delno West of Northern Arizona University obtained a copy of *Raccolta* from the Firestone Library at Princeton University in 1984, for the purpose of translating the *Libro de las profecías* into English, the pages of the book were still uncut—it had sat unopened on the shelves of the library for ninety years. The first English translation and commentary, as well as a publicly available Spanish translation, were not published until 1991, just in time for the five hundredth anniversary of Columbus's First Voyage.

Most historians are comfortable writing about Columbus's skill as a mariner and his weaknesses as a colonial administrator but are considerably less comfortable writing about his deeply held religious beliefs and his scriptural insights, which portray a divine plan of history with Columbus as a central player. Between 1836 and 1839, Alexander von Humboldt published a five-volume history of the European discovery and exploration of America. Humboldt recognized what he characterized as the "persuasive force" of a "mystical theology" that motived Columbus but expressed puzzlement at the

> strange combination of ideas and sentiments in a superior man gifted with a high intelligence and an invincible courage in adversity, nourished on scholastic theology but very apt in the management of business, of an ardent and sometimes disorderly imagination, unexpectedly ascending from the simple and naïve language of a sailor to felicitous poetic inspirations—in short, reflecting in himself at the same time, so to speak, everything sublime and bizarre that the Middle Ages produced.[10]

Historians have generally struggled with these seemingly incompatible characteristics in Columbus—the astute and capable mariner and captain and the mystical and visionary man of faith. In the late twentieth century, it became common for historians to assert that many of Columbus's writings were a cynical attempt to obtain titles and wealth by portraying himself as the instrument of God. In the introduction to his biography of Columbus, Fernandez-Armesto decries the "imaginative reconstructions of what Columbus 'must' have been thinking or doing at moments when the sources are silent or ignored [that] are made the basis for vacuous conclusions."[11] Then, paradoxically, Fernandez-Armesto declares that his book is "not so much about what happened to Columbus as about what was going on in his mind." Rather than accepting Columbus's statements at face value, he engages in imaginative reconstructions of what Columbus must have *really* been thinking as opposed to what he actually said. The result is a description of Columbus as the "socially ambitious, socially awkward parvenu; the autodidact, intellectually aggressive but easily cowed; the embittered escapee from distressing realities; the adventurer inhibited by fear of failure."[12] More recently, Stephen Bown concludes, "Reading the accounts of Columbus's life one can't avoid the impression that he was vain, arrogant, fanatical and power hungry, and that he later evolved into a religious fanatic."[13] That is an accurate summary of the characterization of Columbus that has become prevalent in modern histories and biographies.

But it is a particularly modern view. Anyone writing today what Columbus wrote five hundred years ago would likely be viewed as having selfish ulterior motives. But Columbus didn't write today—he was born and raised and lived most of his life in fifteenth-century Europe, a time and place in many ways foreign to our modern culture and mentality. Furthermore, he wrote in a foreign language that he learned as an adult, and the nuances of his wording and phrasing may not have accurately reflected the nuances of contemporary Spanish, let alone modern Spanish. Interestingly, his contemporary biographers did not seem to have any difficulty with Columbus's claims of divine guidance—they never dispute them. Yet nearly every modern scholar who has written about Columbus tends to "project a modern consciousness onto him,"[14] which includes a deep skepticism of his claims to spiritual guidance and insight. Among modern biographers, only Delaney seems to view Columbus through a fifteenth-century lens: she was trained not as a historian but as a cultural anthropologist.

Fernandez-Armesto's work exemplifies two themes found in much of the scholarly writing on Columbus. First, Fernandez-Armesto and others assert that Columbus's achievements were less the work of divine guidance than of skill and environmental influences—he was simply the right man in the right place at the right time. Second, since most of Columbus's extensive writings about divine guidance and spiritual experiences were written later in his life, they argue that those writings can accurately be viewed as a calculated attempt to claim the honor, wealth, and prestige that he felt was due him by casting himself as God's emissary. Fernandez-Armesto comes to the conclusion that Columbus "claimed to have been divinely inspired—which is a curiously egotistical form of self-effacement" and that the Admiral's claim to divine guidance was a late addition "to his mental baggage. Spirituality was embraced, as we shall see, as a refuge from adversity."[15]

Similar arguments can be—and have been—made about Joseph Smith. What may be considered the most significant spiritual manifestation of the Prophet's life, the First Vision, was not recorded by him until 1832, twelve years after the event, and an account of the vision was not published until 1840. Critics might easily argue that the story of the First Vision was a belated attempt to add credibility to subsequent events in his life.

There has been no dearth of arguments that Joseph Smith's body of work was in large measure the product of his environment—he was a boy whose father and grandfather both claimed heavenly visions, was a youth in the "burned over" district of religious revivals, and was associated early with Oliver Cowdery and Sidney Rigdon.

If one does not accept the reality of revelation and a divine plan of history, then it is difficult to make sense of the writings and actions of either Joseph Smith or Christopher Columbus. And in the case of Columbus, there is no modern scholarly treatment of his life that embraces the notion of a divine plan and the reality of revelation to individuals to empower them to carry out that plan.

In this work, I have endeavored to tell the story of Columbus as factually as possible and to convey to a wider audience some of the recent research that has been largely confined to academia. I have made every effort to tell the story based on what is verifiable and to be clear when an event or incident is not documented. The facts, I have found, are much more compelling than the myths.

Second, I have endeavored to tell the story of Columbus without imposing on his own words any unstated meaning or ulterior motive. I have attempted to read and report his words without suggesting any hidden motivation or calculated objective on his part. In every case, I read Spanish transcriptions of Columbus's writings and compared the original Spanish to English translations, where translations are available.

Finally, I have attempted to add something new to the vast literature of Columbus by including unique source material from latter-day revelation. To my knowledge, no historian has used these sources in a serious biography of the discoverer of America. These materials, though limited, clarify and resolve questions of intent surrounding much of what Columbus wrote. Hugh Nibley observes: "Most of what is mysterious and contradictory in the story of Columbus comes from the refusal of the experts to believe what he tells them. They say he was an outrageous liar when he was actually telling the truth!"[16] When one accepts his words at face value, the Columbus who emerges is very different from the vain, arrogant, greedy, and self-promoting man portrayed in so much of the current literature. What emerges is a man who, rather than arrogant, is unwavering in his convictions; a man not so much greedy and vain as interested in fairness and justice; an immigrant who makes an inestimable contribution to his adopted country, suffering great personal risk to do so, yet who never achieves the acceptance afforded to native sons who did more harm than good. More than anything, the man who emerges is a man of great faith.

Such a reading—and subsequent telling—requires accepting Columbus's frequently stated view that he had a divinely inspired role in history. Columbus's assertions corroborate the prophecy of Nephi, and if one accepts the vision and prophecy of Nephi, the mystery surrounding Columbus disappears and his writings become plain and simple to understand:

> The Lord purposed that there should be something clearly miraculous in this matter of the voyage to the Indies . . . I spent seven years here in your royal court discussing this subject with the leading persons in all the learned arts, and their conclusion was that all was in vain. That was the end, and they gave it up. But afterwards it all turned out just as *our redeemer Jesus Christ had said, and as he had spoken earlier by the mouth of his holy prophets.*[17]

Columbus did not have access to the prophecy of Nephi: that prophecy was written in a lost language on gold plates buried in a hillside on a continent that Columbus was yet to discover. Columbus's understanding of his mission came through diligent personal study of the Bible, the fire of the Holy Ghost, and, on a few occasions, direct revelation. Perhaps the most remarkable aspect of the life of this remarkable man is the degree to which he understood his prophetic mission and his place in history.

PROLOGUE

This night of October 11–12 was one big with
destiny for the human race, the most momentous ever
experienced aboard any ship in any sea.[1]

SAMUEL ELIOT MORISON

s the sun sank below the western horizon of the Atlantic Ocean on the evening of 11 October 1492, it left three small wooden ships surrounded by the gathering darkness. The ships were located at a latitude of about 24 degrees, slightly south of Key West, Florida, and a longitude of about 73 degrees, some 3,500 miles west of the Canary Islands.

The two smaller ships, the *Niña* and the *Pinta,* were captained respectively by Vicente Yáñez Pinzón and Martín Alonso Pinzón, two brothers from Andalusia who were experienced captains. The third and largest of the ships, sometimes known as *La Gallega* (having been constructed in Galicia) but christened the *Santa María* by her devout captain, was under the command of a forty-one-year-old Genoese seaman who used the Spanish version of his name, Cristóbal Colón.

In English-speaking countries he was, and is, known as Christopher Columbus.

As darkness set in, the ships were at full sail in gale-force winds, traveling due west at about nine knots. Their last landfall was thirty-three days before, at San Sebastian in the Canary Islands, where they had repaired a damaged rudder on the *Pinta*. The voyage had already become the longest known journey through open ocean.

About 10:00 o'clock in the evening, an hour before moonrise, Columbus was standing on the sterncastle of the *Santa María,* scanning the dark horizon, when he thought he saw a faint light in the distance, "like a small wax candle that rose and lifted up."[2] Not certain in the darkness if it might be land, he did not inform his crew, but he mentioned it to an aide, Pedro Gutierrez, who thought he saw it too. The little fleet continued to sail west under full sail.

At 2:00 A.M. on 12 October, the moon was high over Orion and Jupiter was rising in the east as the three little ships, with the *Pinta* in the lead, sped through the night. Rodrigo de Triana, a twenty-three-year-old sailor from Seville, was atop the lookout on the *Pinta.* His eye fixed on the western horizon, he saw "something like a white sand cliff gleaming in the moonlight on the western horizon, then another, and a dark line of land connecting them."[3] Recognizing land, he cried out to the deck below, *"Tierra! Tierra!"*

In that moment the world changed. One era—an era that covered over four millennia of recorded history—ended, and a new era began. The discovery would arguably have a more profound impact on the world than any discovery before or since. Though he could not know it at the time, Rodrigo de Triana saw not just a slip of land on the horizon in the dim light of the moon on that fateful morning of 12 October 1492 but the dawn of a new age.

Chapter 1

THE PROPHECY OF NEPHI

Surely the Lord God will do nothing, but he
revealeth his secret unto his servants the prophets.

AMOS 3:9

he written story of Columbus begins two thousand years
before his great voyage of discovery with the record of a
remarkable event that took place somewhere in the deserts
of Arabia, "in a valley by the side of a river of water."[1]

The prophet Lehi fled Jerusalem in the year 600 B.C. It was a time
of political, social, and religious turmoil in the land of Judah. A century earlier, the great prophet Isaiah had died after a forty-year ministry
during which, among other things, he had warned both Judah and
Israel that they would be smitten and scattered if they did not repent.
Many of Isaiah's prophecies were fulfilled when the kingdom of Israel
fell to the armies of the Assyrian king Shalmaneser, and "the king of
Assyria took Samaria, and carried Israel away into Assyria."[2]

The fall of Samaria in 721 B.C. was still relatively recent history in
600 B.C. when Lehi and others preached in Jerusalem. The writings of

Isaiah contained ample warnings that the people of Judah, if they did not repent, would suffer a fate similar to that of the Samaritans. In the century after the fall of Samaria, the political and military balance had shifted; Assyria declined while Babylon became more powerful, and in 606 B.C. the great Assyrian capital of Nineveh was captured by the Babylonians. Two years later, Nebuchadnezzar ascended to the throne of Babylon and began to consolidate his kingdom by putting military and political pressure on Syria, Egypt, and Judah. In that uncertain political scene, the century-old prophecies of Isaiah cast an ominous shadow:

> For, behold, the Lord, the Lord of hosts, doth take away from Jerusalem and from Judah the stay and the staff . . . And I will give children to be their princes, and babes shall rule over them. And the people shall be oppressed, every one by another, . . . For Jerusalem is ruined, and Judah is fallen.[3]

That was the Jerusalem of Lehi and his family. With Jeremiah and others, Lehi prophesied anew the impending destruction of Jerusalem and called upon the people to repent so that the hand of the Lord might be stayed. Writing about these events some thirty years later,[4] Lehi's son Nephi records that "there came many prophets, prophesying unto the people that they must repent, or that great city Jerusalem must be destroyed."[5] But their warnings and counsel went unheeded. Lehi's life was threatened, and he was commanded in a dream to take his family and flee into the wilderness.

We do not know when Nephi was born or how old he was when his father took his family from their comfortable home and moved to the desert. We do know that Nephi was the third of four sons (two more would be born in the desert), that he was "exceedingly young" at the time of their move, that neither he nor his brothers were yet married, and that he died sometime after 544 B.C. We know that Nephi had "great desires to know of the mysteries of God," that he "did cry unto the Lord," and that, as a result, the Lord visited him and softened his heart so that he believed "all the words which had been spoken" by his father.[6]

So it was that sometime in 600 B.C. or shortly thereafter, the young Nephi was living with his father in a tent in a remote location somewhere near the Gulf of Aqaba. While in these circumstances, Lehi had a great vision known as the vision of the tree of life. Having heard his father's description of this vision (which he records in 1 Nephi 8–10), the young Nephi tells us that he "desired to know the things that my father had seen, and believing that the Lord was able to make them known unto me, as I sat pondering in mine heart I was caught away in the Spirit of the Lord."[7] He was then shown the things that his father had seen, portions of which he recorded in what is now 1 Nephi, chapters 11 through 14.

In this great vision, Nephi is shown the history of his descendants as well as the descendants of his brothers and a broad view of history that extended beyond the destruction of the Nephites to the Restoration and the end of the world. He records only a few highlights for us in his brief account of the vision. Eight verses of that record deal with key events leading up to the Restoration and the coming forth of the Book of Mormon. He begins this abbreviated account of latter-day events with this interesting verse:

> And I looked and beheld a man among the Gentiles, who was separated from the seed of my brethren by the many waters; and I beheld the Spirit of God, that it came down and wrought upon the man; and he went forth upon the many waters, even unto the seed of my brethren, who were in the promised land.[8]

With the perspective of history, the "man among the Gentiles" whom Nephi saw is easily identified as Christopher Columbus.[9] One of the best-known facts of history is that Columbus did exactly what Nephi saw him do: he sailed across the ocean that separated the

Gentiles of the Old World from the land of Lehi's seed in the New World, ushering in a new era in world history.

But Nephi also tells us why Columbus would cross the ocean: "I beheld the Spirit of God, that it came down and wrought upon the man." Columbus himself knew exactly why he was compelled, against all odds, to do what he did. He described his motivation in these remarkable words:

> With a hand that could be felt, the Lord opened my mind to the fact that it would be possible to sail and he opened my will to desire to accomplish the project . . . This was the fire that burned within me . . . Who can doubt that this fire was not merely mine, but also of the Holy Spirit . . . urging me to press forward?[10]

The story of Columbus is, among many other things, a story of the fulfillment of prophecy. More than two thousand years passed from the time that simple prophecy was recorded by Nephi in the wilderness of Arabia until the fulfillment of that prophecy with Columbus's successful voyage of discovery. And without access to Nephi's prophecy, Columbus himself described its perfect and exact fulfillment.

Chapter 2

FROM WEAVER'S SON TO MARINER

Since thou wast born, ever has He had thee in His watchful care.[1]

CELESTIAL VOICE TO CHRISTOPHER COLUMBUS, 1503

O ver the centuries there has grown up a mountain of myths and legends regarding the birth and ancestry of Columbus. Claims have been made that he was Jewish, Portuguese, Catalan, Corsican, Majorcan, French, German, Greek, Armenian, even English.[2] The claim that Columbus was actually of Catalan-Jewish origin is still actively promoted by some scholars.[3] Perhaps no other aspect of the Discoverer has been so hotly debated and contested as the simple fact of his origins. Yet Columbus himself was very clear about those origins: writing in his will in 1498, Columbus states simply, *"siendo yo nacido en Génoba,"* "being born in Genoa."[4] Columbus's simple and straightforward statement is supported by numerous documents in the municipal archives of Genoa regarding the Colombo family, several of which mention Christopher Columbus by name. Based on these records, we know that his paternal grandfather, Giovanni Colombo, was from the area around Fontanabuona and lived later in Quinto (so called because it is located at the fifth milestone east of Genoa), both cities of Liguria in what is now Italy. Giovanni Colombo first appears in the municipal records in 1429 when he apprenticed his eleven-year-old son, Domenico, to a weaver in Genoa. Apparently the young Domenico learned the trade well, for the records show that ten years later, in 1439, he leased a house in which he set up shop, weaving and selling cloth from wool, and obtained his own apprentice to assist him. About five years later, in 1445, Domenico married Susanna Fontanarossa. Sometime in the late summer or early fall of 1451, probably in September or October, their son Christopher was born. St. Christopher's day was celebrated on 25 July, and one biographer speculates that Columbus may have been born on or near that date.[5] Whatever the reasons for the choice of the name, it proved to be prophetic.

According to legend, St. Christopher was originally known as Offerus. He was born in the third century to a pagan king in Canaan and grew to be a very large man, some legends suggesting he was over six feet tall. He desired to find and serve the greatest king of all and became a servant of a king reputed to be the most powerful king in the world. One day, however, he saw the king cross himself at the mention of the devil. Seeing that his master feared the devil, he departed to look for the devil. He met up with a band of marauders, one of whom declared himself to be the devil, so Offerus became his servant. But when he saw his new master avoid a wayside cross, suggesting that the devil feared Christ, Offerus left him and inquired where to find Christ. He was directed to a hermit who instructed him in the Christian faith. Offerus asked how he could serve Christ, but when the hermit suggested fasting and prayer, Offerus replied that he was unable to perform that service. The hermit then suggested that because of his size and strength he could serve Christ by assisting people to cross a dangerous river, where they often perished in the attempt, promising that this service would be pleasing to Christ. After performing this service for some time, a small child asked Offerus to carry him across the river. During the crossing, the river became swollen and the child seemed as heavy as lead, so much so that Offerus could scarcely carry him and found himself in great peril. When he finally reached the other side, he said to the child: "You have put me in the greatest danger. I do not think the whole world could have been as heavy on my shoulders as you were." The child replied: "You had on your shoulders not only the whole world but Him who made it. I am Christ your king, whom you are serving by this work." The child then vanished. Offerus became known as Christopher, literally Christ-bearer.[6]

Columbus's son Fernando wrote, "Just as St. Christopher is said to have been so named because he carried Christ over deep waters with great danger . . . so the Admiral Christopher Columbus, invoking the aid of Christ in the perilous voyage, completed the journey to convert the *indios* into members and inhabitants of the triumphant church of heaven."[7] Christopher Columbus came to see his name as prophetic and viewed himself as the bearer of Christ to the peoples of the New World.

The weavers guild of Genoa ran a small primary school that would have provided instruction in the Latin used in daily religious practice as well as the practical Latin used for business, letter writing, and book-keeping. It is probable that the young Christopher attended this school, although there is no direct evidence that he did. He almost certainly received some basic education as a youth[8] and was a natural student who later in life read voraciously and wrote prolifically. He learned to read and write both Latin and Castilian (Spanish). It does not appear that he ever became proficient in written Italian, however; except for a few words or phrases, Columbus's later writings contain no Italian but are written in Spanish or Latin. Even letters written to friends in Genoa and to the Bank of St. George in Genoa are written in Spanish, a language he probably learned as an adult in Portugal. He did make notations in the margins of an Italian translation of Pliny's *Natural History*, but all except one of these notes are in Spanish.

In 1470, when Columbus was about eighteen and his brother Bartholomew in his early teens, their father was appointed to a committee to examine the guild rules of Savona. Domenico apparently was favorably impressed by what he saw and by March 1470 had moved from Genoa to Savona, about 35 miles down the coast. Christopher's name appears in a document dated 31 October 1470, acknowledging a debt for a shipment of wine delivered to him and his father in Savona, suggesting that Domenico had expanded his business interests beyond weaving. The document notes that Christopher was "over 19 years of age."[9] Christopher's name shows up in documents in Savona in 1472, in a document regarding the sale of the house in Genoa in 1473, and in a lease in Savona in 1474. Columbus's statement that he was born in Genoa is well corroborated by the documentary evidence.

How did the eldest son of a wool weaver become the greatest sailor of his age? Though Christopher came from a family of cloth weavers, Genoa was first and foremost a seafaring city. The city and its semicircular harbor are framed by the Apennine Mountains. From the shore to the mountaintops is a distance of less than two miles, and Genoa's connection to the rich valley of the Po River is restricted to steep mountain passes. As a result, Genoa has always looked to the sea for its wealth and for its fame. Columbus himself described his native Genoa as that "noble and powerful city by the sea."[10] Even for the son of a weaver, the sea would have been an ever-present reality.

Shipbuilding took place in harbors and coves all along the Ligurian coast. The Romans called the Mediterranean simply *Mare Nostrum*, "Our Sea," and it was the great highway that linked the empire. In the fifteenth century, Genoa and Venice vied with each other for control of trade through the Mediterranean, and the young Columbus would have frequently seen great ships sailing to and from North Africa, the Levant, and the ports of the Aegean Sea. Genoese captains were generally recognized as the best mariners in Europe and were in demand in Portugal, Castile, and other places. Certainly it would not have been unusual for a young boy in Genoa with an interest in sailing to find opportunities to learn the trade in what was one of the great maritime cities of the world.

During the Crusades, Genoa had played a major role as a point of departure for Christian fleets and benefited from the wealth that came back from war. Columbus was eight years old when Pope Pius II called for a new crusade, and talk of armed ships filled with knights may have stirred the boy's imagination.

A young boy in Genoa would almost certainly have heard stories of the Venetian explorer Marco Polo, who had been held prisoner in Genoa in 1298. He was imprisoned in the Palazzo San Giorgio, a building with which Columbus would have been familiar, and to pass the time of day while in custody, Polo regaled his fellow prisoner, Rusticello, with stories of his travels to Asia and his years of service to Kublai Khan, the Great Khan of the Mongol Empire. Rusticello later wrote down those stories. His manuscript was copied many times and translated into several languages, but copies were relatively rare during Columbus's youth, and most Europeans heard the stories rather than read them. Such stories could certainly fire the imagination of a young boy living on the edge of the sea.

Yet for all this, it seems unusual that the oldest son of a cloth weaver would break tradition by not following the trade of his father. In a letter to Ferdinand and Isabella written about 1501, Columbus says simply, "At a very early age I began to navigate upon the seas, which I have continued to this day."[11] According to his son Fernando, Columbus first went to sea at age fourteen.[12]

But Columbus does give a clue about his transformation from weaver to mariner. In a letter to the monarchs of Spain dated 7 July 1503, Columbus records hearing a divine voice declaring that "since thou wast born, ever has He [God] had thee in His watchful care" and that when he had reached an age which pleased God, "of the barriers of the Ocean Sea, which were closed with such mighty chains, He gave thee the key."[13]

Most scholars note that this statement by Columbus is an allusion to one of his favorite passages from Seneca's *Medea*. But while Seneca portrays the sea as bound by chains, the image of a key to unlock those chains is added by Columbus. The imagery of keys representing divine authority was an integral part of the Christian theology that was the fabric of Columbus's life. This principle is portrayed graphically on the monumental frieze adorning the front of the Basilica of St. Peter in Rome, on which construction began in 1506, the year of Columbus's death. The sculpture portrays Peter holding a great ring of keys, representing the keys given him by Christ: "And I will give unto thee the keys of the kingdom of heaven."[14]

How or when Columbus received the keys to the Ocean Sea is unknown, but his claim that he had been given such keys is wholly consistent with, and gives credence to, the narrative of Columbus's life and his frequent declaration that what he did was under the guidance, inspiration, and urging of the Holy Spirit.[15] Las Casas, who was eight years old when Columbus returned from the First Voyage, observes in his *Historia:* "God granted to this man the keys to the awesome seas, and deemed that he and no other would unlock the darkness."[16]

What we know from Columbus's statements is simply this: God watched over him from his birth; at some point he was given the keys to unlock the Ocean Sea; and "at a very early age," probably fourteen, he went to sea.

Little is known about the voyages Columbus made as a youth

except that he spent considerable time at sea. He mentions sailing with a crew to Tunis and then to Marseille and may have participated in several voyages from Genoa to central Mediterranean ports. It is clear that sailing became his primary occupation and that as a young man he followed in the tradition of many great Genoese sea captains, ultimately becoming the greatest of them all.

Columbus became acquainted with the influential Centurione, Spinola, and Di Negro families who ran merchant banking and trading businesses with branches in Spain, Portugal, and throughout the Mediterranean. At times he was employed by these families. In 1474, when Columbus was twenty-three, they sent a ship from Savona to Chios, an island controlled by Genoa in the Aegean Sea. The purpose of the voyage was to obtain mastic, an aromatic resinous gum that was used for a variety of applications in Europe. The ship records indicate that in addition to seamen and soldiers, she was manned by a number of workmen of Savona, including weavers, and it is likely that Columbus sailed on this and other voyages sponsored by these important merchants. During such voyages, he would have developed his skills as a sailor and learned how to estimate distances, to weigh anchor, to read the winds and currents, to predict the weather, and to manage a sometimes unruly crew.

Two years after the voyage to Chios, the same Genoese merchants organized a convoy to ship and market mastic from Chios in Portugal, England, and Flanders. The fleet was composed of three large three-masted galleys, a large armed ship, and a Flemish cargo ship named the *Bechalla,* which was manned largely by sailors from Savona. The fleet set sail on 31 May 1476 from the port of Noli, just south of Savona, and sailed west, passing through the Pillars of Hercules into the Atlantic Ocean.

On 13 August, off the southern coast of Portugal, the fleet was attacked by thirteen or more vessels of a Franco-Portuguese war fleet.

Genoa and France were theoretically at peace, but the *Bechalla* was flying the flag of Burgundy, with which Louis XI was at war. Though outnumbered and outgunned, the Genoese put up a fierce fight. The battle raged throughout the day, and by sundown four French and three Genoese ships had gone down, including the *Bechalla.*

There is no documentation verifying that Columbus was on the *Bechalla,* but Fernando reports that at about this same time and near this same location, Columbus was aboard a ship that was attacked and began to burn as it sank. As his ship went down, Columbus leaped into the sea, where he clung onto an oar that had floated free. Resting on the oar as he swam, he was able to reach the Portuguese town of Lagos, some 6 miles distant. His son later wrote, "It pleased God, who was preserving him for greater things, to give him strength to reach the shore."[17]

In Lagos the survivors were aided by the local residents. As soon as he was strong enough to travel, Columbus made his way to Lisbon, where he was taken in and cared for by the local Genoese community until he had fully recovered. [18]

What could have been a disaster—what was a disaster in many respects—proved to be providential in the life of Christopher Columbus. He was twenty-four years old, single, virtually uneducated, unemployed, and shipwrecked in a foreign country. But the future Admiral of the Ocean Sea could not have been in a better spot at a better time. His fortuitous shipwreck and miraculous survival placed him at a crossroads that shaped history.

Fifteenth-century Europe was permeated by an air of pessimism, but if there was a bright spot in Europe, it was Portugal. Portugal's resurgence began with the remarkable career of the third son of King João I. Born in 1394, Infante Henrique, Duke of Viseu, is more commonly known today as Prince Henry the Navigator. At age twenty-one, Henry led an expedition that captured the Moroccan port of Ceuta.

The North African city was a haven for pirates who attacked southern Portugal, capturing the citizens and selling them as slaves in Africa. Henry's conquest of Ceuta gave Portugal not just improved security but a colony and a keen interest in Africa. Importantly, it helped Portugal look outward with an expansionary view. In the fifteenth century, while much of Europe was losing territory, Portugal was expanding.

At age twenty-six, Henry was appointed governor of the wealthy Order of Christ, the Portuguese successor to the Knights Templar, and he used the Order to establish a foundation to train sea captains and finance exploration. Until the time of Henry, nearly all voyages were made in traditional *barques,* the standard cargo ship of the Mediterranean. These *barques* were relatively large ships, usually with a single rectangular sail and a flat bottom. Though useful for shipping cargo around the Mediterranean, they were slow and difficult to maneuver, particularly in the Atlantic Ocean. Henry and his sailors developed a new ship design that represented a significant improvement in technology. Based on fishing boats rather than cargo ships, the new caravels were smaller, lighter, and faster. They generally were built with three masts and used triangular sails, which enabled them to tack against the wind much more efficiently than the *barques.*

Henry put his new technology to work, with his captains—some of whom were Genoese—venturing south along the coast of Africa in hopes of finding a new route to Asia and its valuable spices. In 1427 one of his expeditions discovered the Azores, and Portugal colonized the islands in 1430. But no ship had successfully sailed south of Cape Bajador on the coast of the western Sahara. Currents and winds off the Cape were treacherous, and several ships had been lost in attempts to sail around the Cape. Sailors, by nature a superstitious lot, claimed that the region was inhabited by sea monsters. The Cape had become both a physical and psychological barrier to further exploration. A Portuguese mariner, Gil Eanes, attempted but failed to round the Cape in 1433.

Henry sent him on a second expedition the following year, and on this second attempt Eanes succeeded in rounding the Cape and sailing south. Eanes's achievement was important not just for its sailing merits but for dispelling fears about unknown seas.

Having successfully rounded Cape Bajador, Portuguese sailors continued to inch their way southward along the African coast. By 1445 they had reached the mouth of the Senegal River; in 1458 they discovered and colonized the Cape Verde Islands; by 1462 they had reached Sierra Leone; and in 1473 the Portuguese mariner Lopo Goncalves crossed the equator.

Alone among European nations, Portugal was extending its boundaries and its influence and pushing exploration into uncharted seas and unknown lands. Morison puts it this way:

> This lucky landing in Portugal was the turning point in Christopher's career, for chance had washed him ashore in the world-center of oceanic voyaging and discovery. He was among people who could teach him everything he was eager to learn: Portuguese and Castilian, the languages of far-ranging seamen; Latin to read the geographical works of the past; mathematics and astronomy for celestial navigation; shipbuilding and rigging; and above all, discovery.[19]

This was the Portugal upon whose shores the young Christopher Columbus miraculously found himself in 1476.

Chapter 3

IN PORTUGAL

*Thus in that dark and gloomy sea burned a light which
would illuminate the way for the young mariner.*[1]

HIERRO AND PEREDA

enniless and in a foreign country, Columbus was soon back at work as a seaman. Genoese mariners were highly employable in Portugal, and Columbus was already well connected to the Spinola and Di Negro families, who had a business presence in Lisbon. Soon after his arrival in Lisbon, Columbus signed on for a voyage to England. His ship docked in London and then in Bristol. British ships from the port of Bristol sailed regularly as far as Iceland, and Columbus, who already was familiar with the Mediterranean Sea and the Atlantic Ocean from Lisbon north to England, signed on for a voyage to the most distant part of the known world:

> I sailed in the year 1477, in the month of February, a hundred leagues beyond the island of Tile [or Thule, as Iceland was then known] . . . And to this island, which is as big as England,

come English with their merchandise, especially they of Bristol. And at the season when I was there the sea was not frozen, but the tides were so great that in some places they rose 26 *braccia* [about 49 feet].[2]

On this or a subsequent voyage Columbus also visited Galway in Ireland. In the margin of his copy of *Historia rerum ubique gestarum*, by Aeneas Sylvius Piccolonmini (Pope Pius II), is a note that reads, "Men of Cathay, which is toward the Orient, have come hither. We have seen many remarkable things, especially in Galway of Ireland, a man and a woman of extraordinary appearance in two boats adrift."[3]

Columbus was a keen observer of currents, winds, and weather patterns, and these voyages would have added to his store of knowledge. Sailing north into the Gulf Stream, he would have noticed the east-flowing currents in the North Atlantic. These westerly currents and the even stronger westerly trade winds would make it possible for a ship that sailed west in the Atlantic to return to Europe at a more northerly latitude.

Columbus remained in Portugal from 1476 until 1485, nearly nine years. These years in Portugal were busy and productive years for him. His brother Bartholomew joined him in Lisbon[4] and was engaged in making and selling maps, and Columbus probably worked in the map-making business when not at sea. In Portugal he learned to speak, read, and write Castilian, which was the preferred language of the Portuguese nobility. He began to acquire a library and read voraciously. He married and had a child. And it was there that his great plan, which he called the Enterprise of the Indies, began to take shape.

In 1478, Columbus was engaged by Paulo di Negro of Genoa to sail to the North Atlantic island of Madeira, pick up a load of sugar, and deliver it back to Genoa. To be entrusted to carry out this transaction, valued at several thousand dollars, suggests that the twenty-seven-year-old Columbus had established a solid reputation among the businessmen of Genoa. It also indicates that Columbus continued to be actively engaged in sailing during his years in Portugal, improving his maritime skills as well as his knowledge of currents and prevailing winds in the Atlantic.

These voyages through the known parts of the ocean provided Columbus not only with experience but with evidence that suggested to him that Asia was not far off. During Columbus's time in Portugal, a Portuguese sailor by the name of Vicente reported picking up "a piece of wood ingeniously wrought but not with iron" somewhere beyond the Azores.[5] Pedro Correa da Cunha, Columbus's brother-in-law, found a similar piece of driftwood on the island of Porto Santo, northeast of Madeira. It had the appearance of cane or bamboo, but of a variety much larger than anything known in Africa. On the island of Flores in the Azores, two bodies washed up on the beach that did not have the appearance of Europeans but had very broad faces, not unlike those Columbus reported seeing in Galway. All of these finds suggested to Columbus that the ocean could not be as broad as commonly believed.

Samuel Eliot Morison points out that the reports of driftwood were an important and reliable clue. As the Gulf Stream fans out northwest of the Azores, the current becomes so weak that very little flotsam reaches either the Azores or the Madeiras, except for exceptionally light, buoyant pieces which can be driven by the westerly winds. After heavy storms, residents of the Azores and Madeiras often pick up along the shore chestnut-like seeds they call *fava do mar,* "sea beans." They are the seedpods of *entada gigas,* a plant common along the shores of the Caribbean. Morison reports receiving a *fava do mar* from a fisherman in the Azores and, four months later, while sailing along the coast of Panama, finding hundreds of similar beans on the beach.[6]

Sometime after his voyage to Madeira, Columbus met Doña Felipa Perestrello e Moniz. According to his son Fernando, Columbus met his future wife while attending mass at the Convento dos Santos in Lisbon.

The convent served as a boarding school for daughters of the Portuguese aristocracy and so was undoubtedly considered by eligible bachelors to be a particularly good location to attend to their religious duties. How the two met or became acquainted is not known; Fernando says only, "Inasmuch as he behaved very honorably, and was a man of such fine presence and consistently good conduct," Felipa "took notice of him and developed such a friendship with him that she became his wife."[7]

Felipa was the daughter of Bartholomew Perestrello by his third wife, Isabel Moniz. Bartholomew had participated in a colonizing voyage to the islands of Porto Santo and Madeira in 1425 and was granted the hereditary governorship of the island of Porto Santo by Prince Henry. Columbus and Felipa lived at first with Felipa's mother, and she shared with her new son-in-law stories of her husband's adventures. Seeing that "these stories and voyages pleased the Admiral much," relates Fernando, Isabel "gave him the writings and sea-charts left by her husband. The Admiral found these items exciting, and he educated himself on other voyages and navigations that the Portuguese made to La Mina on the coast of Guinea."[8] After living a short time with Isabel in Lisbon, the young couple moved to the island of Porto Santo where their son, Diego, was born.

The papers of his father-in-law influenced Columbus and added to the knowledge that would assist him in his enterprise. But Columbus's marriage to Felipa proved providential in another important aspect: it took him into the ranks of nobility and ultimately made it possible for him to present his plan to the Portuguese monarch. His marriage to Felipa suggests that Columbus was not just a common sailor, a foreigner who had literally washed up on the shores of Portugal a few years earlier, but was a respected and highly regarded Genoese sea captain.

Along with changes in Columbus's personal life, political events were unfolding across the Iberian Peninsula that would affect Columbus and set the stage for his Voyage of Discovery. Henry IV of

Castile died in 1474, and the Castilian crown was disputed between the king's half sister, Isabella, married to Prince Ferdinand of Aragon, and the king's daughter, Juana de Trastamara. In 1475, Alfonso V of Portugal married Juana and invaded Castile. After fierce naval battles in 1476 and 1478, the dispute was finally settled in the Treaty of Alcáçovas, signed on 4 September 1479.

The treaty had far-reaching implications. First, Alfonso and Juana renounced their claims to the throne of Castile, making Isabella and Ferdinand the undisputed monarchs of Castile and Aragon. Second, Castile retained control over the Canary Islands, and Portugal was granted control over the Azores, Madeira, Cape Verde, and everything south of the Canaries, including Africa. The Portuguese ventures down the coast of Africa had taken them to Guinea and its gold, and this was becoming a significant source of Portuguese wealth. The treaty and its subsequent affirmation by papal bull in 1481 (*Aeterni regis,* by Pope Sixtus IV) established a historical precedent by giving European monarchies defined rights for exploration, colonization, and trade in the expanding world. This precedent would become even more important after Columbus's First Voyage.

The affirmation of Portuguese control of navigation and exploration along the African coast accelerated Portuguese trade in Africa. Columbus participated in at least one voyage as far south as São Jorge da Mina in present-day Ghana. The Portuguese constructed a fortress and expanded their trading establishment at São Jorge da Mina in 1482. Columbus made two references to visiting this fortress. In his copy of Pierre d'Ailly's *Imago mundi* at the place d'Ailly states that the Torrid Zone was uninhabitable because of the tremendous heat, Columbus added this note in the margin: "The Torrid Zone is not uninhabitable, since the Portuguese navigate there today, but it is very populated, and below the equinoctial line is found the fortress of La Mina of the most serene King of Portugal, which we have seen."[9]

He wrote a similar note in his copy of Aeneas Sylvius's *Historia rerum,* opposite a passage where Eratosthenes is quoted as to the climate below the equator being temperate: "Under the equator . . . is found the fortress of La Mina of the most serene King of Portugal, which we have seen."[10]

Additionally, in a note in the margin of his copy of Pierre d'Ailly's *Imago mundi,* Columbus wrote: "Note that sailing frequently from Lisbon south to Guinea, I observed carefully the course."[11]

We do not know the circumstances nor the exact dates of Columbus's voyages to Portuguese Guinea, but they were probably sometime between 1482 and 1484. Fernando wrote, "I do not know, to tell the truth, if during his marriage the Admiral reached La Mina or Guinea."[12] Though he was unsure of the dates, however, he was certain about the effect on Columbus: "Being in Portugal, he began to reason that if the Portuguese had reached so far south, by the same token he could travel towards the west, and that he was likely to find land in that direction."[13]

These trips to Guinea not only increased Columbus's confidence in his own enterprise (if he ever had any doubt) but also contributed significantly to his knowledge of the ocean. Sailing south of the Canaries, he would have observed the easterly currents and winds, suggesting that this would be a good place to begin a westward crossing of the Ocean Sea. Combining these with his earlier observations in the North Atlantic, he may have begun to realize the existence of the Atlantic trade winds.

The presence of gold in the Torrid Zone of Africa was also significant. According to Aristotle, gold was most likely to form in the latitudes around the equator, and this theory seemed to be validated by the abundance of gold in Guinea, an area that would later be known as the Gold Coast. Accordingly, then, gold was expected to be found in abundance at that same latitude everywhere on the planet.

When Columbus was not sailing, he was reading and studying. He learned Castilian, began to acquire a library, and poured a great deal of time and energy into studying and formulating his plan to open the gates of the ocean. Nine books known to have been owned and read by Columbus survive and are housed in the Biblioteca Colombina in the Cathedral of Seville. Of the nine volumes, only two were published after Columbus's years in Portugal. He made extensive postils, or notes, in the margins of his books—a total of over twenty-five hundred hand-written notes, of which two thousand were made in the seven volumes that were published either before or while he was in Portugal.

A significant focus of his study was to determine the circumference of the earth, the size of the Asian land mass, and consequently, the width of the Ocean Sea, or the Atlantic Ocean. Key to the success of the Enterprise of the Indies was determining the width of the ocean—and determining that it was narrow enough to accommodate a complete crossing in a reasonable time with the relatively primitive technology of the day. Columbus studied the writings of Aristotle, Pliny, Ptolemy, Strabo, Eratosthenes, the Muslim geographer Alfragan, Marco Polo, and Marinus of Tyre and used them to make his own calculations. In every instance he adopted assumptions that made the crossing narrower. He consistently underestimated the circumference of the earth and overestimated the size of Asia. Morison calculates that Columbus estimated the distance from the Canaries to Japan to be 2,400 miles. The actual distance by air is 10,600 miles. During his First Voyage, Columbus would travel over 3,500 miles from the Canary Islands before making his first landfall in the New World.

How could he have been so far off? Morison observes simply, "He *knew* he could make it, and the figures had to fit."[14] Columbus's highly optimistic calculations appear to be based more on the need to convince others of the feasibility of the project; he himself had no doubts. 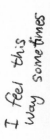 "With a hand that could be felt, the Lord opened my mind to the fact that it would be possible to sail from here to the Indies, and opened my will to desire to accomplish the project." Having that knowledge, he "prayed to the most merciful Lord concerning my desire [to sail across the Atlantic], and he gave me the spirit and the intelligence for it."[15] Las Casas wrote, "He was as sure he would discover what he did discover, and find what he did find, as if he held it in a chamber under lock and key."[16] In Columbus's mind, he was a man with a mission, prepared by God to open the gates of the Ocean Sea, and he simply knew that he could and would accomplish that mission. So unwavering was his certainty that one historian argued that Columbus had already crossed the ocean secretly and needed the support of a sovereign prince to allow him to lay claim to his discovery.[17] The most plausible explanation is that his miscalculations "were the means for justifying the end, and the end was to gain consent for his own seafaring plan. Events were to demonstrate, amply, that the plan was valid."[18]

For those without his spiritual fire and unwavering certainty, Columbus needed to provide convincing evidence that his enterprise could be accomplished. He found confirmation of his calculations from a respected Florentine physician and mathematician by the name of Paolo dal Pozzo Toscanelli. Toscanelli was a well-known intellectual. In 1458 he carefully observed a comet that, when its 1759 return was predicted by Edmund Halley, became known as Halley's comet. He designed a device that was installed in the dome of the Cathedral of Santa María del Fiore in Florence and marked the summer solstice to within half a second. It remained in use for centuries.

Toscanelli wrote to King Alfonso V of Portugal in 1474 or 1475, suggesting that the Portuguese should consider reaching the Orient by sailing west. Toscanelli claimed that the realm of the Grand Khan covered "nearly one third of the globe,"[19] making the ocean narrower than most people thought. He suggested that Alfonso send an expedition westward, arguing that it would be "shorter than the one which you are pursing by way of Guinea." Toscanelli estimated the distance from Lisbon to the capital of China to be 6,500 miles but added that "from the island of Antilla . . . to the very noble island of Cipango [Japan]" was a journey of only 2,500 miles. That no one had ever been to the mythical island of Antilla did not seem to be of significance.

Columbus learned of this letter and obtained an introduction to Toscanelli through a Florentine acquaintance in Lisbon. He wrote the scholar requesting more details. Toscanelli responded by enclosing a copy of his 1474 letter, together with a chart or map. The map, which has been lost, is described in some detail in the letter and proved to be of particular interest to Columbus. It was a map of the world which was divided into grids—that is, it showed both latitudinal and longitudinal lines, with each space in the grid representing a distance of 250 miles. Though Toscanelli was not the first to use a grid system, such maps were not yet commonplace. The power of Toscanelli's map was that it reduced the unknown ocean to a finite series of measured grid spaces. Writing to Pope Alexander VI in 1502, Columbus would describe his voyage in terms of this grid system: "I traveled ten lines into the other hemisphere."[20]

Columbus requested more details and received a second letter from Toscanelli. It contained little additional information but much encouragement:

> I confirm the feasibility of your noble and grand desire, your aspiration to reach the east by sailing west as you indicate in the letter you sent me . . . I believe that such a voyage is not only possible but true and certain and of inestimable honor and worth, as well as great fame among all Christians . . . When you carry out this voyage, you will find powerful kingdoms and noble cities and provinces, abundantly rich in all that we need, that is to say, an abundance of all manner of spices and great quantities of jewels.[21]

He went on to assure Columbus that he would be well received by the Oriental princes, who were eager to open up trade with the Christians. "For these, and many other reasons that I could name, it does not surprise me that you, who are so valiant, and the entire Portuguese nation, that has always relied on signal men in all its endeavors, are filled with enthusiasm and great desires to carry out such a voyage."

The Toscanelli correspondence was valuable to Columbus in at least three ways. First, it provided corroboration of his theories from a respected mathematician and scientist. Second, the grid system shown on Toscanelli's map gave a sense of definition and finiteness to the otherwise blank and unknown ocean. And finally, not only did Toscanelli validate Columbus's proposal with his own calculations and data but he gave an enthusiastic endorsement of the proposed enterprise.

In addition to his studies of geography, Columbus was an avid student of the Bible. Biblical study by a layman was unusual, but Columbus engaged in it with a passion. On a blank page of his copy of Pope Pius's *Historia rerum*, Columbus copied three scriptures under the heading *Auctoritates in Brevia* ("Brief Authoritative Statements"):

> They shall lift up their voices in praise; when the Lord shall be glorified, their rejoicing shall sound across the sea. Give glory to God because of these teachings, as the name of the God of Israel is among the islands of the sea. We have recognized his praises coming from the uttermost parts of the earth, the songs of triumphs of his Righteous one [Isaiah 24:14–16].
>
> Once every three years the king's [Solomon's] fleet would sail to Tharsis, with the servants of Hiram, and from there they would bring back gold, and silver, and ivory, and apes, and peacocks [II Chronicles 9:21].
>
> Ours is a God who, before time began, accomplished his saving work to be in the middle of the earth [Psalm 74:12]. Note that this should be understood as "in the middle of the land of promise."[22]

These quotations, noted by Columbus in 1481 when he was twenty-nine or thirty years old, deal with subjects that appear with frequency in Columbus's later writings. First, all people everywhere—across the sea and on the isles of the sea and in the uttermost parts of the earth—must hear the gospel. Second, Solomon had with regularity sent his fleets across the sea and brought back great wealth that he used to build the temple. Third, the great work of salvation in the last days would be centered in the promised land. Columbus's note on Psalm 74:12 is particularly interesting: he opines that the phrase "middle of the earth"—or "midst of the earth," as it reads in the King James translation—refers to the land of promise. Columbus believed that his great mission in life was to open the way across the sea to the promised land.

Columbus had a particular interest in eschatology. There was a growing sense in his age that the end of the world was near. In 1481, Columbus made his own calculation regarding when the end would come and recorded his analysis on a blank page in his copy of *Historia rerum*. Using the genealogies of the patriarchs in Genesis, the years of captivity in Egypt, the completion of the temple, the Babylonian captivity, the construction of the second temple, and modern history, he noted that "from the beginning of the world until this year 1481, there are 5,241 years."[23] Assuming a total expanse of 7,000 years from the Creation to the Second Coming, that left 1,759 years—ample time for all the remaining required events of prophecy to unfold.

Twenty years later, however, Columbus revised his calculations and determined that only 155 years remained,[24] a calculation that gave great urgency to his work. His writings reveal two great motivations for his voyage: the preaching of the gospel to all people, and the recapture of Jerusalem and the rebuilding of its temple. Both were necessary steps before the end could come, and he saw his voyages as the key to taking the gospel to all the world while at the same time providing the wealth necessary to recapture Jerusalem and rebuild the temple. For Columbus, time was of the essence.

By 1484, Columbus had sailed all the known seas of his age: the

[handwritten margin note: Some sort of direct revelation gave him this notion.]

Mediterranean, the Atlantic north to Iceland and south nearly to the equator. He felt that he had done the necessary research to support his grand enterprise and gain the all-important support of the monarchy. He was, as Morison wrote, "ready to make an amazing proposition to the king of Portugal."[25]

Alfonso V, to whom Toscanelli had proposed a voyage westward across the Ocean Sea to Asia, had succeeded to the throne of Portugal at the tender age of six upon the death of his father, Edward, in 1438. His mother, Eleanor of Aragon, served as regent for the young king. Alfonso continued to support the work of his uncle, Prince Henry the Navigator, but after Henry's death did little to further his work. In 1477, disillusioned and discouraged by military losses to Castile (which would result in the Treaty of Alcáçovas) Alfonso abdicated the throne to his son João II and retired to a monastery.

João II found himself king of a country on the verge of bankruptcy and rife with conspirators who opposed his reign. One of them, the duke of Bragança, was executed for treason in May of 1483. In August of 1484, the king invited the duke of Viseu, who was both his cousin and his brother-in-law and whom he suspected of conspiracy, to the palace. There the king personally stabbed and killed the duke. João's position and authority thus ruthlessly secured, he renewed the emphasis on exploration that had paid such dividends before the death of Prince Henry. The king appointed a council of advisors known as the *Junta de los Matemáticos*—literally, the "Council of Mathematicians," though it is generally referred to as the Maritime Advisory Committee—to oversee and support navigation and exploration, and he resumed the effort to find a way around Africa and from there to the Indies.

Thus it was that late in 1484 or early 1485, the Genoese mariner Christopher Columbus approached King João II of Portugal and proposed an expedition to reach Asia by sailing west—*buscar el Levante por el Poniente,* as he phrased it—arguing that it would be shorter and easier than going around Africa. He asked the king to provide ships for a journey to the island of Cipango (Japan), a land described in glowing terms by Marco Polo. What else he requested is not known, although his son Fernando indicates that he may have asked for terms similar to those he later received from the Spanish monarchs, including a hereditary title. The bestowal of titular honors on successful Portuguese navigators had precedent, and the hereditary nature of the title would ensure Columbus's young son both position and economic security. What is certain is that Columbus requested multiple ships and that Japan was his proposed destination.

That Columbus made a favorable impression on the king is evidenced by later correspondence. The king agreed to put the proposal before the Maritime Advisory Committee. The committee reviewed Columbus's proposal without delay and, just as promptly, rejected it. We have no record of their deliberations, but almost certainly they disagreed with Columbus's estimates on the width of the ocean and, hence, the feasibility of crossing it. As it turned out, Toscanelli was wrong: "the entire Portuguese nation" was *not* "filled with enthusiasm and great desires to carry out such a voyage."

The rejection of his proposal was not the only blow Columbus suffered at this time. His wife, Felipa, died, leaving him with a young son to care for.[26] He was in debt (three years later he wrote King João II asking for immunity from arrest, presumably for unpaid debts, if he returned to Portugal), perhaps from the expenses of preparing and presenting his proposal to the king as well as the cost of giving his wife a burial appropriate for her status. Widowed, in debt, and his grand enterprise rejected by the one country that had seemed most likely to accept it, he was thirty-three years old, the age of Christ at the time of His betrayal and crucifixion, a detail that would not have been lost on the devout Columbus. But "the great idea was by now an obsession."[27]

The kingdoms of the Iberian Peninsula, about 1492.

Chapter 4

TAKING THE QUEST TO CASTILE

Divine plans mature slowly. In this case, certainly,
God seems to have been in no hurry.[1]

FELIPE FERNANDEZ-ARMESTO

he village of Palos, known today as Palos de la Frontera, Spain, is situated on the coastal plain of Andalusia where the Rio Tinto joins the Rio Odiel and flows into the Atlantic. The small port had thrived on the trade with Africa, its ships and sailors making their way as far as Guinea, but the Treaty of Alcáçovas had given the African trade to Portugal with a corresponding decline in the fortunes of Palos.

When Columbus and his young and motherless son, Diego, arrived there in 1485, the little town—its population probably well under three thousand—must have seemed a somewhat drab and sleepy village compared to the life and color of Lisbon, one of the great seaports of the age. Exactly why Columbus chose to go to Palos is not known.[2] It is clear that he went to Castile intending to offer his proposed Enterprise of the Indies to the Spanish monarchs. Perhaps he chose Palos as his entry point because his only acquaintances in Spain—the Molyarts, his sister-in-law and her husband—lived in nearby Huelva.

Little is known of the sister of Felipa Perestrello, Violante, and her husband, Miguel Molyart (or Moliart). After the success of the First Voyage, the Molyarts moved to Seville with Columbus, and Violante maintained his home there during his frequent absences. Miguel accompanied Columbus on at least one of his later voyages. But there is no evidence that Columbus had even alerted his deceased wife's relatives that he was traveling to Spain. Instead, his arrival at Palos had much in common with his arrival in Portugal eight years earlier. There he had swum to shore, a refugee from a sinking ship. In Palos he arrived widowed, in debt, with a five-year-old son to care for, and with his great enterprise rejected by some of the best minds in Europe. But like his arrival in Lagos, his new beginning in Palos would prove providential.

Spain as we know it today did not exist in 1485. The people and cities of the Iberian Peninsula enter into written history with mentions of the semimythical city of Tartessos in the first millennium before Christ. Sometime between 210 B.C. and 205 B.C., the legions of Rome captured the Carthaginian cities of Iberia, and the Roman Empire soon spread its influence across the peninsula. Tarraco (present-day Tarragona) was a great Roman capital, the winter home of Caesar Augustus and the birthplace of Pontius Pilate. According to legend, the Apostle Paul visited Tarragona in A.D. 63 (see Romans 15:28), taking Christianity to Roman Iberia. Although there is no convincing evidence of such a visit, behind the cathedral in Tarragona a modern statue of the Apostle, dated 1963, bears the following inscription:

> *Al apóstol San Pablo*
> *en la XIX centenario*
> *de su venida a España*
> *y de su estancia en Tarragona*

"To the Apostle St. Paul,
on the 1900th anniversary
of his arrival in Spain
and his stay in Tarragona."

As the Roman Empire crumbled, Roman Iberia broke up into numerous Christian kingdoms and fiefdoms, most of which were conquered by Muslim forces in the eighth century. The great Muslim capital of Córdoba became the largest and wealthiest city in Europe. But little by little over the years, Christian forces engaged in the Reconquista, the reconquest of Iberia, won control of various regions, and Christian kingdoms were established in Navarre, Aragon, and Catalonia in the northeast, followed by Castile and León in the central areas of the peninsula.

By the time Isabella of Castile married Prince Ferdinand of Aragon in 1469, Castile and Aragon controlled most of what is now present-day Spain—the sovereign of Castile controlled the territory from Galicia in the northwest corner of the Iberian peninsula eastward to the Basque country, then southward to La Mancha, Murcia, and Extremadura; the sovereign of Aragon ruled the territory of Aragon, Catalonia, Valencia, as well as the Balearic Islands, Sardinia, and the kingdom of Naples. The Muslim kingdom of Granada, with more than fourteen cities, including Granada and Málaga, was the last Moorish stronghold in Western Europe. Ferdinand ascended to the throne of Aragon in 1479, and by 1482 Ferdinand and Isabella were ready to begin their campaign against the Emirate of Granada in hopes of completing the centuries-old Reconquista. Isabella had obtained a bull of crusade from the Pope, elevating the campaign to a holy war and making it part of the great effort to bring all the world into Christianity. When Granada finally fell to the armies of Castile in 1492, Christopher Columbus witnessed the surrender.

But in 1485 that historic event was still seven years away.

Columbus had come to Castile obsessed by a single vision: to obtain royal permission and the financial backing necessary to unlock the gate of the Ocean Sea. All his time and energy were devoted to this cause. As far as is known, the man who had made his living as a sea captain did not go to sea from the time of his arrival in Palos until he sailed again from Palos aboard the *Santa María* seven years later.

Homeless and in a foreign country for the second time in his life, Columbus found shelter for himself and young Diego in a Franciscan monastery just outside Palos, the Convento de Santa María de la Rábida. Founded in 1261, La Rábida is located on a high bluff overlooking the Rio Tinto, about a 4-mile walk from the port of Palos. It is possible that Columbus already had some association with the Order of St. Francis, as there was a Franciscan monastery on the island of Porto Santo where he and Felipa had lived as newlyweds and where Diego was born.

Several of the rooms at La Rábida remain almost unchanged from the time of Columbus. The refectory where meals were served still has rough-hewn, narrow wooden tables surrounded by wooden benches along three sides. A simple iron candleholder hangs from the ceiling. Monks today point out a small room with thick, whitewashed walls and large wooden beams in the ceiling as the place where Columbus studied, discussed his ideas, and prepared his proposal.

It was probably during these first days at La Rábida that Columbus met Fray Antonio de Marchena, a prominent Franciscan scholar who later that year would be appointed to supervise the Franciscan order throughout the Seville area. Marchena had studied theology and astronomy, and his interest in the latter earned him the sobriquet "*Estrellero*" ("Stargazer"). He was well connected with many influential leaders of Castile, and the ideas and fervor of the Genoese mariner newly arrived from Portugal intrigued him. He became Columbus's most ardent supporter. As Columbus later declared:

In all this time [seven years pleading his case in Spain] every mariner, pilot, philosopher and every other man of learning deemed my enterprise to be false; never did I get help from anyone except Father Antonio de Marchena, barring that from God . . . Everyone regarded it [his enterprise] as folly except Father Antonio de Marchena.[3]

Marchena was impressed by both Columbus and his bold idea and not only encouraged him to present his proposal to the monarchs but facilitated the means to do it through his acquaintances and contacts. The Spanish court did not have a permanent home until Philip II moved the court to Madrid in 1561, and in the spring and summer of 1485 the court was in the city of Córdoba. With a letter of introduction from Father Marchena, Columbus traveled to Córdoba, a distance of about 160 miles, where he met with Fernando de Talavera. Talavera, Columbus's senior by twenty-four years, was the confessor of the queen and a most respected and influential member of the court. He had studied theology at the University of Salamanca and after the fall of Granada in 1492 was named archbishop of Granada. It is likely that Talavera brought Columbus to the attention of the queen. Law number 27 of the Cortes of Toledo provided that petitions could be sent directly to the monarchs but was clear that most matters would be referred by them to the royal council, which was composed of wealthy grandees and ecclesiastical leaders. In 1485, the monarchs were fully occupied with the war against Granada and unlikely to divert time and energy to hearing the petition of a foreigner who "proposed a strange, incredible enterprise."[4] Columbus's request was delegated to the royal council. Dutifully, the council reviewed the proposal and took the unrequired step of hearing from Columbus, probably due to the influence of Marchena and Talavera. The council then responded quickly and negatively. They rejected the proposal, probably on the same grounds that it had been rejected by King João II's committee in Portugal:

Columbus's estimated distances for the proposed voyage seemed overly optimistic.

Córdoba, though not still the great world capital that it had been in the Moorish empire, was nonetheless an intellectually and visually stimulating city when Columbus arrived there in 1485. He almost certainly would have visited the Mezquita, the great mosque built in 785 and transformed into a cathedral in 1236; it remains one of the great attractions of the city. It may have been during this visit to Córdoba that Columbus purchased his copy of *Medea,* whose author, the Roman poet and philosopher Seneca, had been born in Córdoba. A verse from *Medea* had particular significance for Columbus:

> *Venient anns*
> *Secula seris, quibus Oceanus*
> *Vincjula rerum laxete, et ingens*
> *Pateat telus tiphisque novos*
> *Detegat orbes nec sit terries*
> *Vltima tille.*

> *An age will come*
> *after many years when the Ocean*
> *will loose its chains,*
> *and a huge land lie revealed,*
> *when Tiphys will disclose new worlds*
> *and Thule no more be the ultimate.*

Columbus, who had sailed to Thule (Iceland) some years earlier, was now preparing to turn the keys that would loose the chains of the Ocean Sea. Years later, Columbus quoted these lines from Seneca, giving his own translation and interpretation:

> In the last days certain times will come in which the Ocean Sea will loosen its bands, and a great land will open up, and a new mariner like the pilot of Jason, whose name was Typhys, will

discover a new world, and then will the isle of Thule no longer be the farthest land.[5]

Columbus saw himself as that "new mariner" prophesied by Seneca. When his proposal was rejected by the royal council, he was not deterred. Castilian law provided an appeal process: if a petitioner was declined by the council, the petitioner could appeal directly to the sovereigns, requesting that the council reexamine the request.

Exactly how Columbus obtained an audience with the queen is unknown, but his relationship with Fathers Marchena and Talavera were probably essential. A younger Columbus had washed up on the shores of Portugal as a castaway and within a few years had been granted an audience with the king of that country to discuss his enterprise. Now, less than a year after arriving in Castile as a foreigner and refugee, he was granted an audience with the Spanish sovereigns. Columbus was clearly a man of destiny.

Queen Isabella was the daughter of John II by his second wife, Isabella of Portugal. Upon the death of her father, her older half-brother, Henry, was crowned as Henry IV, and Isabella and her younger brother, Alfonso, were put under his care and protection. Henry was childless, which made Alfonso heir to the throne. However, shortly after Alfonso was named Prince of Asturias—the official title of the heir to the throne—he died of the plague,[6] opening the way for Isabella to become queen. Henry IV arranged for Isabella to marry the brother of Louis XI of France to create an alliance with the French kingdom. But Isabella, who had told Henry she would marry only by her own choice, refused. She had been approached in secret by King John II of Aragon to marry his son, Prince Ferdinand, and she preferred Ferdinand over the French prince. In the end, Isabella took leave of Henry with the excuse of visiting her younger brother's grave in Ávila. Meanwhile, Prince Ferdinand entered Castile disguised as a servant, and the two were married by a priest in Valladolid. Isabella was seventeen; Ferdinand, sixteen. Five years later, in 1474, upon the death of Henry, Isabella ascended to the throne of Castile.

Columbus and Isabella were certainly different in many ways. A child of royalty, Isabella had grown up in wealth and spent most of her youth in a castle in Segovia; Columbus was the son of a weaver and had spent most of his adult life on the deck of a ship. Isabella was known for elaborate gowns—court records reveal that she spent nearly 806,000 *maravedis* in one year on clothing for her son, an amount about sixty-seven times the annual salary of a sea captain; Columbus, even after the success of his First Voyage, often appeared in public wearing the simple brown habit of a Franciscan monk.

Yet they had much in common. Born the same year, Isabella was Columbus's senior by only a few months. Both were charismatic, religiously devout, and committed to spreading Christianity. And both were determined and driven to achieve their goals. Columbus was committed to reaching the East by sailing west and then using the wealth obtained from his Enterprise of the Indies to fund a new crusade that would win Jerusalem for Christendom. Isabella was committed to the full Christianization of what is now Spain, including the reconquest of Muslim-held territories on the Iberian peninsula and the conversion of her kingdom's large Jewish population. Her zeal would haunt her legacy; she is nearly as well remembered today for the excesses of the Spanish Inquisition as she is for her support of Columbus.

Columbus's first audience with Queen Isabella probably took place on 20 January 1486 at the palace of the archbishop in Alcalá de Henares, near Madrid. Just five weeks earlier, on 16 December 1485, the queen had given birth to her youngest daughter, Catherine of Aragon, in that same palace.[7]

Alcalá de Henares was the seat of the archbishop of Toledo and, as such, one of the most important cities of Castile. The University of Álcala, founded in 1293, is one of the oldest universities in the world.

The central part of the city was recognized in 1998 as a World Heritage Site. The palace of the archbishop remains a popular tourist site and is called the *Casa de la entrevista,* "the house of the interview," referring to the first meeting between Columbus and Queen Isabella in January of 1486.

No record of that meeting has survived.[8] Columbus may have appealed to the queen's religious devotion by tying his enterprise with the spreading of Christianity to the people of the East and the possible conversion of the Grand Khan. He likely emphasized the potential wealth that could flow to Castile, and he may have presented the idea that such wealth could finance a new and successful crusade to bring Jerusalem back into Christian hands and rebuild the temple. All we know is that the queen was favorably impressed with the Genoese sea captain and his visionary proposal and that this was the first of several meetings in which they would discuss his Enterprise of the Indies.

We also know that the timing of this first encounter between Columbus and the monarchs was less than ideal. The sovereigns were occupied with an expensive and protracted war against the Moors. The campaign against Granada was in its third year and would drag on for nearly seven more years, straining the financial resources of the monarchs. As Morison put it, "It was as if a polar explorer had tried to interest Lincoln in the conquest of the Antarctic about the time of the Battle of Gettysburg."[9]

The sovereigns declined Columbus's proposal, at least for the time being. But Father Marchena met with the queen the following month in Madrid and defended Columbus's proposal and urged the monarchs to give it serious consideration. They agreed to establish a special commission to study the proposal and appointed Fernando de Talavera to head the commission. Such special commissions were not uncommon and were specifically provided for in the law to deal with petitions that could not be properly decided by the royal council. Marchena may have argued that the very unusual nature of Columbus's proposal was beyond the expertise of the council and that an appropriate group of specialists should consider his request.

It was certainly not the outcome that Columbus had hoped for. In his first year in Castile, his proposal had been rejected by the royal council and by the sovereigns themselves. But the appointment of a special committee kept the door open, and apparently the door was open wide enough that Columbus was invited to spend considerable time with the court. He was with the court for several days during April in Guadalupe and may have traveled with them during much of the remainder of the year. His time with the court enabled him to begin to build a small network of influential friends. He was given a place to stay for a time in the home of Alonso de Quintanilla, the queen's treasurer, who introduced him to Don Pedro Gonzales de Mendoza, the archbishop of Toledo and grand cardinal of Spain. Much has been said about Columbus's skill as a mariner, but his ultimate success would also require that he become a skilled, persistent, and tenacious lobbyist. Though he could not know it at the time, an agonizing seven years of constant effort would be required to finally obtain the backing he needed to bring the Enterprise of the Indies to its marvelous and astounding reality.

The Talavera commission, appointed by the queen to study Columbus's proposal, met from 7 November 1486 to 30 January 1487, nearly three months, at the College of St. Stephen in Salamanca. Salamanca was and is a college town. Its university, founded in 1218, is the third oldest in Europe. In the fifteenth century it was already well established as a center of learning, and today it boasts an enrollment of thirty thousand students. Like other universities of its time (and like Cambridge and Oxford today), the university consisted of a number of resident colleges, one of which was the College of St. Stephen. It is likely that Columbus traveled to Salamanca to testify before the commission and that while there he stayed at the Dominican Convent of St. Stephen with Father Diego de Deza, tutor of Don Juan, the heir to the throne of Castile. A confidant of the sovereigns, Deza would succeed the infamous Tomás de Torquemada as the leader of the Spanish Inquisition.

In early May of 1487, Columbus received a stipend, or retainer, of 3,000 *maravedis* from the court, probably to reimburse him for his expenses in appearing before the commission in Salamanca. This initial payment was followed by three more payments of 3,000 *maravedis* each on 3 July, 27 August, and 15 October. The stipend was not insignificant—12,000 *maravedis* was the equivalent of the annual salary of a ship's captain—and this financial support was undoubtedly needed as Columbus prepared for and testified before hearings of the Talavera commission. It does not appear that Columbus had a home or any other source of income during these early years in Castile—he often stayed for extended periods in monasteries and was supported by stipends from the court and the generosity of friends. There is no evidence that he left his pursuit of the Enterprise of the Indies to do what he loved and what had earned him his living—sailing the seas.

Having seen his proposed enterprise summarily rejected by the Maritime Advisory Council in Portugal, it is likely that Columbus devoted a great deal of time and effort to refining his proposal and making his arguments before the Talavera commission. Notes in the margins of books that remain from his personal library suggest that he read many of the volumes multiple times as he honed his arguments. Based on the handwriting, some of these notes may have been made by his brother Bartholomew, suggesting that the two brothers worked closely together on this project.

Among Columbus's most heavily annotated books is his copy of *Imago mundi,* by the French geographer Pierre d'Ailly. The book is a comprehensive text on world geography, written about 1410, before the reappearance of Ptolemy's *Geography* in Western Europe. D'Ailly's picture of the world was a very extensive Asian landmass separated from Europe by a relatively narrow Atlantic, a view which, though incorrect, appealed to Columbus as it helped him make his argument:

> For, according to the philosophers and Pliny, the ocean which stretches between the extremity of further Spain and the eastern edge of India is of no great width. For it is evident that this sea is navigable in a very few days if the wind be fair, whence it follows that the sea is not so great that it can cover three quarters of the globe, as certain people figure it.[10]

The passage is underlined and annotated. Columbus made several additional notes in *Imago mundi* that reflect his view of the size of the Ocean Sea:

> Aristotle [says] between the end of Spain and the beginning of India is a small sea navigable in a few days.
>
> The end of Spain and the beginning of India are not far distant but close to one another. It is evident, that this sea can be crossed in a few days with a fair wind.
>
> Julius [Solinus] teaches that the entire sea from India up to Spain behind Africa is navigable.

Columbus's notes in *Imago mundi* also reflect his view that the Asian landmass was larger than most people believed:

> From the end of the Occident to the end of India by land it is much more than one half the [circumference of the] earth, that is 180° . . . [India] embraces a third of the habitable world.
>
> Esdras [says] six parts [of the globe] are habitable and the seventh is covered with water. Observe that the blessed Ambrose and Austin and many others considered Esdras a prophet.

Columbus's arguments had been "denounced" and "ridiculed"[11] and ultimately rejected by the Portuguese Maritime Advisory Committee and by the royal council of Castile. His proposal was now to be studied by a special committee appointed by the queen, and he would sharpen and augment his arguments, citing sources both secular and religious that seemed irrefutable.

Except for their meeting in Salamanca, we have no record of the proceedings or deliberations of the Talavera commission, nor do we know when the members of the commission issued their findings and recommendation to the sovereigns. Many historians assume that they did not make their report until the fall of Granada in 1492. It seems unlikely, however, that they would have deliberated for five years.[12] On 18 August 1487, the city of Málaga fell to the armies of Castile. On that same day, Columbus received a second stipend with an order to appear before the court at the royal camp in Málaga. It is probable that the commission made its report to the sovereigns at Málaga sometime before the fall of the city and that Columbus was summoned to Málaga to be informed of the recommendation of the commission.

The report of the commission was uniformly negative. According to Las Casas, the commission reported that Columbus's proposal was "impossible and vain and worthy of rejection" and advised the monarchs "that it was not a proper object for their royal authority to favor an affair that rested on such weak foundations, and which appeared uncertain and impossible to any educated person, however little learning he might have."[13] The commission enumerated its various arguments against Columbus's proposed enterprise:

- A voyage to Asia would take three years, not a matter of a few weeks.
- The Western Ocean is infinite and probably un-navigable.
- If Columbus were successful in reaching the Antipodes—the land opposite Europe on the globe—he could never get back.

- There are no antipodes, because, according to St. Augustine, the greater part of the globe is covered by water, not by land (the commission clearly gave the opinion of St. Augustine greater weight than they gave to that of Esdras).
- Of the five zones of earth, only three are inhabitable.
- If, in fact, there were unknown lands of value or unknown ways to reach them, they would have been discovered after so many centuries since the Creation.

The logic of the commission may not seem consistent or sound, certainly with the perspective of history, but their recommendation was clear and certain: the proposal was foolishness. Las Casas opined that the members of the commission failed to see the merits in Columbus's proposal because their minds were so full of incorrect notions:

> As it was said of Timothy, the famous flautist, if a student came to him, having studied and learned from another teacher, he charged that student double those that he taught from the beginning, because, he said, he had to teach them twice: first to unlearn what they knew, which was the hardest task, and then teach them the music and skill of the master.[14]

When Columbus met in Málaga with the sovereigns, they informed him that they were not willing to approve his proposal, but remarkably and for reasons about which we can only speculate, they indicated they might reconsider their decision once the campaign against the Moors reached a successful conclusion.

Once again, it was a blow but not a complete rejection. The willingness of the monarchs to consider his proposal at some later date suggests that although the Talavera commission characterized the proposal as far-fetched, unlikely to succeed, and certainly not worthy of a financial investment at a time when the resources of the kingdom were being strained by the prolonged war, there was something about the earnestness and determination of the man that convinced the sovereigns to keep the door open.

The fall of Málaga, the second largest city of the kingdom of Granada, gave hope that the long and expensive campaign of reconquest was nearing a successful conclusion. Columbus returned to Córdoba or Seville, where he received the last installment of his stipend in October.

Sometime during this period, Columbus became acquainted with Diego de Harana in Córdoba. Diego's father took care of Beatriz Enriquez de Harana, Diego's second cousin, who had been orphaned as a child. Columbus and the young Beatriz—she would have been about twenty years old and Columbus nearly thirty-four—were obviously attracted to each other: their son, Fernando, was born in August 1488. This was not, however, a fleeting relationship. Although it is clear that Columbus never married Beatriz, he remained close to her and her family throughout his life, and their relationship extended even beyond Columbus's death—his will and testament ensures her financial security. Diego de Harana accompanied Columbus on his First Voyage, and Beatriz's brother Pedro commanded a caravel on the Third Voyage. In a codicil to his will in 1506, Columbus instructed his legitimate son and heir, Diego, to ensure "that Beatriz Enriquez, mother of Don Fernando my son, is put in a way to live honorably, as a person to whom I am in so great debt, and thus for discharge of my conscience, because it weigheth much on my mind."[15]

When seen in the context of the times, Columbus's relationship with Beatriz was not unusual, nor was it considered particularly inappropriate. In an era when both political and ecclesiastical leaders openly bestowed wealth and title on their mistresses and illegitimate children, no one seems to have criticized Columbus for not marrying the mother of his son Fernando. Columbus's legitimate son, Diego, not only honored his father's wishes to provide financially for Beatriz but remembered her in his own will. And the illegitimate Fernando, who became his father's biographer, argued hard and successfully to protect the hereditary rights of his half brother, Diego.

But as for his Enterprise of the Indies, Columbus was playing a long and discouraging waiting game. Victory over the Moors was not coming quickly, and as a result the needed support of the sovereigns was not forthcoming. Columbus decided to take his proposal back to Portugal. He wrote King João II in late 1487 or early 1488, and the king responded warmly, even enthusiastically, calling Columbus "our particular friend" and praising his "industry and good talent."[16] The king guaranteed his safety and freedom from arrest (for whatever cause) upon his return to Portugal.

The Portuguese had continued to push their way south along the coast of Africa in hopes of finding a way around the continent and from there to the Indies. Bartholomew Dias, a Portuguese sailor about the same age as Columbus, had sailed from Portugal in October 1487 in an attempt to reach the Indies. His was only the latest attempt in numerous voyages to seek the elusive southern latitude that would at last allow passage around Africa and on to India, and the king may have been hedging his bets by inviting the Genoese mariner with the bold proposal to *buscar el Levante por el Poniente* to return to Lisbon.

Dias, in command of three ships, reached the furthest point of prior voyages (the twenty-second southern parallel) and continued to inch his way south, keeping the coast of Africa in sight. By Christmas of 1487 he had reached the mouth of the Orange River, the border between present-day Namibia and South Africa. He left a supply ship in a harbor on the coast and continued the voyage with two caravels. Sometime near year-end they were caught in a heavy gale from the northwest that drove the ships south, and on 6 January 1488, they lost sight of land. When the storm passed, Dias turned east in search of the coast, and when he failed to see land after several days, he altered his course to the north. On 3 February 1488, the lookouts spotted land to the northwest. The ships were about 150 miles east of the Cape of Good Hope at Mossel Bay. The first Europeans to round the southern tip of Africa, Dias and his crew continued up the African coast, Dias with the intent of pushing all the way to India, but the crew was unwilling to continue. The two ships reversed course and sailed back to the Cape, that rocky spit of land where three oceans—Atlantic, Indian, and Antarctic—meet. Then they made their long and weary way up the coast of Africa and back to Lisbon to report that they had successfully sailed around the tip of Africa.

King João II, of course, had no way of knowing of Dias's success, or even his survival, when he invited Columbus back to Lisbon. Columbus's presence in Portugal (or that of his brother Bartholomew—there is some disagreement about the handwriting) is evidenced by a note in the margin of Columbus's copy of *Imago mundi:*

> Note that in this year '88 in the month of December arrived in Lisbon Bartholomaeus Didacus captain of three caravels which the most serene king of Portugal had sent to try out the land in Guinea. He reported . . . that he had reached a promontory which he called *Cabo de Boa Esperança,* which we believe to be in Agesinba [Abyssinia/Ethiopia]. He says that in this place he discovered by the astrolabe that he was 45° below the equator [the actual latitude is 34° 21']. He has described his voyage and plotted it league by league on a marine chart in order to place it under the eyes of the said king. I was present in all of this.[17]

Dias originally named the cape *Cabo das Tormentas,* "Cape of Storms," for the storm that blew him around the tip of the continent, but the king quickly changed the name to Cape of Good Hope, for its discovery was indeed good hope for Portugal. At long last, the Portuguese had found their way around the African continent and a sea route to the Indies was within their grasp. For Columbus, the return of Dias dashed any hope that the Portuguese monarch would accept Columbus's proposal to reach the Indies by sailing west. Dias's success was, for Columbus, yet another *tormenta* that would hinder and delay the Enterprise of the Indies.

Discouraged as he might have been, Columbus refused to give up. He spent some time in Seville with his faithful supporter, Father Marchena, who by then was the guardian of all the Franciscan monasteries in the region. Sometime between October of 1488 and May of 1489, Marchena introduced Columbus to the duke of Medina Sidonia, Don Enrique de Guzman. The second duke of Medina Sidonia, Guzman had inherited his fortune from his father and was considered the wealthiest man in Spain. When Isabella visited Seville in 1477, she entered the city on an ornate barge draped with tapestries and gold ornaments owned by the duke, who met her at the dock and gave her the keys to the Alcazar. Guzman was a man of wealth and influence.[18] He had substantial maritime interests and had sent trade expeditions to the Canaries and Guinea, but he showed no interest in the proposal of the Genoese sea captain. A close ally of Isabella, he would have been aware that the queen had already deferred Columbus's proposal and saw no benefit in supporting a foreigner with a far-fetched scheme that had already been rejected by the best minds of the kingdom.

Columbus then approached the count of Medina Celi, Don Luis de la Cerda Medinaceli. The count owned a large merchant fleet at Puerto Santa María, across the harbor from Cádiz. In Medinaceli, Columbus found a sympathetic listener. The count was in the business of sponsoring commercial voyages and saw a chance to make a small investment that could yield a great return, although the chance may have been small. He provided Columbus with the necessities of life and proposed outfitting, at his own expense, three ships for the enterprise.

But Columbus's proposed expedition would go beyond known waters, and for that, royal approval was required. Medinaceli "urged the

King and Queen to approve the favors and the assistance that he, with his own funds and those of his family, was granting to a man who furnished so much good evidence that he would succeed in discovering such great things and riches."[19] The queen declined. If such an enterprise were to be undertaken, it would be undertaken by the crown. The Treaty of Alcáçovas had established the precedent that the rights to unknown lands belonged to the state, not to private investors. Medinaceli certainly understood that, and it is likely that his proposal to the queen was his way of helping Columbus to move the plan forward.

And Medinaceli's intervention did help move things forward. Las Casas states that Cardinal Mendoza, primate of Spain, approached the queen at the request of Medinaceli, and no more powerful or influential backer could have been found. Columbus had already enlisted the help of Father Diego Deza, tutor of the prince, and Alfonso de Quintanilla, treasurer of the court, and his lobbying efforts were beginning to show some results. On 12 May 1489, the sovereigns issued to Columbus a royal summons to appear once again in court:

> The King and Queen to the members of the Councils, ministers of justice, administrators, knights, squires, and honest men in all cities and villages of our kingdoms and possessions: Christopher Columbus must come to this court and to other places of our realm, to concern himself with some affairs to be concluded in our service; whereby we command you that when he should pass through said cities and villages, he be given hospitality and food, lodgings for himself and those with him, as well as maintenance. And you must not quarrel with him or with the others who may be with him. And you must do nothing to hinder him in any way, under pain of our justice and a fine of 10,000 *maravedis*. Given in the city of Córdoba the 12 May 1489. I the King. I the Queen. By order of the King and the Queen. Juan de Coloma.[20]

In the spring of 1489, the army was preparing to take the city of Baza, and the court had moved to Jaén, where it would be close to the army. King Ferdinand was with the army outside Baza, but Isabella received Columbus in Jaén. Her message was a repetition of what she had told Columbus earlier: once Granada was under the control of the sovereigns, she would turn her attention to his proposal. He was invited to remain with the court, and it appears that Quintanilla provided him with room and board.

While Columbus was with the court in Jaén, two Franciscan friars arrived from Jerusalem. They had been sent to Rome with a message for the Pope from Saladin of Egypt: unless the war against the Moors in the Iberian Peninsula were suspended and captured lands in Andalusia returned to the Moors, Saladin would take reprisals against the Christians and their property in Palestine. The Pope referred the friars to Isabella and Ferdinand, since it was they and not he who was at war with the Moors. The friars took their message to the sovereigns in July of 1489. Columbus almost certainly would have met and spoken with the friars, one of whom was from Italy, and the incident undoubtedly created in him an even greater sense of urgency regarding his enterprise, one of the objectives of which was to obtain the wealth necessary to mount a successful crusade, bring Jerusalem into Christian hands, and rebuild the temple. In Columbus's mind, his success would ultimately bring the Holy Land back under the control of Christianity.

How long Columbus remained with the court is unknown. Baza fell on 4 December; on the 22nd the monarchs entered Almería, and on the 30th they were in possession of Guadix. This should have brought the war to a quick conclusion, for the sovereigns had entered into an agreement in 1487 with Boabdil, the sultan of Granada, that he would hand over Granada upon the capitulation of his rivals in Almería. For Columbus, it must have seemed that his moment—after five long years in Castile—had at last arrived.

But Boabdil recanted and refused to surrender Granada, and the war resumed. With a quick victory now delayed, Columbus left the court. It was a time of bitter disappointment and distress. We can only guess where he went or what he did or how he managed to live. One chronicler claims he went to a monastery under the supervision of Father Marchena. He might have stayed with the Haranas in Córdoba. He might have returned to Puerto de Santa María and stayed with Medinaceli. Columbus himself gives no indication of where he was or what he was doing. It appears that it was a period of time that he preferred to forget.

The siege of Granada proved to be a lengthy affair. The court relocated to Seville in 1490, but as the months dragged on, Columbus became more frustrated. He had enlisted the help of many of the most influential men in the kingdom, but his proposal was of far less immediate interest to the monarchs than the conquest of Granada, and he could do no more. Las Casas says that he suffered

> a terrible, continued, painful and prolonged battle; a material one of weapons would not have been so sharp and horrendous as that which he had to endure from informing so many people of no understanding, although they presumed to know all about it, and replying patiently to many people who did not know him or had any respect for his person [and] receiving insulting speeches which afflicted his soul.[21]

Columbus was in his fortieth year and already beginning to suffer some health issues, primarily a painful form of arthritis that would afflict him until his death. He had devoted at least a decade to his enterprise. He had not been to sea since arriving in Castile six years earlier; for a sailor with the dream of a grand voyage, it must have been agony.

Discouraged, downhearted, but still determined, he returned to La Rábida in the summer of 1491 with the intent to go to France and present his case to the French king. At some point—either in 1491 or perhaps earlier—he asked his brother Bartholomew to go to London and solicit the support of Henry VII. If neither Portugal nor Castile would support his enterprise, he would find a sovereign somewhere who would.

At La Rábida, Columbus met Friar Juan Perez, the former confessor to the queen. Now the guardian of La Rábida, Perez urged Columbus not to give up on Castile yet and offered to approach the queen and request another audience for Columbus.

In July of 1491, the court moved to Santa Fe, a fortified camp constructed by the army as the headquarters for the siege of Granada. Perez sent a letter to the queen at Santa Fe and quickly received a response inviting him to the court to discuss the matter. Perez made the journey from Palos to Santa Fe, a distance of over 200 miles, by mule in the heat of the Andalusian summer. Columbus would later say, as he did of Marchena, that Perez was one of the few who truly believed in him and supported him in his enterprise.

At the urging of Perez, the queen wrote directly to Columbus, summoning him once again to court. She sent him a stipend of 20,000 *maravedis* that he might have suitable attire and transportation. It was probably August when Columbus arrived in Santa Fe. Once again, Columbus's proposal was submitted to a group of counselors who once again reviewed Columbus's calculations and plans and passed their recommendations to the royal council. Both Fernando and Las Casas report that Columbus presented his terms to the council. This suggests that, for the first time, his proposal may have passed the technical review, as the discussion now centered on the costs of the project and the titles and rights to be granted to Columbus. One senses a certain amount of frustration reflected in Columbus's demands: a hereditary title of nobility, governorship of all newly discovered lands, and a significant percentage of the wealth discovered. It is hard to escape the notion that Columbus was seeking redress for years of sustained insult and rejection. It is also a reflection of his own certainty in the success of his proposed enterprise. Still, his boldness is stunning. Essentially he said to the monarchs that if they would grant him the titles and honors to establish a noble family, together with the wealth to support and endow such a family, he would sail for Castile and Aragon. If not, he would go to France or England.

Fall passed into the mild Andalusian winter. While some of the defenders of Granada appeared willing to fight to the death, there was a growing sense within the walls that without the possibility of reinforcements, victory was impossible. Food supplies were running low in the city as a result of the prolonged siege by the armies of Castile. Finally, on 2 January 1492, Boabdil surrendered the city.

Columbus was still in Santa Fe and witnessed the victory. King Ferdinand entered the city in a formal procession, carrying a large silver cross from Pope Sixtus IV. Columbus participated in the procession:

> On the second day of the month of January I saw the Royal Standards of Your Highnesses placed by force of arms on the towers of the Alhambra, which is the fortress of the said city; and I saw the Moorish King come out to the gates of the city and kiss the Royal Hands of Your Highnesses.[22]

The war was over, and the Reconquista complete. Over the ramparts of the Alhambra flew the standard of Castile with its motto, *Unum ovile et unus pastor* ("one flock and one shepherd"). The sovereigns now turned their attention, as promised, to Columbus's proposal. Within days of the surrender of Granada, Columbus was informed that his proposed Enterprise of the Indies was, firmly and finally, declined. The monarchs confirmed the decision in a personal audience with Columbus, an audience which they no doubt intended to be their last with him.

So that was it. For nearly seven years Columbus had been in Castile, lobbying the royal court, defending his proposal again and again, and meeting on multiple occasions with the sovereigns themselves, always with a glimmer of hope. Now it was over. Columbus packed up his maps and books, saddled up his mule, and headed towards Córdoba with the intent of going to France.

Then, suddenly, everything changed. No sooner had Columbus left the queen's presence than Luis de Santángel, *escribano de ración*—"keeper of the privy purse," meaning that he looked after the sovereigns' personal financial affairs—approached the queen and urged her to reconsider. It is likely that Talavera, Deza, and other supporters of Columbus participated in the conversation.[23] No one present made a record of the discussion, so we are left to guess at the arguments presented. Santángel and the others may have reasoned that while the scientists had recommended rejection of the foreigner's proposal, they had not been able refute many of his arguments. They may have noted that not everyone familiar with the project opposed it—several powerful, knowledgeable, and reliable individuals supported Columbus. Furthermore, the expense of the venture was modest, and, aside from the funds necessary to mount the expedition, Columbus asked nothing unless he was successful. If he was successful, his price was small compared to the wealth and glory that would flow to the sovereigns. Suppose he really did go to France, and sailed for France, and was successful?

Santángel, accountant that he was, may have reminded the sovereigns that the town of Palos owed the crown a fine that could be satisfied by providing two of the three ships requested by Columbus. Columbus himself had offered to provide one-eighth of the cost of the voyage, and though he was poor and without income, he seemed to be well connected to such wealthy Genoese families as the Spinolas and Di Negros.

Then there was the persona of Columbus himself. More powerful than his maps and reasoned arguments was the calm and unwavering assurance of a man who had no doubts. While the scientists and mathematicians applied logic, Columbus was a man of the sea, a man who had personally sailed all the seas that had been sailed. Unlike the members of the court, who had for the most part spent their lives in Castile and Aragon, Columbus had traveled far and wide. He had seen Africa, the Atlantic islands, the islands of the Aegean Sea, England, Ireland, and even Iceland. And he exuded a supreme confidence that he could yet travel to new and unknown lands.

Whatever the arguments, the queen revisited her decision. She dispatched a royal messenger who overtook Columbus just four miles beyond Santa Fe and presented him with a summons to return to the court. Columbus turned his mule around and returned for one more audience with the queen whose name would ever after be associated with his.

Chapter 5

PREPARATIONS

With this authority Columbus departed, as has been said, and went to
the village of Palos de Moguer, where he prepared for his voyage.[1]

GONZALO FERNÁNDEZ DE OVIEDO

It took most of the next three months, from mid-January to mid-April 1492, to negotiate and finalize the details of the agreement between Columbus and the crown. The cost of outfitting the expedition was about 2 million *maravedis,* the equivalent of approximately half a million dollars today.[2] In addition, payroll costs were about 250,000 *maravedis* a month. It seems a relatively modest sum for an enterprise with such promise. The monarchs had spent much more than that on the wedding of their daughter Isabella to Prince Afonso of Portugal in 1490; in 1501 they spent an estimated 60 million *maravedis* on the marriage of their daughter Catherine to Arthur, Prince of Wales. But in 1492 the protracted war with the Moors had depleted the treasury of Castile. Luis de Santángel, in addition to being the queen's accountant, was treasurer of Santa Hermandad, a quasipublic police force with its own substantial endowment, and he borrowed 1,140,000 *maravedis* from the endowment (which was later repaid through the sale of indulgences). A consortium put together by Quintanilla raised an additional 500,000 *maravedis;* Columbus was a part of this consortium and probably contributed 250,000 *maravedis,* which he may have borrowed from friends in Genoa or perhaps from Medinaceli. The remaining funds were provided from the payment in kind of the fine of Palos.[3]

The primary document outlining the agreement between the crown and Columbus is known as the Capitulations of Santa Fe. Friar Juan Perez represented Columbus in the negotiations and Juan de Coloma, secretary to the sovereigns, represented the monarchs. The document was signed on 17 April. A second document, known as the Title or the Commission, was signed on 30 April. Columbus received everything he had asked for. The sovereigns agreed to grant Columbus, subject to his successful return, the title of Admiral of the Ocean Sea and Viceroy and Governor of all islands and any mainland that he discovered. These titles were to be hereditary. In addition, he was granted free of tax one-tenth of all gold, silver, pearls, gems, spices, and other merchandise obtained from the newly discovered lands. He was also granted the option of paying an eighth part of all subsequent voyages to the new lands in exchange for taking an eighth part of the profits from such voyages.

The concessions made by the crown were extraordinary. The title of viceroy was unprecedented in Castile, but the title of Admiral of Castile belonged to the house of Mendoza. As Admiral of the Ocean Sea, Columbus, the immigrant son of a weaver, would be elevated to a position on a par with that of one of the wealthiest and most powerful noble families of the kingdom.

In addition to the Capitulations of Santa Fe and the Title, the sovereigns provided Columbus with three identical letters that he could use as a means of introduction to the sovereigns of foreign lands:[4]

To the most serene prince _____ Our very dear friend,

Ferdinand and Isabella, King and Queen of Castile, Aragon, León, Sicily, etc. greetings and increase of good fortune. . . . We have learned with joy of Your esteem and high regard for Us and Our Nation and of Your great eagerness to be informed about things with Us. Wherefore, we have resolved to send you Our Noble Captain, Christopherus Colon, bearer of these, from whom You may learn of Our good health and Our prosperity.

I the King   I the Queen

It was anticipated that one of these letters would be given to the Grand Khan, whom Columbus mentions specifically in the introduction to his journal of the First Voyage.

Formalities concluded and documents in hand, Columbus left Granada on 12 May 1492 and headed for Palos, the place where he had first entered Spain nearly seven years earlier. He spent the summer preparing, at last, for the great voyage: obtaining ships, supplies, captains, and crew. The sovereigns sent a letter to the mayor of Palos instructing the citizens to provide two ships at their expense. Those two ships, the *Niña* and *Pinta,* would go down in history. For his flagship, Columbus chartered a somewhat larger ship, known as a *nao,* that had been built in Galicia. Columbus named it the *Santa María.*

No contemporary drawings or plans exist of Columbus's ships, so scholars have been left to rely on comments made by Columbus and others, together with information about similar ships of the time, to approximate the size and construction of these famous ships. The *Niña* was the smallest of the ships and probably had a deck fifty to sixty feet long. The *Pinta* was slightly larger, and the deck of the *Santa María* was perhaps seventy-five feet in length.[5] The ships had open decks, with the exception of a captain's quarters on the *Santa María,* and the space in the hold was taken up with the storage of supplies. The men typically slept on deck in the open. Because the decks were cambered to allow

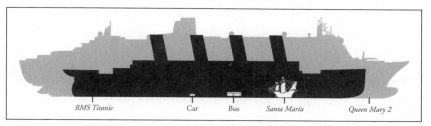

The Santa María *compared to later ships and other means of transportation.*

water to run off, the only flat spot for sleeping was typically on top of the main hatch in the center of the deck, a spot that was often crowded with sailors trying to get some rest. The discovery of Indian hammocks during the First Voyage would prove a boon to sailors for centuries to come.

Like all ships of that era, these were single-hull ships. All that separated the men and supplies from the sea was the thickness of a single set of wooden planks with caulking in the seams and joints. Termites, poor caulking, sharp rocks, and a dozen other dangers could be deadly. On his Fourth Voyage, Columbus's ships became so damaged from shipworms—a form of clam that burrows into wood—that he could not keep them afloat.

Columbus never liked the *Santa María.* It was the slowest of the three ships and difficult to maneuver. He wrote in the journal of the First Voyage that it was "very sluggish and not suited to the work of exploration."[6] The *Niña* became his favorite of the three ships, and he took it on both the Second and Third Voyages. Morison estimates that the *Niña* logged more than 25,000 miles under the command of Columbus.[7]

But despite Columbus's complaints about the *Santa María,* all three ships were sound and solidly built. In his introduction to the journal of the First Voyage, Columbus writes that the ships were *muy aptos para semejante fecho,* "well suited for such an undertaking."[8]

Recruiting officers and sailors was probably a much more difficult task than obtaining the ships. Columbus was relatively unknown in Palos, at least among the common sailors. He was a foreigner recruiting sailors for a voyage to an unknown destination for an uncertain duration. Columbus would captain the flagship and serve as captain general of the little fleet, but he needed locally known and respected captains for the other ships. He found his captains in the Pinzón brothers of Palos. Martín Alonso Pinzón was between forty-six and fifty years old in 1492, a few years older than Columbus. He was "an able person, known to be knowledgeable and expert in matters of navigation. He was also well-to-do, with good family connections and one of the most illustrious people of that time."[9] He signed on as captain of the *Pinta,* and his younger brother, Vicente Yáñez Pinzón, age thirty, captained the *Niña*. Two other family members joined the crew—a brother, Francisco, was master of the *Pinta,* and a cousin, Diego, sailed on the *Pinta.* The Pinzóns were well known and well respected. Without their support, Columbus would have had great difficulty recruiting sailors. Although an enduring conflict would arise between them and Columbus, their participation made the First Voyage possible.

In addition to the Pinzón family of Palos, Columbus garnered support from the Niños, a seafaring family of nearby Moguer. At least three members of the Niño family sailed on the First Voyage. Juan, the oldest brother, owned the *Niña* and sailed as its master. Peralonso Niño was pilot of the *Santa María,* and nineteen-year-old Francisco joined his older brothers for the voyage. Two other relatives of the Niño family also joined the crew: Cristóbal Quintero was the owner of the *Pinta,* and Juan Quintero sailed as boatswain on the *Pinta.* Juan Quintero is the only member of the crew known to have sailed on all four of Columbus's voyages.

The three ships had a combined crew of ninety men. Painstaking research has identified the names of eighty-seven of these original crew members.[10] Four of them, in addition to Columbus, were foreigners:

a Genoese, a Venetian, a Portuguese, and a Calabrian. At least eight of the crew were from the Basque country, including Juan de la Cosa, who was the owner and master of the *Santa María*. But the ships were largely manned by local sailors from Palos and nearby towns, a tribute to the local reputation of the Pinzón brothers.[11]

The royal court moved to Barcelona in the summer of 1492, and Columbus may have traveled to Barcelona to review and finalize some details of the expedition, for he had knowledge of a letter delivered that summer to the sovereigns from the Genoese deputies. He quoted from the letter several years later: "I call earnestly to the attention of you, the most noble sovereigns, some very important things that are to be observed, since indeed we did read that Joachim the Abbot of Southern Italy has foretold that he is to come from Spain who is to recover again the fortunes of Zion."[12] For Columbus, this was additional confirmation that his journey was the fulfillment of prophecy.

It is unlikely that the rest of the crew shared Columbus's absolute confidence in the ultimate success of the voyage. While there would certainly have been a sense of excitement and adventure about undertaking a voyage to parts unknown, doubts and dissension would arise before they reached the Indies. The men were all experienced sailors, but none—including Columbus—had ever sailed as far into the unknown as they were about to go. Their fears were likely three-fold. First, that the ocean was much wider than the captain general estimated (it was). Second, that they would therefore run out of food and fresh water (they didn't). Third, that even if they made a successful crossing from west to east, they might not be able to make the return journey east (and not all of them did).

The success of their voyage, especially the safe return home of two of the three ships, attests to the competency of the crew and their officers. Several of the original crew members sailed with Columbus on later voyages, suggesting their confidence in him.

By the end of July, all was ready for the great Enterprise of the Indies to begin. Columbus had spent at least eight years trying to get royal approval for his proposal, first in Portugal and then in Castile. Just four months elapsed between the signing of the Capitulations of Santa Fe and the eve of the voyage. One can only imagine the thoughts and feelings of Columbus on the night of 2 August 1492 as the three little ships sat in in the harbor at Palos ready to begin their journey before sunrise the next morning. After so many years of rejection and ridicule, he was about to turn the key and unlock the chains of the Ocean Sea.

For the ninety men sailing with Columbus, that last night in Palos would have been a restless night. In early August the temperatures in Palos average in the low 90s Fahrenheit during the day and fall below 70 at night—the heat of the Andalusian summer moderated by the sea breezes. What thoughts crossed the minds of these men that summer night? Did they wonder about the dangers of the journey, about the leadership of the charismatic foreigner whose idea this was? Did they think of family, of children, and the possibility that they would never see them again?

What we can assume with a high degree of certainty is that none of these men comprehended the impact that this voyage, just the latest of many voyages for most of the crew, would have on the world. It is unlikely that even Columbus, with his spiritual steadfastness in his mission, could really comprehend its impact. No voyage of any man in all of recorded history since Noah would change the world as certainly and completely as the voyage that this Genoese mariner was about to undertake.

THE FIRST CROSSING

There are tides in the affairs of men, and this was one of them.[1]

SAMUEL ELIOT MORISON

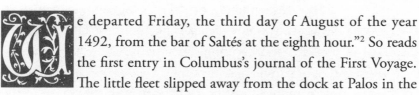e departed Friday, the third day of August of the year 1492, from the bar of Saltés at the eighth hour."[2] So reads the first entry in Columbus's journal of the First Voyage. The little fleet slipped away from the dock at Palos in the predawn light, about half an hour before sunrise. It was a still morning with no wind, and they floated with the outgoing tide down the Río Tinto to its confluence with the Rio Saltés (now known as the Odiel). They would have passed La Rábida about the time the friars were chanting their morning prayers:

> *Deo Patri sit gloria,*
> *eiusque soli filio,*
> *cum Spritu Paraclito*
> *et nunc et in perpetuum.*

"May the glory of God the Father
and His only Son
with the Spirit of the Comforter
be with us for ever and ever."

At eight in the morning the tide carried them over the sand bar at the entrance to the Saltés, where they entered the open sea, caught a "strong sea breeze," and set their course for the Canary Islands.

It was not yet a common practice for ship captains to maintain a daily log of travel and position. Nevertheless, Columbus maintained a daily journal, generally referred to now as the *Diario.*[3] The *Diario* was much more than a traditional log recording weather, position, distances, and speed. It was a journal in the broader sense—a daily record not just of what happened on board ship but of Columbus's thoughts and observations. Fernandez-Armesto opined that the *Diario* alone is sufficient "to establish Columbus as a man of extraordinary character and exceptional gifts." He added that it is "unique in the annals of the sea; no master ever compiled so detailed a log; no commander of the day ever wrote such copious reports; no navigator of that era . . . displayed such talent for observation, such sensitivity to the elements, such appreciation of nature."[4]

The original manuscript of the *Diario* was probably given to the sovereigns at Barcelona after the voyage, and at least one copy was made shortly thereafter. Bartolomé de Las Casas had a copy, from which he made an abstract, often quoting long passages from the original in his *History of the Indies.* Fernando Columbus also had a copy of the *Diario,* which he used in writing his *History of the Admiral.* Regrettably, neither the original nor any copy has survived. The abstract made by Las Casas is housed in the National Library in Madrid and has been translated into several languages and published. Most of what we know about Columbus's great voyage of discovery comes from this document.

Columbus begins his *Diario* with an introduction, or preface, directed to the monarchs. This introduction tells us a great deal about the man, his vision, and his objectives, as well as about the times in which he lived:

In the Name of Our Lord Jesus Christ

Whereas, most Christian and very noble and excellent and powerful princes, King and Queen of the Spains and of the islands of the sea, our Lords: This present year of 1492, after Your Highnesses had brought to an end the war with the Moors who ruled in Europe and had concluded the war in the very great city of Granada, where this present year on the second day of the month of January I saw the Royal Standards of Your Highnesses placed by force of arms on the towers of the Alhambra, which is the fortress of the said city; and I saw the Moorish King come out to the gates of the city and kiss the Royal Hands of Your Highnesses and of the Prince my Lord; and later in that same month, because of the report that I had given to Your Highnesses about the lands of India and about a prince who is called "Grand Khan," which means in our Spanish language "King of Kings"; how, many times he and his predecessors had sent to Rome to ask for men learned in our Holy Faith in order that they might instruct him in it and how the Holy Father had never provided them; and thus so many peoples were lost, falling into idolatry and accepting false and harmful religions; and Your Highnesses, as Catholic Christians and Princes, overseers and promoters of the Holy Christian Faith, and enemies of the false doctrine of Mahomet and of all idolatries and heresies, you thought of sending me, Christopher Columbus, to the said regions of India to see the said princes and the peoples and the lands, and the characteristics of the lands and of everything, and to see how their conversion to our Holy Faith might be undertaken. And you commanded that I should not go to the East by land, by which way it is customary to go, but by the route to the West, by which route we do now know for certain that anyone previously has passed. So . . . in the same month of January Your Highnesses commanded me to go, with a suitable fleet, to the said regions of India. . . . And for this purpose I thought of writing on this whole voyage, very diligently, all that I would do and see and experience, as will be seen further along. Also, my Lord Princes, besides writing down each night whatever I experience during the day and each day what I sail during the night, I intend to make a new sailing chart. In it I will locate all of the sea and the lands of the Ocean Sea in their proper places under their compass bearings and, moreover, compose a book and similarly record all of the same in a drawing, by latitude from the equinoctial line by longitude from the west; and above all it is important that I forget sleep and pay much attention to navigation in order thus to carry out these purposes, which will be great labor.[5]

The introduction makes it clear that Columbus's destination was the Orient, the kingdom of the Grand Khan, and that the purpose of the voyage was not just to find the great Oriental kingdoms but "to see how their conversion to our Holy Faith might be undertaken." Taking the gospel to other lands and the isles of the sea would continue to be one of the great objectives of Columbus's life. His introduction and his taking the time and making the effort to write the *Diario* indicate that he had a great sense of occasion, that he knew this voyage would matter, and that keeping a careful record would, as the Spanish say, *vale la pena*—"be worth the effort."

Part of the genius of Columbus's voyage was his decision to sail to the Canary Islands. The Portuguese had attempted to cross the Ocean Sea by setting out from the Azores, a logical point of embarkation because the islands are at the westernmost edge of Europe. Furthermore, at the latitude of the Azores, the prevailing winds are from the west, providing sailors assurance that, once across the ocean, they could safely return. But every such attempt had failed. In fact, there is evidence that King João II, after rejecting Columbus's proposal, authorized an expedition to sail west across the ocean. The documents relating to that journey make it clear that the attempt was launched from the Azores and failed. The Azores were controlled by Portugal, and had King João II and the Maritime Advisory Council approved Columbus's proposal in 1484, it is likely that Columbus would have sailed from the Azores. And he too would have failed.

The Azores are located at about the thirty-eighth parallel, while the Canaries are nearly ten degrees further south, a distance of nearly 700 miles. At this lower latitude, the easterly trade winds begin, and those winds would propel Columbus's little fleet across the Ocean Sea. Columbus makes no mention of the prevailing winds in his writings prior to the First Voyage, but he was a keen observer of winds and currents, and having sailed down the coast of Africa as far as the fifth parallel, it is likely that he planned the route of the First Voyage to take advantage of the easterlies that blow at more southern latitudes and the westerlies (for the return voyage) that are found further north. In any event, the existence of the trade winds and the political affiliation of the Atlantic islands combined to make possible this momentous voyage.

The trip between Spain and the Canaries generally required about eight to ten days and was known for its rough seas. It provided Columbus's little fleet with a good "shakedown" cruise, always valuable to determine weaknesses in the ships and the crew. The fleet made good time—they sighted the nearest of the Canary Islands with only six days at sea. The crew proved able but the ships less so. On 6 August, just three days out from Palos, the rudder of the *Pinta* broke. A day at sea was spent with the crew making some temporary repairs, and Columbus determined to set a course for Grand Canary, where he was likely to find facilities to repair the rudder or perhaps find a new ship. The ships were becalmed for two days as they neared Las Palmas, and when the wind finally picked up, Columbus decided to take the *Santa*

María and the *Niña* further west to the island of Gomera while the *Pinta* made its way to Las Palmas for repairs.

When the *Pinta* did not show up at Gomera after several days, the *Santa María* and the *Niña* returned to Las Palmas. The crippled *Pinta* had arrived only the previous day, and while her rudder was being repaired, Columbus decided to alter *Niña's* large lateen (triangular) sails to square sails. The change made the *Niña's* speed more nearly equal to that of the other ships, and the smaller square sails were less dangerous for the crew to maneuver. Repairs on the *Pinta* were finished, the new sails were in place on the *Niña,* and the three ships sailed again on 1 September, arriving at San Sebastian in Gomera on 2 September. They spent four days at San Sebastian taking on additional supplies, including water and firewood, anticipating that their next landfall would be in the Orient. Early on the morning of 6 September, the fleet weighed anchor for the last time in the Old World and set out upon the unknown sea bound for unknown lands. Three days later, on 9 September, the last view of the ancient volcano of Tenerife disappeared below the eastern horizon, and the three small ships had the uncharted ocean to themselves.

Columbus's navigational technology on the open sea was primitive at best. The most useful instrument was the compass, which consisted of a magnetized needle on a circular card marked with thirty-two directional points. Second only to the compass was a sand glass, which marked each half-hour. The glass was usually hung from a beam so that the flow of sand would not be affected by the rocking of the ship. Once the last grain of sand slid into the bottom of the glass, a ship's boy would turn the glass and the officer on deck would mark a stroke on a slate. This was not a particularly accurate way to keep time, but it was the best technology available on a ship—no mechanical clocks were reliable enough to keep time on a moving ship. Theoretically, corrections could be made by determining noon from observing the sun, but this too was prone to error as the ship rocked back and forth.

Columbus also carried with him a common quadrant, designed to help determine latitude. It consisted of a quarter-circle made from wood with sights along one edge through which the user would line up a heavenly body (usually the North Star), a 90-degree scale on the arc, and a silk plumb line that hung from the angle and marked the degrees, enabling the user to determine how high the star was above the horizon. The angle at which the star appeared could be used to calculate the latitude. The quadrant was a primitive tool and was not designed for use on a rolling ship. Rather, it was intended for use on land with a tripod or similar support in order to locate positions for mapping. Columbus was not particularly skilled at making accurate readings with a quadrant. In his note regarding São Jorge da Mina in Guinea, he states that São Jorge lies below the equator when, in fact, it lies five degrees above the equator. During his voyages in the Caribbean, his quadrant readings were equally inaccurate.[6]

Determining longitude was even more problematic. The only known scientific methodology for determining longitude at the time was to observe the timing of an eclipse. Almanacs were available that gave the predicted hours of total eclipses at Nuremburg and Salamanca. By observing the local time of an eclipse, one could determine the distance from Nuremburg or Salamanca, as each hour of difference equates to fifteen degrees of longitude. But as a practical matter, it was difficult to use this method to make an accurate determination of longitude. It required knowing with some precision the time of day at which the eclipse was observed, and the lack of accurate clocks compromised the calculations. Columbus had two opportunities in the New World to determine his longitude using this method—first in 1494 and again in 1503—and was wrong in both cases.

He was not alone in finding it difficult to use this methodology with any degree of accuracy. Scholars in Mexico City used two eclipses of the moon in 1541 to determine the longitude of the city and established the longitude at 120° 38'—an error of about 25½°, or 1,450 miles. The problem of determining longitude was not solved until the late eighteenth century when John Harrison, an English clockmaker, developed a clock that could accurately keep time on a moving ship. By carrying two clocks, one set on Greenwich time and the other adjusted daily with a noon reading of the sun, a reasonably accurate estimate of longitude could be made. But that breakthrough was still two centuries distant.

How, then, did Columbus navigate? It was one thing to sail west until he found land but quite another to return home and then repeat the journey a second, third, and fourth time. Columbus depended primarily on a method used by sailors of all time and the only workable method in the fifteenth century: dead reckoning. Dead reckoning consists of simply laying down the course traveled each day on a chart by estimating the distance traveled and using the compass to determine the direction of travel. Sailing in uncharted seas, Columbus had little more than a blank sheet of paper as his initial chart. He had his compass to determine the direction of travel, the sand glass to estimate the time, and his best guess to determine his speed. Estimating time and speed, he simply multiplied the two estimates to obtain distance traveled and marked it on his chart.

In 1939, Samuel Eliot Morison and a team from Harvard University attempted to trace the route of the First Voyage using only the primitive technology and methods available to Columbus. Morison opined, "No man alive [today], limited to the instruments and means at Columbus's disposal, could obtain anything near the accuracy of his results."[7] While sailors even today continue to use dead reckoning, they can make adjustments with modern technology. Columbus had no means to check or adjust his dead reckoning, and on an ocean crossing, an error of half a degree can mean a landfall 250 miles off course. In 1991, a careful reconstruction of the First Voyage based on the information in the *Diario* concluded that Columbus's dead reckoning on both the outward and return passages was 99.7 percent accurate.[8] His ability to find his way in an open ocean with no landmarks, no accurate clock, and no fixed point against which to estimate speed was remarkable. Las Casas declared, "Christopher Columbus surpassed all of his contemporaries in the art of navigation," and virtually all students of Columbus since Las Casas agree. Paolo Taviani says simply, "He was an exceptionally gifted sailor."[9] Michele da Cuneo, who accompanied Columbus on the Second Voyage, wrote, "By a simple look at the night sky, he would know what route to follow or what weather to expect."[10] He had what the great French explorer Jean-Baptiste Charcot called *le sens marin*—"that mysterious and inborn gift that allows you to pick the right route in the middle of the ocean."[11]

Where did Columbus get this *sens marin,* this uncanny and seemingly unequaled ability to navigate an uncharted sea, not just once but over and over again? Orson Hyde, speaking in the old Salt Lake Tabernacle on 4 July 1854, declared that Moroni "was with him [Columbus] on the stormy deep, calmed the troubled elements, and guided his frail vessel to the desired haven."[12] Columbus himself declared, "I prayed to the most merciful Lord concerning my desire, and he gave me the spirit and the intelligence for it. He gave me abundant skill in the mariner's arts, an adequate understanding of the stars, and of geometry and arithmetic."[13] His understanding of the stars, geometry, and arithmetic were adequate at best, but his skill in the mariner's arts was unsurpassed.

The little fleet kept a steady course due west from the Canaries, and while Columbus does not give any indication that he was "racing against the clock," the fleet moved with remarkable speed. Ships in that era typically made 3 to 5 knots (about 5 to 6 miles per hour) in a mild breeze and 9 knots with a strong breeze. For five consecutive days in October, Columbus averaged just under 6 knots (142 miles per day) and on one day averaged nearly 8 knots (182 miles per day). While it

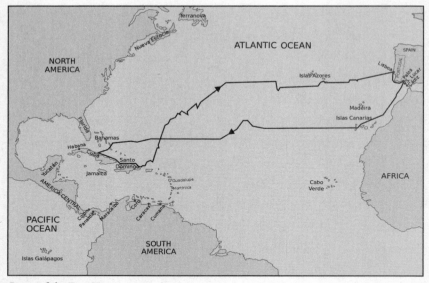

Route of the First Voyage.

was common for captains to reduce speed after dark, Columbus seems to have kept his ships moving as fast as possible around the clock. He had limited supplies and an unknown distance to travel.

Ten days out from San Sebastian, the fleet entered an area known as the Saragasso Sea—a broad section of the Atlantic where the surface is covered with gulf weed (saragassum). For several days the gulf weed was so thick that the surface of the ocean appeared solid, and the appearance gave concern to the captains and sailors. But the little ships cut through without hindrance. Columbus's *Diario* contains the first record of this unusual feature of the Atlantic Ocean.

On 23 September, a Sunday, Columbus noted, "Since the sea had been calm and smooth the men complained, saying that since in that region there were no rough seas, it would never blow for a return to Spain." It would not be the last complaint of the men, who would become increasingly wary of their chances of seeing home again. But soon after they voiced their complaints, the sea rose up in large swells, which Columbus viewed as a gift from heaven. The appearance of the high seas quieted the men's complaints, and the journey continued. Columbus recorded that "the high sea was very necessary for me" and considered it as significant to his success as the signs given to Israel when they complained about Moses.[14]

At about sunset on 25 September, nineteen days out from San Sebastian, Martín Pinzón cried out that he could see land from the deck of the *Pinta*. Men on all three ships "climbed the masts and into the rigging and all affirmed that it was land, and so it appeared to the Admiral, and that it was about 25 leagues off."[15] By the next day, however, they realized that what they had seen were clouds on the horizon. They sailed on. "The sea was like a river; the breezes sweet and very soft."[16]

By the end of September the fleet and its crew had been beyond sight of land for over three weeks. It is highly unlikely that anyone on board the ships had ever been in the open ocean so long. A sailor might go for three or four days without seeing land while sailing from Spain to the Canaries, but anything more than a few days was unusual, particularly in uncharted waters. The great Portuguese explorers rarely lost sight of land on their voyages down the coast of Africa. Not surprisingly, tensions were beginning to mount.

On 1 October there was a heavy rain, and the crews were able to refill the water barrels. On 6 October, Martín Pinzón advised Columbus to change the course to the southwest, for he was certain the island of Japan lay in that direction. But Columbus continued due west. On 7 October, the *Niña,* which was running ahead of the other ships, raised a flag and fired a gun, the prearranged signal for land. But it proved to be another false landfall. Later that same day large flocks of birds were seen overhead, flying to the southwest. "Because the Admiral knew that most of the islands that the Portuguese hold they discovered by birds, the Admiral agreed to leave the route west and head west-southwest."[17] The course change was made an hour before sunset.

Since leaving the Canary Islands, Columbus had recorded two figures in the *Diario* for the distance traveled each day. Las Casas, puzzled
by the two sets of figures, opined that Columbus fabricated the lower
figures and disclosed them to the crew in hopes of avoiding a mutiny
that might ensue if the crew members felt they were getting too far
from Europe. However, Las Casas was almost certainly mistaken in
his explanation. The reduced set of figures in the *Diario* appears to be
simply a conversion of the original distance estimates into Portuguese
maritime leagues, a measure with which the crew would have been
more familiar.[18]

By any reckoning, however, they had sailed much, much further
than any known ship, and the men were becoming increasingly restless.
On 9 or 10 October the concerns of the men flared into the open.
Columbus records simply that "the men could no longer stand it; they
complained of the long voyage."[19] But it was far more than complain-
ing. He referred again to the event on the return voyage when it appeared that a hurricane-force gale would destroy the ships before their
return. On that occasion he wrote in the *Diario* that God "had delivered him on the outward voyage, when he had greater reason to fear
from his troubles with the sailors and people that he took with him,
who all, with one voice, were determined to go back and to rise against
him in protest."[20]

A series of depositions given many years later, part of the lawsuits
between the crown and the heirs of Columbus in which the descendants of Martín Pinzón claimed that Pinzón should be given full credit
for the discovery of the New World, give conflicting accounts of the
events of 9–10 October 1492, particularly with regard to a council
held among the captains of the three ships. Sorting through the conflicting stories and accounts, Morison concludes that on 9 October,
when the winds were light and the ships were traveling at only about
2 knots, the Pinzón brothers came aboard the *Santa María,* where they

"held a more or less stormy conference with Columbus in his cabin, demanded that the search for land be abandoned, and that advantage be taken of the southerly breeze to start home." Morison concludes that Columbus convinced his captains to carry on for three more days and that the captains returned to their respective ships. On the morning of 10 October the wind picked up and the ships sped along at 7 knots. The renewed easterly winds fueled fears among the crew that a return voyage would be impossible, and the men confronted Columbus "with one voice" demanding that he turn back.[21]

This was where the enterprise came the closest to failure—a similar revolt by Dias's crew had forced him to turn back rather than sail on to India after rounding the Cape of Good Hope. Columbus's record of how he dealt with the crisis is simple and straightforward: he "encouraged them as best he could, giving them good hope of the benefits that they would be able to secure."[22] It appears from later reports that he gave the men the same promise he had made to the Pinzón brothers: he agreed that if land were not found in three more days, he would turn back. But "then he added that it was useless to complain since he had come to find the Indies and thus had to continue the voyage until he found them, with the help of Our Lord." A contemporary noted that Columbus "was charming when he wished to be and very testy when annoyed."[23] No doubt both of these characteristics were manifested in his exchange with the mutinous sailors. In any event, he was immovable.

One can hardly blame the sailors for their concerns nor consider them cowardly for their desire to turn around and head home. They had experienced two false landfalls, they had been in open ocean at least twice as long as any previous expedition, and by every reasonable measure they were beyond where they had been told they would find land. They had passed the 65th meridian and were north of Puerto Rico. If one looks at a map today and blocks out the Americas—unknown to

Columbus and his crew—one might begin to sense the growing despair, even fear, felt by the crew. Morison characterized the attempted mutiny with these observations:

> It was . . . the inevitable conflict between a man of one great, compelling idea and those who did not share it in anything like the same degree . . . Their issue with their commander was the eternal one between imagination and doubt, between the spirit that creates and the spirit that denies.[24]

Faith vs. doubt

Columbus was unwavering, and his vision prevailed. When Orson Hyde said that Moroni "calmed the troubled elements," he might well have been referring to the events of 9–10 October 1492.

The three days which Columbus bought from the Pinzón brothers on 9 October proved to be exactly what he needed, and the change of course on the evening of 7 October proved critical. Had Columbus continued due west, he would not have seen land for at least an additional day. The new course brought them to landfall on 12 October.

Much has been written about why Columbus changed course. Martin Pinzón had suggested the change on the 6th; Columbus mentions seeing the flocks of birds flying to the southwest on the 7th and changed course that evening. Was he following Pinzón's advice? Was he following the birds? In any event, the change in course was providential. Without it, Columbus would not have sighted land until his three-day window with the men had passed, and the voyage might well have failed.

On Thursday the 11th the wind picked up, and the little fleet sped along, logging 78 miles during daylight hours. The men saw several signs that gave them encouragement that land was near. The crew of the *Pinta* saw what they described as a "small stick that appeared to have been worked with iron." From the *Niña* they sighted a "small stick loaded with barnacles." These and a few other items were sufficient to keep the men satisfied that the end of the westward journey was near:

"With these signs everyone breathed more easily and cheered up."[25] By evening the winds had reached gale force, and the ships sped along at almost 9 knots. With the encouraging signs of land seen during the day, it would have made sense to follow the common practice of reducing sail after dark to lessen the risk of approaching an unseen reef or offshore rocks not visible in the darkness. But Columbus kept the fleet at full sail in gale-force winds. He had promised landfall within three days, and time was running short.

Sunset was about 5:30 P.M. on 11 October. As usual, the crew gathered for evening prayers and sang *Salve Regina*, "Hail, Holy Queen." Columbus gave a short speech to the men on the *Santa María*, "admonishing them to keep a good lookout on the forecastle and to watch carefully for land; and that to the man who first told him that he saw land he would later give a silk jacket in addition to the other rewards that the sovereigns had promised, which were ten thousand *maravedis* as an annuity to whoever should see it first."[26] At sunset Columbus changed the course back to due west, a change for which he gives no explanation, but it put him directly on course for the most significant encounter in modern history. At 10:00 P.M. he thought he saw a flickering light on the horizon but was uncertain that it was land. At 2:00 A.M. on 12 October, Rodrigo de Triana spotted land from the forecastle of the *Pinta*. Martín Pinzón waited until he could verify the landfall and then fired the cannon to alert the other ships. Columbus drew the *Santa María* near the *Pinta* and ordered the ships to lower sail. The three ships jogged on and off throughout the night, drifting to the southwest, until there was enough daylight that they could safely approach the island.

Although there has been much discussion over the years, it is generally agreed that Columbus's landfall was the island now known as San Salvador or Watlings Island. A small coral island located on the eastern edge of the Bahamas north of the westernmost tip of Cuba, San

Salvador is only 13 miles long and 6 miles wide, with the highest point being only 140 feet above sea level. The island is nearly surrounded by a coral reef, and after daybreak on 12 October the men on the three little ships began looking for a break in the reef. Sailing up the western side of the island, they found an opening into what is now called Fernández or Long Bay. They sailed the ships into the bay, lowered the boats, and rowed to the beach. Columbus carried the banner of the expedition, which depicted a large green cross with an F (for Ferdinand) on one side of the cross and a Y (for Isabella) on the other. A crown was emblazoned above each letter. With the two other captains and the fleet *escribano,* the official recorder, present, Columbus named the island *San Salvador,* "Holy Savior," and officially took "possession of the said island for the king and for the queen his lords, making the declarations that were required."[27] The Ocean Sea had been crossed.

Chapter 7

IN THE NEW WORLD

It is a land to be desired, and once seen, never to be left.[1]

CHRISTOPHER COLUMBUS

Columbus records his first encounter with the people of the New World in some detail in the *Diario*. As always, missionary work was on his mind:

> In order that they would be friendly to us—because I recognized that they were people who would be better freed [from error] and converted to our holy faith by love than by force—to some of them I gave red caps, and glass beads which they put on their chests, and many other things of small value, in which they took so much pleasure and became so much our friends that it was a marvel.[2]

Later in the day some of the natives swam out to the boats, carrying parrots, balls of cotton thread, and other items they wanted to trade. Columbus includes in the *Diario* a detailed description of his first observations of the inhabitants of the New World. They appeared to be "very poor in everything," and he noted that they were all young, suggesting a short life span. "All of them go around as naked as their mothers bore them . . . They wear their hair down over their eyebrows except for a little in the back which they wear long and never cut." He also noted that they carried wooden javelins but had no iron—in admiring the Spanish swords, some of them "took them by the edge and through ignorance cut themselves." And, importantly, he observed that they seemed to have no religion and felt "that they would become Christians very easily." He decided to take six of them with him "in order that they may learn to speak [Spanish]."[3] These people were the peaceful Tainos, one of two peoples indigenous to the Caribbean Islands.

The next day, several of the natives came out to the ship in dugouts—Columbus used the word *almadías,* which referred to West African dugouts. They were "made from the trunk of one tree, like a long boat, and all of one piece, and worked marvelously in the fashion of the land, and so big that in some of them 40 and 45 men came."[4] Within two weeks he would use the native word *canoa* rather than *almadías* in the *Diario,* and the modern word *canoe* would enter European languages.

It was clear to Columbus that this was not the island of Cipango (Japan) that he was looking for, and after spending the night at this first anchorage in the New World, he set off in search of the more advanced civilization he hoped to find. He carried with him the letter of introduction from Queen Isabella and King Ferdinand to the Grand Khan, and he had every hope of being able to deliver it. During the next week—from 15 October to 23 October—he visited three more small islands, which he named, successively, Santa María de la Concepción, Fernandina, and Isabella. Two of these islands were probably the modern-day Crooked Island and Long Island, although there remains disagreement among scholars: the sailing directions and descriptions that have survived through various transcriptions are uncertain and difficult to follow.

On 24 October, Columbus's hopes rose as he anchored off the island of Cuba. "I believe this is the island of Cipango, of which marvelous things are told."[5] Not only was the island much larger than others he had visited but its people seemed more highly civilized. He dispatched three men, including the official interpreter (who spoke Hebrew, Chaldean, and some Arabic), to move inland in search of the capital and the Grand Khan, instructing them to return within six days. What they found was a village with fifty thatched-roof huts, but they were received with great honor. "The Indians touched them and kissed their hands and feet, marveling and believing that the Spaniards came from the heavens." This first encounter was with the male leaders of the village, but the Spaniards reported that later "the women came in and seated themselves in the same way around them, kissing their hands and feet and feeling them, attempting to see if they were, like themselves, of flesh and bone. They begged them to stay there with them for at least five days."[6] It was the first record of a scene that would be repeated over and over again in the New World as the Spaniards encountered native peoples: they were viewed by the natives as messengers from heaven.

Finding neither a great city nor the Grand Khan, the emissaries returned. Still, Columbus was impressed by the abundant resources and beauty of the island, and he foresaw an opportunity to create an idyllic Christian kingdom "free of heresy and malice"[7] in the lush forests and meadows of Cuba.

Martín Pinzón, however, was less interested in conversion or the establishment of a Christian community. He became frustrated with the expedition's failure to locate any significant sources of gold, and on 20 November, without leave, he sailed off in the *Pinta* to follow rumors of gold on other islands. Though Columbus and Pinzón had

had disagreements during the voyage, this was the first clear breaking of ranks. Columbus categorized it as treachery—the desertion of a captain under his command. It was a break that would be carried on by the descendants and friends of both men through a marathon of lawsuits lasting fifty years.

A few days after Pinzón's desertion, Columbus and his men heard the first reports of cannibals. As the ships approached a cape near the eastern end of Cuba, the Indians on board the *Santa María* became very agitated, claiming that the area was inhabited by cannibals. "And when they saw that he was taking this route, he says that they could not talk, because the cannibals eat them, and that they are very well armed."[8] Columbus would hear similar reports from the Indians during his first months in the New World, but he discounted them. On later voyages, however, both Columbus and others traveling with him would give eyewitness reports of cannibalism among the fierce Carib tribe, the mortal enemies of the Tainos.

On 5 December, Columbus took advantage of a change in the wind, which bore him away from Cuba and led him to what would be his most valuable discovery in the New World, the island that was known by the natives as Haiti. Columbus named the island for his adopted homeland, *La Isla de España,* or Hispaniola. On Hispaniola, Columbus found both a more advanced society and greater wealth. Though it was not the fabled Cipango, the Haitians had built impressive stone and wood structures and ball courts similar to those that would be found in Mesoamerica. They also produced a variety of gold artifacts and jewelry. The wealth of Hispaniola would eventually pale in comparison to that found in Mexico and Peru, but it was sufficient to ensure a second voyage for Columbus, and that alone made it a significant and vital discovery.

After reconnoitering along the north coast of the island, Columbus met with a local *cacique,* or chief, near the modern Port Paix. He explained to the *cacique* that "he came from the kings of Castile, who were the greatest princes in the world. But . . . they would only believe that the Spaniards came from heaven and that the realms of Castile were in the heavens and not in this world."[9]

How Columbus and his men communicated with the local inhabitants is a question answered only by speculation. The official translator of the expedition was of no use, and none of the natives whom Columbus brought from his first landfall at San Salvador could have acquired much familiarity with Spanish in a few short weeks. One can only assume that the communication consisted of much gesturing, drawing in the sand, and the effort to pick up meaning from repeated words. On 18 December, Columbus invited a local *cacique* aboard the *Santa María* and served the chief and his counselors dinner in his quarters. He noticed that the chief admired the "coverlet which I had on my bed" and gave it to him as a gift. But "he and his tutor and counselors were very troubled because they did not understand me nor I them."[10]

Columbus was impressed by what he saw of Hispaniola, and the *Santa María* and the *Niña* made their way along the northern coast, stopping in small harbors and trading with the natives. He found the harbors better than any he had known in all of his years of sailing. He was particularly impressed by the landscape:

> There are exceedingly high mountains that seem to reach the heavens . . . and all of them are green and tree covered, which is a thing of wonder. In between the mountains there are very pretty plains, and at the foot of this harbor [Acul Bay], to the south, there is a plain so large that eyes cannot see the end of it. . . . Through it a river comes, and it is all inhabited and cultivated, and it is as green now as if it were in Castile around May or June.[11]

Not only was the landscape impressive but the inhabitants were also:

> May your Highnesses believe that in the whole world there cannot be a better or more gentle people. Your Highnesses should take much joy in that soon you will make them Christians and will have instructed them in the good customs of your realms, for neither better people nor land can there be; and the quantity of people and of land [is] so large that I do not know how to write about it. [12]

Word of the arrival of the Spaniards spread among the natives of Hispaniola, and Columbus received an invitation to visit a senior *cacique*, Guacanagarí, whose realm encompassed the northwestern part of the island. Accordingly, before sunrise on Christmas Eve the ships left the harbor where they had been anchored to sail further west and meet the chief. At about 11:00 P.M., "the Admiral decided to go to sleep because there had been two days and a night when he had not slept."[13] With the Admiral—and presumably most of the crew—fast asleep, the helmsman decided to take a nap as well and turned the tiller over to the ship's boy. Just about midnight, the *Santa María* slid onto a coral reef "so gently that it was hardly felt."[14]

Realizing what had happened, the boy cried out. Columbus and others rushed to the deck. Columbus, quickly assessing the situation, ordered that an anchor be thrown out behind the ship in hopes of lifting the bow and floating the ship off the reef. He dispatched the master of the watch to lower the boat and pull the anchor out to sea. But the men panicked. The master and several of the crew jumped in the boat and rowed instead to the *Niña* in hopes of saving themselves. Captain Yáñez Pinzón of the *Niña,* to his credit, refused to let the deserters board and sent them back. Meanwhile, Columbus ordered the ship lightened and the mast cut, hoping to float her off the reef, but to no avail. The breakers continued to push the *Santa María* higher onto the rocks while the ebbing tide made it impossible to float her off. Before long, the sharp coral broke open the planking, and the *Santa María* was lost. Columbus had his men ferried to the *Niña*.

After daylight, Guacanagarí sent men and canoes, and the first Christmas Day in the New World was spent ferrying the supplies from the *Santa María* to shore. His flagship broken up and the *Pinta* missing, Columbus moved his flag to the little *Niña*.

The loss of a ship, far from its home port and in a place where no other ship had been nor could be expected to come, meant that not everyone who had come on the ocean crossing could return. Columbus was understandably angry and upset, blaming the seaman who had violated orders by letting the ship's boy man the tiller and the insubordination of the ship master and crew for failing to follow his orders and ease off the rocks. In any event, it was too late, and the *Santa María* was irretrievably lost.

But the captain, certain that his expedition was part of God's great plan, soon saw this unwelcome incident in a more positive light. "He recognized that Our Lord had caused the ship to ground there so that he would found a settlement there."[15] The loss of the *Santa María* resulted in the founding of Navidad, the first known European colony in the New World. It also guaranteed a second voyage, if for no other reason than to rescue the men left behind. Columbus expressed his hope that upon his return "he would find a barrel of gold that those who were left would have acquired by exchange; and that they would have found the gold mine and the spicery, and those things in such quantity that the sovereigns . . . will undertake and prepare to go conquer the Holy Sepulcher; for thus I urged Your Highnesses to spend all the profits of this my enterprise on the conquest of Jerusalem."[16]

The damaged ship provided wood and supplies to build a fort and establish the colony. Columbus selected thirty-nine men from the crews of the *Santa María* and the *Niña* (including Luis De Torres, the

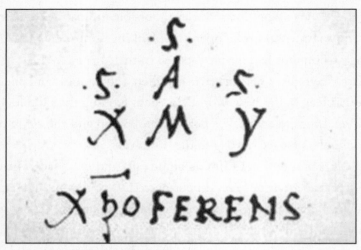

Signature of Christopher Columbus.

translator whose Hebrew was proving to be of little use) to stay behind. He placed his friend Diego de Harana of Córdoba, a cousin of Beatriz, in charge of the new little colony.

Before leaving he gave a letter of instruction to Rodrigo de Escobedo, the *escribano,* charging him to watch over a chest containing gifts that Guacanagarí had given to Columbus. The letter is signed with a signature that Columbus must have designed at some point during the voyage and which he used thereafter on his letters and documents. Later in life, he instructed his son Diego and subsequent heirs to continue using the signature.

The meaning of the letters in the top three rows is unknown, although there has been no lack of speculation on what they might stand for. But the bottom line is clear: *Xpo Ferens,* a Greco-Roman form of Christopher, "Christ-bearer." Having successfully carried the message of Christ across the waters, Columbus now signed his name in a way that clearly identified him with his namesake, St. Christopher.

Columbus and the remaining men on the *Niña* bade farewell to their comrades at sunrise on Friday, 4 January 1493, making their way carefully through a channel in the reef and out to sea. With the *Santa María* shipwrecked and the *Pinta* missing, Columbus did not deem it prudent to spend any additional time exploring the Caribbean. He set a course for home.

Two days later, on Sunday morning, Columbus ordered a sailor to climb the mast and watch for shallow water, and to everyone's great surprise the lookout saw the *Pinta* coming down the east wind. The two ships backtracked to the island of Monte Christo, where Columbus had seen a good harbor. There Martin Pinzón boarded the *Niña* and offered up his excuses for his insubordination and desertion. Columbus refused to buy them and marveled at the arrogance of Pinzón. In Columbus's view, "Martin Alonso left him from 21 November until 6 January without cause or reason, except his disobedient nature."[17] He kept his feelings largely to himself "so as not to give an opening to the evil works of Satan, who desired to impede that voyage."[18] But the Admiral had lost all confidence in Pinzón and was suspicious of his brother, Yáñez, who had captained the *Niña* until the loss of the *Santa María*.

The two ships sailed along the northern coast of Hispaniola. On 10 January, they anchored at a place that Pinzón had visited while he was missing and which he had named after himself. Columbus renamed it *Rio de Gracia* ("River of Grace"), suggesting perhaps that Pinzón had been pardoned. On the same day, however, Columbus recorded that Pinzón's "wickedness was a thing so public that he could not hide it."[19]

On Saturday 12 January, the ships anchored near the mouth of Samaná Bay on the northeastern coast of Hispaniola. In their brief stay there, they had their most dangerous encounter with Indians. Going ashore in hopes of obtaining additional food for the voyage home, they were met by Indians armed with large bows and arrows, the first such weapons they had seen in the New World. A large group of Indians attacked a landing party from the *Niña,* but after the Spaniards wounded two Indians, the situation calmed. The Spaniards were able to conduct some modest trading over the next few days but were wary of the well-armed natives. Both ships were in need of caulking before the voyage home, but the Admiral was so concerned about the sinister nature of these natives that he decided not to risk a prolonged stay.

The two ships took on food, wood, water, and other supplies for the voyage back to Spain. They also had on board a quantity of gold, live parrots, and six natives, and they took with them stories of cannibals, descriptions of flora and fauna, and wondrous tales of a new world. On 16 January, a little over a year from the time the monarchs had authorized the expedition, the two surviving ships of Columbus's little fleet raised anchor for the last time in the New World.

Chapter 8

THE RETURN VOYAGE

*Thus the eternal God, Our Lord, grants to all those who walk
in his way, victory over the seemingly impossible.*[1]

CHRISTOPHER COLUMBUS

he crew wanted to sail directly east, but Columbus
took the ships north in search of the westerly winds he
was certain he would find, knowing those trade winds
would carry them home. He found them the first week of
February, and the ships altered course to the east.

Strong winds from the northwest filled the sails in early February,
and from 4 February to 7 February they averaged nearly 150 miles per
day. Between sunset on 5 February and sunset on the following day,
they covered an impressive 198 miles, the fastest run of the entire voyage. Those small wooden ships of the fifteenth century were racking up
speeds that would be the envy of a modern-day sailor.

After 7 February, however, the winds died down, and Columbus
took advantage of the calm to hold a conference with the captain of
the *Pinta* the next day to discuss their position. Both he and Martin

101

Pinzón kept a dead reckoning chart, as did the pilots of each ship, but there was a wide diversity of opinion regarding their actual location. Columbus estimated that they were due south of Flores, the western-most island of the Azores, and it appears he was reasonably correct. He decided to call at one of the Azores, if possible, to take on fresh water and additional food, as their supplies were low.

So far they had experienced good weather and generally good wind. But the North Atlantic in February can be unpredictable. Cold air masses from the north move south and collide with warm air masses from the tropics moving the opposite direction, and the resulting storms can be fierce. On Tuesday, 12 February, Columbus noted that they began to experience high seas and stormy weather.

By Wednesday night the storm had increased, and the ships went under bare poles—*árbol seco,* as Columbus put it—most of the night.[2] The winds were so strong that it was feared the sails would be destroyed, or worse, the mast would break from the force of the strong wind. "The sea became terrible; the waves crossed one another and tormented the vessels."[3] The storm continued to build. On Thursday night "the wind increased and the waves were frightful, one contrary to the other, so they crossed and held back the vessel which could neither go forward nor get out from between them, and the waves broke on her."[4] In these high seas it was no longer possible to follow a compass course; the helmsman simply did his best to position the ship so it could cut through the next wave without capsizing. With each ship doing its best to stay afloat in the storm, they lost sight of each other in the darkness. "The Admiral made signal lights all night and the other [*Pinta*] answered until it appeared that she could do no more because of the force of the storm and because she was very far off."[5] By daybreak there was no sign of the *Pinta.*

Morning brought no relief from the storm. No one knew if the *Pinta* had simply sailed beyond view or if she had gone down in the night, swamped by powerful waves. What the crew of the *Niña* did know was that they were alone somewhere in the North Atlantic—they were not sure exactly where—and that the next wave could swamp their own little ship. "In their terrible affliction they [the crew] cursed their coming and regretted that they had let me cajole or coerce them into sailing on, when they had so often wished to turn back."[6]

Their captain too despaired. His thoughts turned to his "two boys at school in Córdoba, abandoned without help in a foreign land, before I had accomplished for your Highnesses the service that might dispose you to remember them with favor." His concerns and fears were real. Had Columbus perished at sea before returning to Spain with news of his discoveries, his would have been just another apparently failed attempt to cross the Ocean Sea and simply added emphasis to the impossibility of such a voyage. And two orphans, sons of a foreigner, would be dependent upon other relatives of modest means to care for them.

> I have been near death so often [he wrote] and so close that it seemed that the best step I could take was the one that separated me from it. What made it so unbearable this time was the thought that after our Lord had been pleased to enflame me with faith and trust in this enterprise, and had crowned it with victory . . . His divine Majesty should now choose to jeopardize everything with my death . . . and I tried to console myself with the thought that our Lord would not allow such an enterprise to remain unfinished . . . which I had brought to pass with so much travail in the face of such hostility, nor would He want to break me; yet I realized that He might choose to humble me for my sins, to deprive me of the glory of this world.[7]

The thoughts and feelings recorded by Columbus at this time of great peril are poignant. They reflect themes that would appear again in his writings, sometimes in almost exactly the same words, at times of great stress and discouragement. Although Columbus does not say that these thoughts were given to him by revelation, Fernandez-Armesto asserts that these thoughts of Columbus were "of apparently celestial origin."[8] Columbus would record receiving revelation on two later occasions, and the message would be similar: he would be upbraided for his lack of faith, cautioned about the dangers of pride, reminded that trials are part of the divine plan, and ultimately assured that God was aware of him and watching over him.

we receive the same pattern

Both Columbus and his crew prayed for deliverance and vowed to make pilgrimages of thanksgiving when and if they arrived safely home. Lest the ship and crew perish and their discoveries remain unknown, Columbus

> took a parchment and wrote on it all that he could about everything that he had found, greatly beseeching him who might find it to take it to the sovereigns. He wrapped it in a well-tied, waxed cloth and ordered a large wooden barrel brought and put the parchment in it . . . and he ordered it thrown into the sea.[9]

After sunset on 14 February, the storm began to weaken, and the next morning land was sighted. Because of the uncertainty of their location, "some said it was the island of Madeira, others that it was the Rock of Sintra in Portugal, near Lisbon."[10] Columbus maintained that it was one of the Azores, and, as usual, he was correct. The wind and high seas remained so treacherous that the *Niña* was not able to approach close enough to drop anchor for three days. On Saturday night, "the Admiral rested somewhat because, since Wednesday, he had not slept or been able to sleep and hardly had the use of his legs because of always being exposed to the cold and water and because of eating little."[11] These sleepless nights in the cold and wet exacerbated Columbus's arthritis, which plagued him throughout his life.

After dark on 17 February, an anchor was dropped in sight of some houses on the shore, but the sea was still so rough that the chain gave way, and the weary crew had to continue to man the ship through the night. The next morning they worked their way along the northern coast looking for a suitable anchorage. They again dropped an anchor and sent a boat ashore to talk with the inhabitants of the island and find out where they were. They had reached Santa María, the southernmost island of the Azores. Their initial reception was friendly. The locals reported that they could not remember a tempest of such ferocity and expressed great surprise to see such a small boat survive the storm. They provided the crew with chickens and fresh bread, gifts that were no doubt greatly appreciated.

Columbus had not intended to stop at the Azores on the return voyage for fear that the reception would not be friendly in Portuguese territory. But the weather was still threatening and a treacherous journey lay ahead. The *Santa María* had been lost in Hispaniola, and the fate of the *Pinta* was unknown. They needed wood, water, and fresh food, but mostly they needed rest after their ordeal with the storm.

Still uncertain about the reception he might receive from local Portuguese authorities, Columbus sent just half the men ashore at a spot near a small hermitage, or chapel, where they could offer prayers of thanksgiving for their deliverance. He instructed them to return after offering up their devotions so that the remainder of the crew could then go ashore and do the same. The shore party, in accordance with proper religious tradition, took off their shoes and hose and entered the little chapel dressed only in their long shirts. While the men "were at prayers, the whole town, on foot and on horseback, with the captain [of the island], fell upon them and captured them all."[12]

When the men did not return as expected, Columbus suspected foul play. With the reduced crew on board, he brought the *Niña* around a rocky point where he could get a view of the small hermitage. There "he saw many men on horseback who dismounted and got into the launch with their arms and came to the caravel to capture the Admiral."[13] A stand-off ensued in which Columbus refused to allow the militia to board the *Niña* and likewise refused to leave his ship. It was not until four days later that, having failed in his attempts to capture Columbus, the governor of the island released the captured men and allowed them to return to the *Niña*.

Not only had the reception in the Azores been stormy but the weather itself remained stormy. Columbus expressed surprise "at such bad weather as he was having in those islands and regions, since in the Indies he sailed all winter without anchoring and there was always good weather and not for a single hour did he find the sea when it could not be sailed easily."[14] After spending most of the winter in the Caribbean, the North Atlantic seemed particularly inhospitable. Despite the weather, however, Columbus felt it imprudent to remain in the inhospitable Azores, and on Sunday, 24 February, he left Santa María for the final leg of the trip home. He had spent ten days in and around Santa María, had lost two and possibly three anchors, but had succeeded in replenishing water, wood and ballast.

The ship headed due east, a course that would have taken them directly to Palos and home, a distance of about 800 miles. Under normal circumstances, such a journey would have taken about a week. But on Wednesday, 26 February, the wind shifted and the seas increased—the ship was entering yet another winter storm. Columbus "was very distressed with so much stormy weather now that he was nearly home."[15] By Sunday, 3 March, the seas were so dangerous that all of the men "made a vow to fast on bread and water the first Saturday when they reached land," suggesting the gravity of the situation. The mainsail split in the wind, and they again went under "bare poles because of the great storm of wind and sea, which from two directions was swallowing them up."[16] Once again, fearing the ship would be lost and with it any record of his discoveries, Columbus made another copy of his account of the voyage that he sealed up in a barrel attached to the deck of the ship in such a manner that if the ship went down, the barrel would float free. In 1985, a copy of a letter dated 4 March 1493 surfaced in a private collection and is believed to be a copy of the letter that Columbus sealed in a barrel on the stern of the *Niña*.[17]

On Monday morning "they thought they were lost because of the winds and the seas that came at them from two directions and seemed to lift the caravel in the air. And [they had] rain from the sky and lightning all around. It pleased Our Lord to sustain him, and he went on this way until the first watch when Our Lord showed him land."[18] Worried about approaching an unknown, rocky coast in the storm, Columbus mounted a spare sail that had escaped damage, and the crew tacked back and forth until daylight. "And thus God watched over them until day . . . with infinite trouble and fright."[19]

In the light of dawn Columbus recognized the land as the Rock of Sintra, marking the entrance to the harbor of Lisbon. The storm had blown the ship more than 150 miles north of their desired destination, and Columbus found himself again in Portuguese territory. But with only a single sail left intact and the storm still blowing, attempting to sail north to Galicia or south to Palos along such a rocky coast would have been suicidal. His experience in the Portuguese Azores made him wary of the dangers in putting into port at Lisbon. Nevertheless, he gave orders to take the ship into the Tagus River and the port of Lisbon "because he could not do anything else."[20]

Shortly after dawn, the *Niña* entered the mouth of the river. The citizens of the town of Cascais, at the mouth of the river, were astonished to see such a small vessel emerging from the storm and were so worried for the safety of the ship and crew "that the people of the town spent all that morning in fervent prayer for them, and after they got inside the people came to see them and to marvel at how they had escaped."[21] Columbus learned later that twenty-five ships had been lost near Flanders during the winter storms and that several ships had been trapped by the weather in the Tagus River near Lisbon for four months, unable to get out to sea in the fierce storms.

At 9 A.M. on Monday, 4 March 1493, the *Niña* dropped its remaining anchor at Rostello (now known as Belem), the outer port of Lisbon, about 4 miles below the city. The first recorded round-trip crossing of the Atlantic had been completed.

The journey, however, was not yet over. For the second time in two weeks, Columbus found himself in Portuguese territory. His initial encounter in Santa María had not been positive, and in that little island no one knew who he was or the nature of his voyage. Although he had had a cordial relationship with King João II, he also knew that the king would be aware of his voyage and unhappy with his success. Upon anchoring in the port, he learned that the king was in the country, and he immediately wrote and dispatched a letter requesting permission to proceed upstream to Lisbon. He reminded the Portuguese king that he was sailing under the auspices of Ferdinand and Isabella and that he came from the Indies, not the Portuguese dominion of Guinea.

Having explained himself as best he could to the king, he penned a short postscript to the letter he had written at sea, describing to Ferdinand and Isabella the results of the voyage. He noted the storm that had driven him so far off course and added, "But today, which was the greatest wonder in the world, I made this harbor of Lisbon."[22] He sent the letter by courier to the sovereigns.

Moored near the *Niña* was a large Portuguese man-of-war. Shortly after the *Niña* docked, the master of the navy vessel—none other than Bartholomew Dias, the discoverer of the Cape of Good Hope—approached the *Niña* in an armed boat and ordered Columbus to return with him to the Portuguese war ship. Columbus refused, stating that he was an Admiral of Castile "and that it was the custom of the Admirals of the sovereigns of Castile to die before they gave up themselves or their people." He did allow Dias to review his papers. Dias reported back to the captain of the war ship, who was apparently satisfied. The captain, upon hearing the report, "with great ceremony, and with kettledrums, trumpets, and horns sounding gaily, came to the caravel and talked to the Admiral and offered to do all that he commanded."[23]

Within a few days, Columbus received a response from the king, inviting the Admiral to come and meet with him. The king also gave orders that the *Niña* be supplied with provisions and any necessary repairs be made at his own expense.

We know little of the meeting between Columbus and the king. They had met twice before, and on each occasion the king had rejected Columbus's proposal. Now the Admiral stood before the king, having achieved for Castile what he had originally proposed to do for Portugal. By all accounts it was a cordial meeting, although the king argued that the lands visited by Columbus were within the Portuguese domain as defined by the Treaty of Alcáçovas.

Columbus remained in Portugal eight days. While he was engaged in meetings with the king and others, the crew of the *Niña,* taking up the king's generous offer, had her cleaned and caulked, refilled her ballast, and replaced the torn and tattered sails. The refitted *Niña* weighed anchor at 8 A.M. on 13 March and was carried by the ebb tide down the river and over the bar of Lisbon.

Meanwhile, unbeknownst to Columbus, the *Pinta* had arrived in Galicia sometime near the end of February. Columbus had worried that if the *Pinta* survived and reached Europe ahead of the *Niña,* Pinzón would attempt to report the voyage directly to the sovereigns and claim the success for himself. And that is exactly what Pinzón endeavored to do. From Galicia he sent a message to the sovereigns in Barcelona, requesting an audience to deliver news of the discovery. The sovereigns, to their credit and to Pinzón's dismay, replied by saying they would await word from their Admiral.

At noon on 15 March, exactly thirty-two weeks from the date she sailed from Palos, the *Niña* was carried by the tide across the Saltés bar and into the port of Palos. In his final entry in the *Diario,* Columbus wrote,

> In the circumstances of this voyage, He has miraculously made [his power] . . . manifest, as one may understand through this writing, through the signal miracles that He has performed during the voyage and for me . . . I hope in Our Lord that it will be the greatest honor to Christianity that, unexpectedly, has ever come about. [24]

Las Casas adds: "These are the final words of the Admiral Don Cristóbal Colón concerning his first voyage to the Indies and their discovery."

Not far behind the *Niña* but as yet unseen, the *Pinta* entered the harbor of Palos on the same tide. One can only imagine what Martín Pinzón must have thought when he entered the harbor and saw Columbus's ship already moored. Rejected in his effort to report directly to the sovereigns and suffering from a high fever, it appears that Pinzón neither reported to the Admiral nor visited his brother who was on the *Niña.* He was rowed to shore and taken to his home in the country, where he died a few days later.

Chapter 9
THE WORD SPREADS

Raise your spirits . . . and hear of a new discovery![1]

PETER MARTYR D'ANGHIERA

he entire village of Palos rejoiced at the return of the two ships, "giving great thanks to God, that this great and singular feat had been brought about by people of that village."[2] Columbus immediately dispatched a copy of the letter describing his voyage (which he had already sent to the sovereigns from Lisbon) via Seville, where there was an official courier of the court. The court was meeting in Barcelona, some 800 miles to the northeast. Columbus requested an audience with the sovereigns to report on his voyage directly and in detail and asked that the response be sent to him in Seville. He also sent letters to his family at Córdoba, which he considered his home, and to the city fathers of Córdoba. Before proceeding to Seville, he spent two weeks at Palos recovering from the rigors of the voyage, probably staying with Juan Perez at La Rábida.

Columbus and his entourage, which included several Indians,

entered Seville on the last day of March. Bartolomé de Las Casas, who was eight years old at the time, recalled seeing the Indians, who were housed at the Gate of the Imágenes. He described the green and red parrots, colorful belts, gold jewelry, and other things "never seen nor heard of in Spain."[3]

Columbus did not have to wait long for a response from the sovereigns. Easter Sunday fell on 7 April, and on Easter or shortly thereafter, he received a letter addressed to "Don Cristóbal Colón, their Admiral of the Ocean Sea, Viceroy and Governor of the Islands that he hath discovered in the Indies." The monarchs invited Columbus to come to Barcelona "forthwith" and to "make the best haste you can in your coming."[4] They were as anxious as anyone to hear the full report. In the same letter they also committed to a second voyage, to be undertaken as quickly as preparations could be made.

The newly appointed Admiral of the Ocean Sea had originally intended to sail from Seville to Barcelona, but he had been at sea almost constantly for nearly nine months: he traveled to Barcelona by land. He took with him at least one of his officers, some servants whom he had employed, and six Indians, along with the parrots, clothing, gold, and other artifacts acquired in the New World. The procession made its way across Andalusia in April, a particularly beautiful time of year in southern Spain, stopping in cities and villages along the way. The local citizens came to see both the man and his exotic cargo. "His fame spread like fire across Castile,"[5] and even towns distant from his route emptied out as their inhabitants went to see the wonderful procession. He traveled through Córdoba, on to Murcia, then up the coast via Valencia and Tarragona, and finally to the great Catalan capital of Barcelona, probably arriving between 15 and 20 April. "All the court and the city came out."

At the foot of Las Ramblas, the great central boulevard of modern Barcelona, stands a monumental statue: a 131-foot Corinthian column topped by a 24-foot statue of the discoverer of the New World. It was built in 1888 and completed in time for the celebration of the four hundredth anniversary of Columbus's voyage. One of the eight bronze bas-relief panels surrounding the base depicts Columbus greeting the monarchs in Barcelona upon his return. One can easily walk from the base of the monument through the narrow cobblestone streets of the *Bari Gótic,* the ancient medieval city, to the *Palau del Rei,* where the court was meeting that spring. The palace was a complex of buildings located adjacent to the cathedral and was the customary home of the king of Aragon when the court was in the city. It is not difficult to imagine Ferdinand and Isabella seated at the top of the steps in front of the palace doors as Columbus and his party came through the narrow alley and into the plaza. A visitor today can walk up the same steps that Columbus climbed to greet the king and queen.

No contemporary portrait of Columbus exists, but detailed contemporary descriptions of his appearance were written by four of those who knew him. He was, by these accounts, tall and well built, with a long nose and high cheekbones. His hair had been light red as a youth, but by the time of the First Voyage it had turned silver. He had light blue eyes and a fair, reddish complexion. As he entered the square, filled with the nobility of Castile and Aragon, he looked, according to Las Casas, like a Roman senator.

Ferdinand and Isabella arose from their thrones as Columbus approached them. He knelt to kiss their hands, and they invited him to stand, then ordered that a chair be brought forward and had him sit next to them. The weaver's son from Genoa took his seat at the side of the greatest monarchs of Europe.

The formal report of the voyage was given in the great hall of the palace, known today as the *Saló del Tinell.* There Columbus displayed the gold artifacts he had brought home, reported on the loss of the *Santa María,* and spoke of the need to return quickly to the sailors, now colonists, left behind at Navidad. Afterwards, the party moved to the royal chapel where *Te Deum Laudamus* ("We Praise Thee, O God") was sung while great tears of joy filled the eyes of the monarchs and their admiral. It was the high point of Columbus's life. After many years of discouragement, disappointment, and ridicule, he had successfully turned the key and opened the gates to the Ocean Sea. Columbus was honored by the sovereigns and the nobility of Spain. Columbus's new status as a member of the nobility was confirmed with the official titles Admiral of the Ocean Sea and Viceroy and Governor of the Indies. The titles would be hereditary, ensuring both position and prestige for his son Diego, who at the age of four or five had accompanied his father to Palos from Portugal. In addition, Columbus's brothers Bartholomew and Diego would both be ennobled and were to be addressed as "Don." Diego was invited from Genoa to be present for the granting of the titles, but Bartholomew was still in France, where he had gone from England in an effort to obtain the support of France for Columbus's voyage; he was unaware that his brother had already sailed and returned.

As new members of the nobility, the Columbus family was authorized to bear a coat of arms, the design of which was prescribed by the court. It would consist of four quadrants. The upper two quadrants would contain a lion (representing Aragon) and a castle (representing Castile). The lower quadrants would contain a depiction of several islands (representing the lands discovered and over which the bearer was viceroy) and a number of anchors (symbolizing the rank of admiral).

Soon after his arrival in Barcelona, the six Indians whom Columbus had taken with him to Spain were baptized in the cathedral, the first Native Americans to receive any Christian ordinance. The king, the queen, and their son, Prince Juan, acted as godparents at the ceremony. Visitors to the Barcelona Cathedral can still view a large marble baptistry dating from the fifteenth century and supposed by some to be the very font used to baptize this small group of natives. One can only wonder what those young Caribbean natives might have thought of all they saw and experienced. Of the six Indians baptized in Barcelona, one stayed at the court and died about two years later. The other five left Spain with Columbus on his Second Voyage, but three of them died before reaching the Indies.

Word of Columbus's return to Spain began spreading across Europe within days of his arrival on the continent. A letter dated 19 March 1493, written by the Duke of Medinaceli from his home northeast of Madrid, states that Columbus had arrived in Lisbon after a successful voyage. Because Columbus did not arrive at Palos until 15 March, this letter by the duke must have been written based on information from Lisbon.

The Italian community in Spain was active in sharing news of the voyage with friends back in Italy. A merchant in Barcelona, Hannibal Zenaro, wrote to his brother in Milan on 9 April informing him of the discoveries. A copy of Columbus's letter to Santángel describing the voyage reached Rome prior to 18 April, as it is mentioned in a Venetian chronicle on that day.[6] The letter must have been printed and circulated before Columbus arrived in Barcelona.

During the month of April, Leandro de Cosco, a Catalan, translated the letter into Latin, and it was printed in Rome in pamphlet form. The booklet became a bestseller, going through three printings in Rome in 1493. During 1493 and 1494, six different editions were published, including editions published at Paris, Basle, and Antwerp. A Florentine poet living in Rome, Giuliano Dati, translated the letter into Tuscan verse, and the sixty-eight-stanza poem was printed in Rome on 15 June, with two subsequent printings in Florence during 1493. A German translation and a new Spanish edition were published in 1497. In all, at least seventeen editions of Columbus's letter were published before 1500.

Attending the court of Ferdinand and Isabella when Columbus presented his report to the sovereigns was a young Italian named Peter Martyr d'Anghiera. Several weeks passed before he wrote to a friend in Italy and mentioned the arrival of Columbus. He devotes just a few lines to the event, saying that "a certain Christopher Columbus, a Ligurian, who with barely three ships . . . returned from the Western antipodes."[7] But before long, Peter Martyr began to grasp the importance of what he had recently seen and heard, and he would publish the first history of Columbus and his discoveries.

For Columbus, there was never any doubt about the import of his voyage nor the means by which it was achieved: "For God is wont to listen to His servants who love His precepts, even in impossibilities, as has happened to us on the present occasion, who have attained that which hitherto mortal men have never reached."[8]

As news of the voyage traveled across southern Europe, the fame of Columbus spread and made him the most celebrated man in Spain. He would learn soon enough the harsh veracity of the Latin phrase *sic transit gloria mundi,* "all worldly glory is fleeting," but during the first few weeks after his miraculous return, he was accorded the honor and respect he had duly earned.

Chapter 10

TRIUMPH AND TRAGEDY

To those islands by the goodness of God and by the good judgment of the Admiral, we came as directly as if we had been following a known and accustomed route.[1]

DIEGO ALVAREZ CHANCA

he successful reception of Columbus's report is best evidenced by the swiftness with which the monarchs approved and funded a second voyage. Preparations for the Second Voyage actually began before Columbus left Seville for Barcelona and continued during the weeks that the Admiral remained in Barcelona. The first order of business was to secure Spanish control of Columbus's discoveries through a papal bull. King João II of Portugal had already indicated to Columbus during his stay in Lisbon that he believed the Admiral's discoveries were within Portuguese jurisdiction under the Treaty of Alcáçovas. Queen Isabella requested confirmation from Pope Alexander VI that the new discoveries indisputably belonged to Spain, and the pope, a native of Aragon and former archbishop of Valencia, obliged. On 3 May 1493, he issued the papal bull *Eximiae devotionis,* which affirmed his right to assign newly discovered territories to the discovering nation. He reiterated that Africa and, in particular, Guinea and São Jorge da Mina, were Portuguese territory and that Columbus's discoveries were Spanish territory. The next day the pope followed up with *Inter caetera,* which drew an imaginary line of longitude 100 leagues west of the Azores and Cape Verde Islands and assigned to Spain all discoveries west of that line.

King João II of Portugal, however, was not satisfied. The enmity between Castile and Portugal was more than just a geopolitical feud; it was a family feud. Isabella's half brother, Henry IV of Castile, had married Joan of Portugal, sister to King Afonso V of Portugal. Joan bore Henry IV a daughter, also named Joan, whom Henry wanted to name as his heir. Had the princess Joan become queen, Castile and Portugal would have been united under one ruler. But in the complexities and intrigues that define medieval royalty, Isabella refused to marry the husband chosen for her by her half brother the king, Princess Joan's legitimacy was questioned, Isabella's half brother died (whether from plague or poison), and Isabella eloped with Ferdinand of Aragon and ultimately became queen of Castile. It was a set of tortuous circumstances that had united Castile and Aragon rather than Castile and Portugal, and the competition between Castile and Portugal was keen.

It was one thing for the Pope to declare a line of demarcation in the *Inter caetera* but another to enforce it. Portugal threatened to block further exploration by Castile with naval action. Castile, war weary and without the naval force of Portugal, entered into negotiations. The result was the Treaty of Tordesillas, named for the small village in northern Castile where the document was signed on 7 June 1494. The treaty preserved the concept that the undiscovered world and its oceans would be divided between Castile and Portugal; it simply moved the line of demarcation an additional 170 leagues west of the line declared in *Inter caetera.* As a result, Brazil became a Portuguese-speaking nation.[2]

Having secured the equivalent of an international decree affirming

Spanish control of yet undiscovered lands, the sovereigns appointed Columbus as captain general of the new fleet to be assembled and put Juan de Fonseca, archdeacon of Seville, in charge of making the preparations. The stated objective of the First Voyage had been to reach Japan and from there to make contact with the Grand Khan, but in reality its great achievement was crossing the unknown Ocean Sea and returning. Japan or no Japan, Grand Khan or no Grand Khan, no one suggested that the First Voyage was anything but a great success. The stated objectives of the Second Voyage were conversion and commerce: the conversion of the native people and the establishment of a *factoría,* or trading post, through which gold could be collected and shipped back to Spain.

Columbus felt that the natives he had met in the Indies—with the exception of the fierce Caribs—were excellent prospects for conversion to the Christian faith, and he saw their conversion as the primary purpose of his life and work. His prophetic role was to bear the message of Christ across the sea. He had observed that the natives seemed to have "neither dogma nor doctrine"[3]—much as Nephi described them as having "dwindled in unbelief."[4] The sovereigns instructed Columbus that "by all ways and means he strive and endeavor to win over the inhabitants of the said Islands and Mainland to be converted to our Holy Catholic Faith."[5] To accomplish this conversion, the sovereigns directed Columbus to take six priests on the voyage and appointed Bernardo Buil, a Catalan friar, as the chief cleric. They gave strict instructions to Columbus and those with him

> to treat the said Indians very well and lovingly and abstain from doing them any injury, arranging that both peoples hold much conversation and intimacy, each serving the others to the best of their ability [and if any person] should maltreat the said Indians in any manner whatsoever, the said Admiral, as Viceroy and Governor of their Highnesses, shall punish them severely by

virtue of the authority vested in him by their Majesties for this purpose.[6]

Because of the distance from Spain, the proposed *factoría* was envisioned as a substantial colony. It does not appear that either Columbus or the monarchs intended a large-scale colonization of the newly discovered lands: there was already an indigenous population, and it was assumed that the great empires of Asia were nearby. But a trading outpost so far from the motherland would require farmers, smiths, carpenters, and a host of tradesmen to support it.

It had not been easy to recruit men for the First Voyage, but as Columbus's fame spread, thousands petitioned for the Second Voyage. The expedition included not just sailors but common laborers, priests, administrators, *hidalgos* (lower-ranking nobles), and a contingent of soldiers with their mounts. Although most of the ships' records have been lost, based on what is available, it appears that the expedition included several Genoese mariners and a few Basques, but most of the men came from the towns around Palos and Cádiz.

Several of the men had personal ties to Columbus. Joining Columbus on the Second Voyage were his youngest brother, Diego, a boyhood friend from Savona named Michele da Cuneo (whose account of the voyage is one of the primary sources for what took place), and several veterans of the First Voyage. Five of the six Indians who accompanied Columbus to Spain also sailed with him on this voyage. Other notables on the voyage included Pedro de Las Casas, whose son, Bartolomé, would become the first priest ordained in the New World and would write an extensive history of Columbus's voyages and the exploration and colonization of the Indies; Juan de la Cosa, who made the first maps of the islands of the Caribbean (excluding Columbus's sketch of the north coast of Hispaniola); Diego Alvarez Chanca, a physician from Seville who also wrote a detailed account of the voyage; and

Ponce de León, who would later discover Florida while searching for the mythical Fountain of Youth.

With preparations well underway and Fonseca managing most of the details, Columbus left Barcelona to return to Seville and go from there to Cádiz where the fleet was being readied. From Barcelona he traveled first to the shrine of Guadalupe to fulfill his vow made on the *Niña* during the great storm. His route would have taken him through the green hills of Catalonia, up the broad plain of the Ebro River to Zaragoza and then down through the Sierra Guadarrama to Madrid. From Madrid, the road goes southwest to Talavera de la Reina, crosses the Tagus River, and enters the province of Extremadura. Columbus was the most celebrated person in Spain, and it is likely that among those who came out to see his procession as he passed through the towns of Extremadura was a swineherd's thirteen-year-old son named Francisco Pizarro. Pizarro would accompany Vasco Nuñez de Balboa in his march across the Isthmus of Panama in 1513, and in 1533 he would conquer the great Inca empire and found the city of Lima.

After praying at the shrine of Guadalupe, Columbus and his entourage descended the mountains en route to Córdoba. Passing through the town of Medellín, those who came out to see him may have included the eight-year-old Hernán (or Hernando or Fernando) Cortés. Many years later, Cortés would pray for nine consecutive days at the shrine of Guadalupe in the hope of being forgiven for the sins he committed in the conquest of Mexico.

In Córdoba, Columbus picked up his two sons, Diego and Fernando, and visited with Beatriz. Whether Columbus ever intended to marry the mother of Fernando is unknown, but by that time it was impossible, as members of the nobility were prohibited from marrying commoners.

With his sons at his side, the Admiral proceeded to Seville to determine the progress of Fonseca in preparing the fleet. Wishing to sail in August, as he had found fair winds that time of year on the previous voyage, he was disappointed that preparations were not yet complete. It would be late September before all was ready, but the delay would ensure that the expedition would miss the hurricane season, the danger of which Columbus as yet had no knowledge.

Preparations were completed, and on 24 September the fleet was ready. It must have been an impressive sight. This was no small expeditionary voyage of three ships—seventeen ships lay in the harbor at Cádiz. They carried food and water for six months, horses, chickens, pigs and other livestock, at least twelve hundred men, and a variety of supplies, including complete equipment to set up the first Christian church in the New World. It was the largest expedition ever undertaken by a European nation, and the fact that it had been assembled in just six months is a tribute to Juan de Fonseca and the people of Andalusia, who provided the ships and their cargo.[7]

The fleet departed with great pageantry on the morning of 25 September. The royal standards of Castile flew from the masts, the volunteers lined the decks, and so many additional flags and standards were flown that they became entangled with the rigging. Trumpets played, cannons boomed, and a fleet of Venetian galleys rowed alongside the armada as young Diego and Fernando watched their father sail out of sight.

On 5 October the fleet put in at San Sebastian on the island of Gomera, where Columbus had anchored and resupplied a year earlier. They stayed a few days to take on fresh water and supplies, and on 13 October took their last glance at the Old World fading in the distance. Rather than sailing directly west as he had done on the First Voyage, Columbus took the fleet southwest. He had learned from Indians on the First Voyage of islands further south and east of those

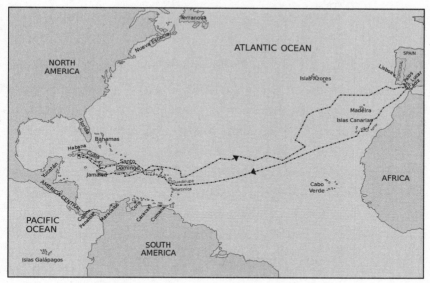

Route of the Second Voyage.

he visited, and he determined to head directly to these new islands. The more southerly course also enabled him to take better advantage of the easterly trade winds.

The crossing proved to be uneventful. With the exception of a squall that split several sails on the night of 26 October, the weather was beautiful and winds steady. They made landfall in a remarkable twenty-one days and pioneered the shortest and best route from Europe to the Caribbean, a route that would be used by sailing ships for the next five hundred years. "Put it down to luck, seamanship or the finger of God, as you will," commented Morison, "it was marvelous." Morison characterized the voyage with this description:

> This second outward passage must have been very near to the mariner's dream of perfect sailing. Running before the trades is a glorious sensation even when you are alone on the ocean; and on this voyage the beauty of deep blue water, flashing flying fish, curling wave crests and changing cloud formations, was enhanced

by seeing sixteen other white-winged ships spread out over the face of the sea.[8]

The lookout on Columbus's flagship, *Mariagalante,* "the Gallant Maria," gave the cry of *"Tierra"* at about 5 A.M. on Sunday, 3 November. They had reached the island of Dominica, which Columbus so named because they had arrived on Sunday. The fleet would spend the next twenty-five days sailing past island after island, stopping occasionally to take on fresh water and bathe in the rivers, and going through the formalities of claiming the islands for Castile and Aragon. On multiple occasions they encountered members of the Carib tribe and recorded evidence of cannibalism. Wherever possible, Columbus freed other Indians held as prisoners by the Caribs and took them on board to return them to their native islands. On at least one island he ordered that all the native Carib canoes be destroyed so they could not prey upon the other tribes who had been so friendly to Columbus. On St. Croix, a landing party had a skirmish with a group of Caribs in which one of Columbus's men was mortally wounded.

For the most part, these were days of beautiful sailing around some of the most picturesque islands in the hemisphere. The Europeans tasted pineapple for the first time, and those new to the islands, which were the vast majority, had their first taste of yam and sweet potato. But this was not a Caribbean pleasure cruise, and Columbus was becoming anxious to get back to the men he had left at Navidad the previous January. The fleet made its way north to Hispaniola, and on 23 November arrived at Samaná Bay, from where the *Niña* and *Pinta* had departed the New World the previous January. The seaman who had been wounded during the skirmish on St. Croix a few days earlier died and was given a proper burial ashore after the first Christian funeral in the New World.

Continuing west along the north shore of Hispaniola, the fleet stopped briefly at Monte Cristi. There a landing party came across two corpses bound with ropes. The next day they found two more. Although the bodies were badly decomposed and unrecognizable, one showed traces of a heavy beard: the bodies were almost certainly those of Spaniards. The high spirits, sense of wonder, and excitement that had characterized the voyage ended abruptly.

The Admiral headed with all speed towards Navidad. They reached the entrance to the harbor after dark on 27 November but stayed anchored at sea, not wishing to experience the fate of the *Santa María* on the previous Christmas Eve. Once the anchors were set, the Admiral ordered that two cannon shots be fired, hoping that the men of Navidad would respond by firing their cannon.[9] There was no response, nor could the men aboard ship see any fires or make out any buildings on the shore. "From this the men were much depressed," wrote Dr. Chanca.[10] About 10 P.M. a canoe with several Indians approached the fleet, calling out for the *Almirante.* They were directed to the *Mariagalante,* and when they recognized Columbus's face in the light of a torch, came aboard. They assured Columbus that the Christians at Navidad were all well except for a few who had died of illness. But during the three hours they remained on board, one of the returning Indians who served as the fleet interpreter (having learned some Spanish during his six months in Spain), extracted the truth: all the men Columbus had left behind were dead.

The Spaniards in the fleet, including Friar Buil, demanded revenge and insisted that Guacanagarí, the chief who had been so friendly to Columbus and who had been charged with the safety of the men left behind, be sought out and executed. But Columbus demonstrated great patience and restraint, insisting that his men not act without knowing the facts. Those facts came out over the next few days. With the help of his interpreter, Columbus learned that the men of Navidad had begun to quarrel and fight among themselves, and several of them had gone on raiding parties into the interior of the island to an area controlled by Caonabó, a rival to Guacanagarí. They had stolen goods from the Indians, raped the women, and carried some of the women back to the settlement as concubines. Caonabó retaliated by attacking the garrison at Navidad, killing the men and burning the fort.

For Columbus, it was a terrible blow. Among the dead was his good friend and Beatriz's cousin, Diego de Harana. He wrote to the sovereigns:

> Though I know it happened through their own fault, there is much to be sad about in such an event, and for me it is a punishment greater than any experienced by their relatives, because I wanted them to win great honor at little danger, which would have been the case had they governed themselves according to my instructions as they pledged to do.[11]

It was a task hard enough to tell surviving family members of the loss of a loved one in a good cause but far more difficult to deliver the news that they died as a result of their own greed and misdeeds.

With a shadow of gloom over the remains of Navidad, Columbus determined to establish a new settlement at a new location. They buried the dead, and the fleet weighed anchor and began sailing east along the coast in search of a new settlement site. They were going against the wind and the currents, and in twenty-five days—four days longer than the Atlantic crossing—they had made only about 32 miles. On 2 January 1494, the fleet dropped anchor in the shelter of a peninsula on which was a small plain. The crew and passengers, most of whom were not seamen and were unaccustomed to life on a small, crowded ship, had been sleeping on the ships for nearly one hundred nights. The men were tired, many were sick, the sailors were worn out from fighting the wind and currents, and the livestock were dying. The fate of Navidad had cast a pall of discouragement over what had been a great adventure. The Admiral determined to halt the voyage and establish a settlement, which he named La Isabela after his patron, the queen. It was not, in retrospect, a particularly good location for a new colony, but at the time everyone was undoubtedly glad for solid ground to sleep on.

Up to this point, the expedition had been a success. Morison writes that Columbus

> had conducted across the Atlantic seventeen vessels, many of them very small, made a perfect landfall, and continued through a chain of uncharted islands, with no accident serious enough to be recorded. He had discovered twenty large islands and over two-score small ones, upon which the eyes of no European had rested before. Over the biggest fleet that had yet crossed deep water, bearing twelve hundred seamen, colonists and men-at-arms, he had kept discipline during a voyage that lasted fourteen weeks. In a region inhabited by fierce man-eating Caribs, he had avoided conflict save for the one brief skirmish, and lost but a single man.[12]

Columbus immediately set the men to laying out and constructing the *factoría*. It would be nothing less than a model Spanish village, complete with a church and governor's palace fronting a central plaza. While some men were felling trees and laying the foundations for the village, Columbus sent a small group of men under the command of Alonso de Hojeda to explore the interior of the island in search of the gold mine which the natives had indicated was located in the mountains. Rainy weather and swollen rivers caused Hojeda to turn back before he found any mines, but he returned with three large gold nuggets given to him by the natives, who assured him that there were more where those came from.

Columbus had hoped to send most of the fleet back with a substantial cargo of gold that was to have been gathered by the men at Navidad, but the three nuggets and a few gold trinkets would have to do. Many of the men were becoming sick. The food supplies they had brought from Europe were nearly exhausted, and the men were not yet accustomed to the native foods, although they were abundant. Keeping five ships, including his flagship *Mariagalante* and his favorite, the *Niña,* he put the remaining twelve vessels under the command of Antonio de Torres, loaded the ships with cotton fabric, native cinnamon, pepper, and sandalwood, sixty parrots, twenty-six Indian slaves, the gold nuggets and artifacts, navigational instructions for the return journey, and the outline of a report which Torres was instructed to give the monarchs. The flotilla of a dozen ships entered the harbor of Cádiz just thirty-five days after leaving Isabela, a record that would stand for many years.

The returning fleet met with a mixed reception. The "cinnamon" taken to Spain by Torres turned out to be a poor substitute for Oriental cinnamon; the pepper too had an odd flavor. The "sandalwood" was not, in fact, sandalwood. But the gold was enticing enough to excite the court. The twelve ships laden with cargo under the command of Torres was the first of hundreds of fleets that would eventually cross the Atlantic laden with cargo from the New World. Over the years, those fleets would bring unimagined wealth back to Spain.

Back in Isabela, conditions were deteriorating rapidly. So many of the laborers and artisans had become sick that Columbus ordered the *hidalgos* to do much of the labor, and they complained bitterly. Many of the men who had come on the voyage had done so with the expectation of reaping great wealth with little effort while living in a tropical paradise. But the reality of establishing a small colony in a distant foreign land turned out to consist mostly of hard manual labor and deprivation. The seeds of rebellion were beginning to swell.

In March, Columbus followed up on Hojeda's initial exploration of the interior by mounting a large, well-outfitted expedition. A small garrison was left behind at Isabela, and Columbus himself led a great overland expedition of men in armor, horses, trumpets and pageantry.

It was the first of the great overland marches that would become a colorful part of the history of Spain in the New World. Although it was a relatively short march, the pattern would be replicated by Cortés, Balboa, Pizarro, Francisco Vásquez de Coronado, and others over the subsequent decades. The cavalcade followed the route of Hojeda into the great central valley of Hispaniola, a long, lush, and stunningly beautiful valley. Columbus christened it the *Vega Real,* "the Royal Plain." He left a group of fifty or more men under the command of Mosén Pedro Margarit to establish the small fort of St. Tomás, which he hoped would become a base for future mining operations. The return trip to Isabela was hindered by bad weather and a lack of food, but after seventeen days on the march, the cavalcade, somewhat ragged and hungry, reentered Isabela to the sound of trumpets and musket shots.

The next day a messenger arrived from Margarit saying that the friendly local Indians had fled at the report that Caonabó, the chief who had killed the men at Navidad, was on the march. Columbus sent four hundred men under the command of Hojeda to provide reinforcements and relief. The plan was to bring Margarit back and allow Hojeda enough men to continue exploring the interior in a series of expeditions during which they would live off the land. In Columbus's view this would have multiple benefits: it would allow further exploration of the island, accustom the men to live off the local food while conserving what little European food was left, and keep some of the worst troublemakers—of whom Hojeda was becoming the most prominent—occupied and away from Isabela.

This new expedition left Isabela on 9 April and marched up to the Vega Real, where they entered a small native village. Upon hearing that some of the Indians had stolen clothing from three Spaniards returning to Isabela and that the chief in the village had taken the clothing for his own, Hojeda—of whom Las Casas said, "he was always the first to draw blood in any fight or argument"[13]—cut off the ears of one of the Indians and sent the chief, his brother, and a nephew back to Isabela in chains to be executed. Fortunately for the prisoners, a chief who had been friendly to Columbus accompanied them to the settlement and persuaded Columbus to release them. But the damage was done. Until this point, except for the behavior of the men at Navidad, the Spaniards had treated the Indians fairly and had been received as messengers from heaven. "This was the first injustice," wrote Las Casas, "which was committed in the Indies against the Indians, and the beginning of the bloodshed that later was so heavy on this island."[14]

Columbus always seemed more comfortable at sea than he was governing on land. He placed his brother Diego in charge of the colony and determined to continue the exploration of the islands. He had visited Cuba during the First Voyage and believed it was a peninsula of the Asian continent. Taking the *Niña* and two smaller ships, he left Isabela on 24 April and sailed for Cuba in hopes of finding the Grand Khan.

One of the most interesting events of the voyage happened while the ships were anchored at or near the fishing port of Batabanó in southwest Cuba. A man who had gone ashore to hunt with a crossbow reported that he had encountered a group of about thirty natives, one of whom was dressed in a white tunic that came down to his feet. The Spaniard at first thought it was the priest from his ship. Then two additional fair-skinned natives in white tunics appeared. Frightened, the Spaniard began running towards the sea. He was followed by one of the white-garbed men, who disappeared when the hunter reached the shore. Upon hearing the report, Columbus thought his man might have encountered the people of Prester John, a legendary priest of Ethiopia who was reported to lead a Christian enclave in the Orient. The Admiral sent men ashore for the next two days hoping to find the white-clothed men, but they encountered no one.

The three ships spent five months exploring Cuba and Jamaica.

They experienced challenging weather and some difficult sailing through shallow waters. They had to thread their way through tangled archipelagos and narrow channels. The *Niña* was stuck in mud for several hours, but the Admiral succeeded in freeing her with no damage. While he may have had difficulty managing affairs on land, Columbus rarely made a mistake at sea.

The return voyage to Hispaniola was difficult, as they were fighting the current and the winds, making progress slow and difficult. The Admiral had little sleep for eight consecutive days and fell ill with "a high fever and drowsiness, and caused a temporary loss of sight, feeling and memory."[15] When they finally anchored at Isabela on 29 September, his men had to carry him to shore. It took him five months to recover.

The best news Columbus received when he returned to Isabela was of the arrival of his brother Bartholomew. His faithful friend and partner in the Enterprise of the Indies, Bartholomew had traveled to England and then to France seeking backing for the bold proposal to sail west across the Ocean Sea. He was still in France when Columbus returned from the First Voyage and did not receive Columbus's letter asking him to come to Spain until late 1493. He had arrived at Seville after the Admiral had sailed from Cádiz. Following instructions Columbus had left for him in Seville, Bartholomew took the Admiral's two sons to court, where the queen agreed to employ them as pages. The sovereigns were well impressed with their Admiral's brother and gave him command of three caravels laden with supplies for the new colony. He had arrived in Isabela with much-needed supplies, additional men, and an encouraging letter from the monarchs.

But Bartholomew's arrival was the only good news Columbus received in Isabela. His youngest brother, Diego, whom he had left in charge of the colony, had been even less able than Columbus to cope with the difficulties and growing discontent. Columbus had left

Margarit with strict instructions to treat the natives kindly, reminding him that "their Highnesses desire more the salvation of this people by making them Christians, than all the riches that can be obtained from them."[16] Margarit did not share the noble views of their Highnesses. He and his band of men roved freely through the Vega Real, extorting gold, stealing food, raping women, and kidnapping natives to be enslaved. When Diego Columbus ordered him to cease and desist, an indignant Margarit, believing that the foreign-born Diego was questioning his honor, returned to Isabela and demanded an apology. When none was forthcoming, he commandeered the three caravels brought by Bartholomew and, with a group of discontents that included Friar Buil, sailed for Spain. Such was the situation when Columbus returned from Cuba.

Columbus remained bedridden for several weeks after his return, but sick as he was, he took over the management of the colony with the hope of bringing some order out of the chaos. There were no good solutions. The first Governor and Viceroy of the Indies undertook several actions in an attempt to salvage the situation, but in some ways his actions only made things worse. Angered by the depredations of Hojeda and Margarit, many of the natives were now openly hostile. Columbus responded by rounding up over fifteen hundred of them and taking them into Isabela. He sent about five hundred to Spain to be sold as slaves, and the remainder were taken by the men of Isabela as slaves. Though the enslavement of non-Christians, particularly those who fought against Christians, was an acceptable practice at the time, it was a decision that would lead to grief for everyone involved, particularly for the poor Tainos of Hispaniola. Few survived the difficult journey to Spain, and those who did soon died. Those who remained behind fared no better.[17]

Columbus's early decision not to retaliate against the natives for the killing of the men at Navidad had been a sore point with many of the men on the Second Voyage. Now that relations with the Indians had unraveled to the point of no recovery, Columbus determined to capture Caonabó. He sent Alonso de Hojeda to make contact with the chief. Hojeda captured him by treachery and took him back to Isabela in chains. Hojeda then took his mounted cavalry and a pack of hunting hounds and traveled through the countryside tormenting, capturing, or killing any natives who resisted. The poorly armed and inexperienced Tainos were no match for armed horsemen and fierce dogs. By the spring of 1496 a series of forts had been built, the resisters had been enslaved or killed, and Columbus had imposed a tax or tribute upon the remaining natives—everyone over fourteen years of age was required to provide the Spaniards with a hawk's bell full of gold dust every two months. The tribute system was undoubtedly designed to ensure the collection of gold without the need for manual labor, but it was a system destined to fail—there simply wasn't enough gold on the island.

Sometime in 1496, either Columbus or his brother Bartholomew implemented the *repartamiento* or *encomienda* system in Hispaniola, under which colonists were given land grants and assigned Indians who lived on their land as laborers. It appears that this was done originally instead of collecting tribute. The practice of *repartamiento* did not originate with the Columbus brothers; it was a well-established system that had been used in Spain during the Reconquista and was governed by a complex set of statutes. The legal strictures of the system, originally centered in providing farm labor, were altered in Hispaniola to allow settlers to use their assigned natives for labor in the mines. In the New World, however, far away from the judicial controls of continental Spain, the system was abused and resulted in the virtual enslavement of many natives. Columbus blamed the early abuses on Francisco Bobadilla, who appointed himself governor in 1500.

The only positive result of Columbus's actions was that by 1496, the island was so peaceful that a lone Spaniard could roam safely anywhere on Hispaniola and be fed freely by any native he encountered. But what a high price was paid for this peace! When Columbus first arrived in Hispaniola in 1492, the native population was between 250,000 and 300,000. By 1508 a census found only 60,000 still alive. By 1548 there were fewer than 500. It was but a shadow and a type of what would befall Native Americans during the next century. As Nephi had foreseen, "they were scattered before the Gentiles and were smitten."[18]

Columbus's shortcomings as a colonizer and governor are one of the few things historians agree on. Many of his problems resulted from trusting men whom he should never have trusted. He seemed to have difficulty accepting that others did not share his passion for converting the natives, and he continued to select and appoint leaders whose interests were often diametrically opposed to his. He clearly felt pressure to provide an economic justification for the colony, and the paucity of gold on Hispaniola led him to make some decisions that ultimately had very negative consequences.

As for the *hidalgos* and others who went to Hispaniola, they were lazy, fractious, and seemingly interested only in obtaining gold with little effort. They resented Columbus and his brothers as foreigners. And there was never enough gold to satisfy their expectations. Las Casas opined that even "the Archangel Gabriel would have been hard put to govern people as greedy, selfish, and egotistical as the early settlers of Hispaniola."[19] Columbus's immediate successors did not fare much better as governors than he had, and they were certainly more cruel. Gonzalo Fernández de Oviedo, whose *History of the Indies* was published in 1535, wrote that any early governor of Hispaniola, "to succeed, must be superhuman."[20] Columbus may have been divinely endowed with "abundant skill in the mariner's arts,"[21] but he was given no such superhuman powers to govern the fractious colonists of the New World.

Unfortunately, many of Columbus's problems as a colonizer were common throughout the European settlement of the Americas. The very site of the first settlement was ill-chosen: it was a poor harbor and had relatively limited and poor agricultural potential. Site selection in a new land was always a problem. Jamestown and Plymouth were equally poor sites; Jamestown would end in tragedy, and Plymouth would survive only with the support of the much better-located Boston. Imposing European norms and culture on native populations was uniformly disastrous. Of the early settlements, perhaps only Plymouth achieved anything like a working peaceful relationship with native peoples, and that was due in part to the fact that so much of the native population had already succumbed to diseases imported from the Old World.

Yet for all of his shortcomings and failures as viceroy and governor, Columbus accomplished much of significance in this first, ill-fated little settlement. He directed the construction of a magnificent customs house, the first church and first hospital in the New World, a governor's mansion, and over two hundred small houses, streets and a central plaza, a sawmill, a kiln for manufacturing tiles and pottery, a fort, and a shipyard with a forge.

Isabela would suffer one last disaster before Columbus returned home. In June 1495, a great storm arose "which the Indians in their language called 'huracán.'"[22] The storm sank three ships anchored in the bay, and the word *hurricane* entered European languages. The little *Niña* survived, but before returning to Spain, Columbus had the shipwrights at Isabela construct a new vessel from the ruins of the sunken ships. The new ship, even smaller than the *Niña,* was christened *Santa Cruz,* but the men nicknamed her *India,* the first ship built in the Indies.

Before he sailed for Spain, Columbus directed his brother Bartholomew to found a new city at a site that looked more promising on the opposite side of the island. Bartholomew began construction of Santo Domingo in 1496 or 1497. It is the oldest continuously occupied European settlement in the New World. Isabela, the little colony that had begun with such high hopes and been the scene of so much disappointment and suffering, was abandoned and soon fell into ruin. Nothing remains today but a few stones that mark the site of what was the first capital of the Spanish Indies.

On 10 March 1496, Columbus left Bartholomew in charge as *Adelantado,* "Governor," and boarded the *Niña.* Over 250 Spaniards and 30 Indians crowded the decks of the two little ships. It was a difficult crossing, and with so many men on board, rations ran low. By early June, the men were so hungry that some proposed throwing the Indians overboard to conserve food, but Columbus refused. The pilots were uncertain about their location, some saying they were near the coast of England and others that they were approaching Galicia. Columbus, however, insisted that they were near Cape St. Vincent (on the southern tip of Portugal) and ordered that the sails be lowered during the night to avoid hitting land in the darkness. Once again, Columbus demonstrated his *sens marin:* at daybreak they saw Cape St. Vincent in the light. "Ever afterwards," wrote Fernando, "the seamen considered him to have heaven-sent wisdom in the art of navigation."[23] On 11 June 1496, almost three years after the gallant departure of the great fleet in 1493, the two small, overcrowded ships arrived in Cádiz.

Navigation gifts from above. But we learned that he is human + somewhat inept w/ weaknesses in other aspects.

Chapter 11

A NEW WORLD, THE GARDEN OF EDEN, AND THE FUTURE OF CHRISTIANITY

There is another preaching of the gospel that is yet to take place,
with such effectiveness that all the gentiles will accept the faith
of Christ; and this shall take place at the end of the age.[1]

NICHOLAS OF LYRA

olumbus's return from the Second Voyage had none of the glory and pageantry of his victorious return from the First Voyage. The disaffected colonists and priests who had preceded his return had already had plenty of time to publish their complaints and disappointments, both to the court and to the public. Columbus's friend Andrés Bernáldez was surprised to discover that the gold artifacts brought back by Columbus were genuine, as his enemies had spread the word that they were all cheap alloys. Fernando Colón reports that his father

> decided to return to Spain to give an account to the monarchs
> of many things he considered important for them to know, espe-
> cially because many individuals malignant and scathing, born of
> envy, ceased not to give a negative report to the kings of the affairs

in the Indies, to the detriment and dishonor of the Admiral and his brothers.[2]

Before going ashore, Columbus donned the simple habit of a Franciscan monk, which would become his common dress when not in court. Though he never explained his reasons for adopting such plain dress, he often expressed concerns that many of the misfortunes in his life befell him as a result of pride, and adopting the dress of his humble Franciscan friends may have been his way of repenting and demonstrating humility.

As soon as the sovereigns received word of the Admiral's return, they invited him to attend them at court at his convenience, noting that "since in what has passed you have had much hardship."[3] Accordingly, Columbus set off from Seville for Burgos, where the court was meeting. To help set the record straight, he traveled again with a cavalcade that included at least two Indians, cages of brightly colored parrots, and enough gold jewelry to convince the public that he had not misled anyone in describing the glory of the Indies.

He was received graciously by the sovereigns and was apparently successful in regaining their full confidence. Among other things, they gave him permission to create a *mejorat,* a will and testament. Such documents could be written only with royal consent, and the *mejorat* of Columbus affirms the titles and rewards granted by the monarchs. Columbus named his son Diego as his heir and instructed Diego to provide for the care of his brother and uncles. In the event of Diego's early death, Fernando would be the heir. Columbus also provided for a fund to be established at the Bank of St. George in Genoa to maintain a permanent home for the Columbus family in that city. He provided for the establishment of a church in Hispaniola with a chapel where masses would be said for his soul, a hospital, and a fund to support four able instructors in sacred theology who could teach Christianity to the native inhabitants.

The sovereigns approved Columbus's request for a third expedition, but it would be two years before he sailed again across the ocean. King Ferdinand had been engaged in repelling a French invasion of Italy and had been in combat with the French along the Pyrenees border. While holding the French at bay militarily, Ferdinand determined to consolidate and expand his influence on other fronts through a series of marriages. The heir to the thrones of Aragon and Castile, Prince Juan, was married to Margarita of Austria; Margarita's brother, Archduke Philip of Hapsburg, married Juana, the second daughter of Ferdinand and Isabella; Juana's elder sister, Isabella, married Manuel, king of Portugal. This last union proved especially useful to Ferdinand. The relationship between Castile and Portugal had been strained during the reign of King João II, as both kingdoms vied for control of newly discovered lands. When João II died in 1495, his nephew Manuel became the new king of Portugal. His marriage to Isabella of Aragon and Castile thus brought an era of détente to the relationship between Portugal and Spain, and the two countries cooperated in a remarkable way in the exploration and colonization of the New World recently discovered by the Genoese mariner who had lived for several years in each country.

The series of marriages was European diplomacy at its best and a tribute to the sagacity of Ferdinand. It was also expensive and time consuming. And, particularly unfortunate for Columbus, it required a large number of ships: Juana was escorted to Flanders for her marriage by a fleet of 130 ships, all elaborately equipped.

Columbus attended the wedding of Prince Juan and Margarita in Burgos in the spring of 1497, and with the wedding complete, the sovereigns began to turn their attention back to Columbus and the Indies. Less than three weeks after the marriage they issued their first orders regarding the Third Voyage. But the excitement of the plans for a new voyage was soon overshadowed by tragedy for the sovereigns: on 4 October 1497, their son, Prince Juan, heir to the thrones of Castile and Aragon, died. He was nineteen years old and a husband of only six months. Columbus's son Diego had served as a page to the prince, and other members of the prince's entourage were strong supporters of Columbus, including the prince's tutor, Diego Deza, and his nurse, Juana de la Torre. "The pain shattered all those present, not just for the sorrowful parents that had just lost their only son, but for the calamity that was bound to come as a result of his death," wrote Peter Martyr to a friend. The widowed princess was pregnant—on 8 December her daughter was stillborn. The grieving monarchs did the only thing they could do—they hid their sorrow and pressed forward.

During late 1497 and early 1498, Columbus carried on a correspondence with an English merchant known as John Day, as evidenced by a letter, almost certainly addressed to Columbus, that surfaced in 1955 in archives at Simancas, Spain. In the letter, Day wrote of the successful voyage of John Cabot, who in 1497 sailed west from Bristol under authority from Henry VII and reached Newfoundland before returning. Day noted that the English were planning a second, larger voyage to begin the following year.

John Cabot was, like Columbus, Genoese,[4] though he had become a citizen of Venice before relocating to Spain, first to Valencia and then to Seville. He was in Valencia in 1493 when Columbus passed through that city on his way to Barcelona and may have begun to develop his own plans for a voyage at that time. During 1494 he was in Seville, where he began construction of a new stone bridge across the Guadalquivir. When the city ceased work on the bridge project in December 1494, Cabot apparently went to London with the idea of obtaining the backing of Henry VII for a trans-Atlantic voyage of his own. He sailed with a single ship on 2 May 1497 and returned on 6 August 1497, ten months before Columbus would leave on his Third Voyage.[5]

The knowledge that England was venturing across the Ocean Sea may have given new impetus to Columbus and the Spanish sovereigns. Columbus's Third Voyage would not compare to the Second Voyage in size and scope: a large expedition was less necessary because ships were now beginning to sail with greater frequency between Cádiz and Hispaniola. There was a need to provide additional supplies to Hispaniola, and the *Niña* and *India* sailed on 23 January 1498 with instructions to go directly to the colony. Columbus sailed with six additional ships, leaving the last week of May.

One of Columbus's objectives of the Third Voyage was to seek out a continent rumored to be found at more southerly latitudes than had yet been explored. Columbus believed that King João II of Portugal had insisted that the line of demarcation be moved further west because he was of the opinion that there was a large continent near the equator, and Columbus wanted to test the king's theory. In addition, Columbus had received a letter from Jaime Ferrer, a Catalan scholar who was a consultant to the court, urging him to explore further south to the equator, convinced that gold would be more abundant at that latitude.

The fleet sailed, as usual, to the Canaries. From there, Columbus sent three ships with instructions to proceed directly to Santo Domingo and deliver their supplies; he would take the other three and explore further south. Because of the improved relationship between Castile and Portugal (as a result of the marriage between the Spanish princess and the new king of Portugal), Columbus was able to go to the Portuguese islands of Cape Verde and start his westward crossing at a much more southerly latitude than the Canaries.[6] He departed the Cape Verde Islands on 4 July 1498 and set a southwesterly course. A week out from Cape Verde the wind ceased and the ships were becalmed for eight consecutive days in an area of the Atlantic that was later dubbed the doldrums.[7] The heat became almost intolerable—casks of wine and water burst open, the bacon and meat putrefied, and the wheat spoiled. Columbus records that had it not been for some cloud cover on several of those days, many of the crew might have perished.

But the wind ultimately returned, and the fleet sailed onward. Looking back over the centuries, it is sometimes difficult to remember that it was not just the first great voyage that was daunting and difficult but every ocean crossing. On this latest crossing the men also began to despair, thinking they were lost and would never return home. Much of their water, wine, and food had spoiled in the heat. As they continued west, the pilots could not agree on their location, giving widely varying opinions. But Columbus informed the crew that he believed they were just south of the Lesser Antilles, or Caribbee islands, he had explored in the fall of 1493. He altered course to the northeast, and at noon the same day a lookout spotted three hills or mountains in the distance. Once again, Columbus's dead reckoning was on target. Columbus named the island Trinidad, not just for its three mountains but because he had previously decided to name their first landfall after the Holy Trinity. Las Casas, in his account of this voyage, which he took from the Admiral's journal, notes that when Columbus left Spain "he departed . . . in the name of the Holy Trinity, as he says, *and as he was always wont to say.*"[8]

After taking on fresh water and giving the men a chance to bathe, the ships continued along the southern coast of Trinidad. To their left they could see what they thought was another island and named it *Isla Sancta,* "Holy Isle." It was, in fact, the coast of South America. At the southwestern tip of Trinidad, the strait narrows, and the ships needed to turn north to continue around the island. In a letter to the sovereigns written three months after the fact, Columbus describes what happened:

> I saw some lines of waves crossing this estuary with a great roaring sound, which made me think that there was a reef here

with rocks and shallows which would prevent us from entering. Beyond this line of waves was another and yet another, which made a great noise like seas breaking on a rocky beach. I anchored here . . . and observed that the water was flowing from east to west as furiously as the Guadalquivir [the river that flows through Seville] in flood. It flowed continuously both day and night, which made me think I could neither turn back on account of the waves, nor go forward on account of the shallows. Late at night standing on the deck I heard a terrible roar approaching the ship from the south. I remained watching and saw the seas rising from west to east, with a swell as high as the ship, which gradually came nearer. On top was a crest of advancing water which rushed on-wards with a tremendous noise like that of the other waves I had observed before. Even today I can recall the fear in my body that the ship might be swamped when it broke over her.[9]

The little ships were tossed up and over the wave, with the only damage the breaking of an anchor chain. Columbus named the strait *Boca del Sierpe,* "Mouth of the Serpent," a name it still carries. The continuous line of waves and treacherous currents were the result of the enormous volume of water flowing from the Orinoco River into the sea. The little fleet entered the Gulf of Paria and sailed north, exploring the land on the north and west of the gulf. Again assuming this was an island, Columbus named it *Gracia.* On 5 August 1496, the ships lowered anchor in a small bay, at or near present-day Ensenada Yacua on the Paria Peninsula of Venezuela. Here for the first time that can be clearly documented, Europeans set foot on the South American continent.

Though he wanted to spend more time exploring this coast, Columbus felt compelled to push towards Santo Domingo, where his brother Bartholomew awaited him. The ships sailed out of the Gulf of Paria through the northern passage but only after dealing with the treacherous currents created by the conflict of sea tides and fresh water

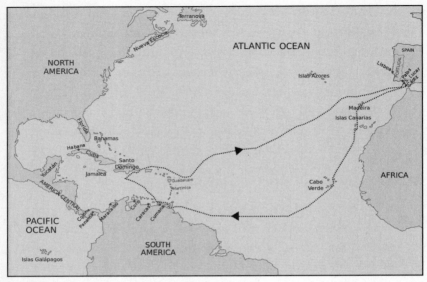

Route of the Third Voyage.

flowing with force from the Orinoco. Columbus named this passage *Boca del Dragón,* "Mouth of Dragon," feeling that the ships had been blessed to escape from the mouth of a dragon.

Even though Columbus had begun this journey with the objective of finding the southern continent rumored to exist near the equator, he seems to have determined that the continent did not exist when he did not find it before arriving at Trinidad. After leaving the Gulf of Paria, the painful eye problem from which the Admiral had suffered in Cuba during the Second Voyage returned, probably due to lack of sleep while negotiating the dangerous coastal waters. Although the expedition learned from local Indians of the rich pearl beds off the coast of Venezuela, Columbus was physically exhausted and felt a pressing need to sail to Hispaniola and the seat of his governorship. His eyes still aflame, he gave orders to head towards Santo Domingo and left the ship in the hands of his officers. As he rested for the first time in weeks, he had time to think about the mysterious currents he had encountered in the Gulf of Paria. Neither Columbus nor any of his crew had ever seen one of the great rivers of the world, and Columbus continued to think about the vast quantity of fresh water being discharged by the Orinoco. As he tried to make sense of so much fresh water flowing into the sea, pushing the salt water miles from shore, he came to the inescapable conclusion that such a river could not be contained on an island—only a large continental land mass could produce such a tremendous flow of water. Yet this continental land mass was clearly not Asia—there were no signs of a highly civilized culture or government. On 13 August 1496, two days after leaving the island he had named *Gracia,* Columbus recorded in his journal what Fernandez-Armesto called "one of the most momentous statements in the history of exploration."[10] The statement is contained in a single sentence in the Admiral's hand: "I believe this is a very large continent which until now has remained unknown."[11]

During these early weeks of August, Columbus had also been thinking about the variations he had observed in his compass readings. He had first noticed a variation between the compass needle and the North Star on the First Voyage, and while sailing through the Gulf of Paria in August 1496 he took several readings. As he thought about the cause of the variations, he concluded that the earth was not a perfect sphere. Though both his data and his logic were flawed, his conclusion was at least partially correct: the earth is not a perfect sphere but is somewhat bulged at the equator.

Having theorized that the earth was not perfectly round, he concluded that, like a pear, it had a protuberance and that where "this protuberance stands is the highest and nearest to the sky. It lies below the equator, and in this ocean, at the farthest point of the east, I mean by the farthest point of the east the place where all land and islands end."[12]

Columbus was familiar with medieval speculation and philosophy regarding the location of the Terrestrial Paradise, or Garden of Eden. In his copy of *Imago mundi,* where D'Ailly discusses a mountain at the far end of the Orient, Columbus had written in the margin, "The

Terrestrial Paradise is there."[13] John Mandeville's *Travels* gives a very specific description of the location of the Garden of Eden:

> The Earthly Paradise, so men say, is the highest land on earth . . . In the middle of Paradise is a spring from which come four rivers . . . with so strong a current, and with such a rush and such waves that no boat can sail against them. There is also such a great noise of waters that one man cannot hear another.[14]

Likewise, Dante recounts the belief that the Garden of Eden was located at the edge of the East and at the highest point on the globe. It was commonly believed to be antipodal to Jerusalem—that is, at a point exactly opposite on the earth from the Holy City. Columbus's study of the Bible convinced him that in the last days both the Old Jerusalem would be restored and the Terrestrial Paradise would be found, and thus two great centers, or capitals, would be created at opposite sides of the globe.

From the variations in the compass, the enormous rush of waters flowing out of the new continent, and the seeming bulge in the surface of the earth, Columbus concluded that he was near the highest point on the globe and hence the Terrestrial Paradise was located on this newly discovered continent. In a letter to the sovereigns, he details his reasoning over several pages, referencing Aristotle, Ptolemy, and Genesis, and describing in detail his celestial observations. He was particularly convinced that the great flow of fresh water coming into the sea must come from the fountain of Paradise. "I have never read or heard," he writes, "of such a quantity of fresh water flowing so close to the salt and flowing into it . . . I do not believe that there is so great and deep a river anywhere in the world."[15] He summarized his conclusion with this statement: "I believe that, if I pass below the Equator, on reaching these higher regions I shall find a much cooler climate and a greater difference in the stars and waters . . . For I believe that the earthly Paradise is there, which no one can enter except by God's will."[16]

Not only had he discovered a hitherto unknown continent but the Garden of Eden itself was located on that new continent! As was true so often with Columbus, he was right for all the wrong reasons. His logic and his observations were faulty—just as they had been when he argued that it was possible to safely sail across the Ocean Sea or that the earth was not a perfect sphere—but his conclusion was correct.

In both his journal and a letter written to the sovereigns a few months later, Columbus expressed his concern that few people apart from the sovereigns themselves seemed to have much faith in the value of his enterprise. He acknowledged the firm support of the monarchs but wrote that he was "worried by what I have heard about certain persons, since constant dripping wears a hole in a stone." He was concerned that so many had complained that "so far no ships have been sent back loaded with gold." He assured his patrons that not only would Christianity be extended but that "great profit will shortly accrue from these lands."[17] He then made this prophetic statement: "Your Highnesses have won these great lands, which are another world [*que es otro mundo*], where Christianity will have much enjoyment and our faith, in time, will have great growth."[18]

It was a bold prophecy and reflected Columbus's unwavering faith in the grand mission of his life—to carry the message of Christianity across the Ocean Sea. Only a relatively few Indians had been baptized in Hispaniola, and it is unlikely that those baptized really understood anything of Christianity. Disgruntled and angry colonists had returned to Spain and were engaged in a campaign to discredit the foreign-born Admiral, a campaign that was meeting with some success. Morison observed:

> At a time when not fifty people of importance in Spain believed in Columbus or valued his discoveries, when the court doubtless hoped that shipwreck or other disaster would rid them forever of this importunate Genoese, when his name was a curse

on the lips of the Spaniards in Hispaniola, he foresaw the vast revenue that his Sovereigns were about to secure. He foretold that Christianity, whose area had been shrinking since the rise of Islam, would here win new converts to the Cross, that the Catholic faith was destined to advance triumphantly into *Otro Mundo,* this Other and New World.[19]

But not even Morison could appreciate the full impact of what Columbus seemed to see with the eye of faith, though through a glass darkly: in this New World, Christianity would be renewed and restored, and a new dispensation would unfold upon the continent where Eden once had flourished.

Chapter 12

EAST OF EDEN

And I saw a new heaven and a new earth; for the first heaven and
the first earth were passed away; and there was no more sea.

REVELATION 21:1

In the same week of August 1498, while the Admiral was pondering on the location of the Terrestrial Paradise, he was also "successfully concluding one of the finest bits of dead reckoning in his maritime career."[1] From a location in the Caribbean north of Trinidad, where neither he nor any other European had ever sailed, he was heading for Santo Domingo, a city on Hispaniola that he had never seen. Since leaving the Cape Verde Islands the first week of July, he had not had the opportunity to verify his position with any known landmark; he was entirely dependent upon his daily estimates of speed, distance, and direction to plot by hand his dead-reckoning course on his chart. On 20 August he anchored between two small islands off the shore of Hispaniola about 100 miles from his target of Santo Domingo. Las Casas, who had access to Columbus's journal of the voyage, notes that "it grieved him to have

149

missed by so much."[2] The somewhat disappointed Admiral correctly surmised that he had underestimated the strong westward currents. By any measure it was an extraordinary piece of navigation.

Nearly two and a half years had passed since Columbus left Hispaniola. Before leaving, he and his brother Bartholomew had pacified the island and established a small chain of forts. He had appointed Bartholomew *Adelantado*[3] and left him in charge of affairs in the New World. He no doubt hoped to find peace and growing prosperity in his viceroyalty, to perhaps have some time to rest his bloodshot and painful eyes, and to recuperate from the arthritis that had begun to plague him since the stormy return home from the First Voyage five years earlier. But if such were his hopes, they were quickly dashed.

Before leaving Hispaniola in 1496, Columbus had appointed Francisco Roldán as *alcalde,* or mayor, of La Isabela. Roldán was able, ambitious, and resented the leadership of the Genoese Columbus brothers. In the absence of the viceroy, he saw an opportunity to obtain both greater power and wealth. Bartholomew, like his brother Christopher, expected the colonists to act in orderly and almost monastic harmony, an expectation that consistently proved disappointingly optimistic. Roldán fomented seeds of rebellion among the men and promised the discontents that he would allow them more food, women, permission to collect gold for themselves, and the option of living anywhere they wanted. With an organized group, he broke into the armory, stole weapons and ammunition, slaughtered the cattle (a particularly odd move, as one of the rebels' complaints was the lack of food), stole the horses, and rode off to the southwest section of the island known as Xaragua. There the rebels formed alliances with the Indians by promising to eliminate the tribute that had been imposed by Columbus. The Indians, however, soon discovered that they had been deceived by Roldán and his men: Roldán kept the tribute for himself and his men quickly engaged in plundering the native villages, raping the women, and enslaving captives.

The three ships that Columbus had sent to Hispaniola directly from the Canaries—carrying additional food, farm implements, and even some musicians whom Columbus hoped would cheer up the settlers and induce them to act in a more civilized manner—lost their way and did not arrive until July. Worse, they landed in Xaragua, and Roldán convinced many of the men on board to join his band of rebels. The ships carried a letter from Columbus to his brother that was properly delivered, and it contained the news that the sovereigns themselves had confirmed Bartholomew's title of *Adelantado*. Upon receipt of the letter, Bartholomew's first official act was to strip Roldán of his title of *alcalde* and threaten prosecution as a rebel to the crown if he continued with his rebellion. But Bartholomew and his men were almost as helpless to stop Roldán as the local Indians: Roldán had guns, and they did not. Such was the news Columbus received when he was greeted by his brother.

Columbus did not want war with Roldán and did everything he could think of to restore the peace and reduce tensions. He offered supplies, free passage back to Spain, letters of commendation, whatever it would take to convince them to leave the island. He offered to meet with Roldán, but Roldán refused. Columbus tried to negotiate, but the months dragged on. In August 1499, Columbus sailed from Santo Domingo to Xaragua and finally negotiated an agreement that Roldán signed but never lived up to.

Meanwhile, back in Spain, Alonso Hojeda, who had done so much damage in the early days at La Isabela, had heard the report sent by Columbus of the pearl fisheries and set sail for Paria in search of pearls. After sailing along the mainland just north of where Columbus had left off the previous year, he arrived at Hispaniola on 5 September 1499 and landed near the area where Roldán and his men had established themselves. Hojeda attempted to displace Roldán and establish himself as the leader of the rebels but ultimately failed and returned safely to Spain.[4]

Roldán soon found himself dealing with rebellions among his own men, including a plot by a rival to assassinate him. And during all this, the rebellious Christians continued to plunder the native population, killing Indians capriciously and capturing both slaves and concubines. If Columbus thought he had found the Terrestrial Paradise a year earlier, Hispaniola must have seemed like the Terrestrial Inferno. It seemed as if all he had hoped for was slipping from his grasp—the conversion of the Indians, the wealth to fund a new crusade, and establishment of a great new Christian civilization. In the midst of these struggles, he found his own life in danger:

> On Christmas Day of 1499, having been abandoned by all, I was attacked by Indians and the wicked Christians. I found myself in such peril that to save my life, I left all, entered a small caravel, and put out to sea. The Lord came to my aid, saying, "O man of little faith, fear not, I am with thee." And he scattered my enemies and showed me how He could fulfill all that was promised me. Alas, sinful man that I am, to have trusted completely in worldly hope.[5]

It was not the first time that Columbus had heard a Divine voice, nor would it be the last. For whatever failings he might have had as a colonial administrator, he was a man of remarkable faith and devotion.

To help resolve matters on the island, Columbus had urged the queen by letter to appoint an investigator to journey to the island under her direct authority (and at Columbus's expense, if necessary) to investigate and resolve the turmoil on the island. She decided to do so and assigned the task to Francisco de Bobadilla, a man who was of noble birth and a native of Aragon. He was the brother of the queen's best friend, Beatriz de Bobadilla, and a commander of the military

Order of Calatrava. In short, he had all the connections and status that Columbus did not have. But as Isabella would find out soon enough, Bobadilla proved to be an incredibly poor choice.

Columbus was inland when Bobadilla arrived at Santo Domingo in August 1500. Upon entering the settlement, Bobadilla was greeted by the sight of two Spaniards hanging from a gallows in public view. They had been executed at Columbus's command for rebellion and for mistreatment of Indians as an example to both the colonists and the Indians that the rule of law applied even in this distant outpost of the kingdom. Bobadilla immediately sympathized with his disaffected countrymen and quickly made his own intentions clear—he declared himself governor, seized Columbus's property, including all his papers, moved into the governor's mansion, and ingratiated himself with the colonists by easing the restrictions on gathering gold and reducing the amount they needed to pay to the crown.

As soon as he received notification of the investigator's arrival, Columbus returned quickly—and, no doubt, hopefully—to Santo Domingo to meet with the man whom he hoped would conduct a fair investigation of the rebellion and help bring order and justice back to the island. But Bobadilla was not interested in an investigation, much less order or justice. He immediately put Columbus in chains and imprisoned him. He took no testimony from Columbus and gave no reason for his actions. When he had ships ready to sail back to Spain, he took Columbus from the dungeon and marched him to one of the departing ships, while the malcontents shouted insults at the chained Admiral as he shuffled from the stockade to the shore.[6]

Five years earlier, Columbus had returned to Spain a hero. Now he was wearing shackles, having been imprisoned by the emissary of the very queen who had been his great supporter. It was a stunning reversal, though not entirely unusual—temporary imprisonment was something of an occupational hazard for prominent nobles in late fifteenth-century Spain. Even so, Las Casas, who greatly admired the Admiral but was very critical of his actions as viceroy and governor, found the treatment of Columbus appalling, cruel, and inhumane. Columbus, understandably, felt betrayed and wronged. "If I had robbed the Indies and the adjoining lands from the altar of St. Peter [that is, from the realm of Christianity] and given them to the Moors," he wrote, "they could not have shown me greater enmity in Spain. Who could believe such a thing from a land of such nobility?"[7]

As was always the case in times of great discouragement, of which Columbus had more than his share during his life, his great faith buoyed him up and carried him through. While a prisoner in chains he wrote to his friend Juana de la Torre, the nanny of Prince Juan, "I have been cruelly cast into the depths, but my hope in Him who created all sustains me; His support has always been swift." He recounted the recent event when the voice of the Lord came to him while alone on a caravel escaping his enemies, saying, "Not long ago when I was cast even lower, He raised me with His right arm, saying, 'Oh man of little faith, arise, it is I, be not afraid!'"[8] He held firm to the knowledge that the Almighty had called him to the work he had undertaken, paraphrasing from Isaiah and the Revelation of John, "Of the new heaven and the new earth, of which Our Lord spoke . . . He made me the messenger and He showed me where to go."[9]

Chapter 13

THE MIND AND HEART OF COLUMBUS

Before thou didst form me in the womb, thou knewest me,
and before I went forth from the womb, thou didst preordain
concerning me whatever was pleasing to thee.[1]

St. Augustine

t was probably early November of 1500 when the ship carrying Columbus arrived in Cádiz. Although the captain had offered to remove the Admiral's chains once they left Hispaniola, Columbus refused: he had been shackled by an emissary of the queen and would remain in chains until she ordered them removed. He added that he would keep the shackles as a reminder of the reward given him for his service to the crown. His son Fernando recalled seeing them years later in the Admiral's bedroom.

Columbus sent a letter to the sovereigns dated 20 November 1500 and three weeks later received a return letter ordering him released and inviting him to court. They also sent him 2,000 ducats, a welcome gift since he had not been able to take any money, gold, or even his papers with him from Hispaniola. On 17 December 1500, Columbus and his brother Diego arrived at the court in the Alhambra at Granada.

"The Admiral kissed the hands of the King and the Queen, and with tears made his apologies as well as he could; and after they had heard him, with great clemency they consoled him and spoke such words that he was somewhat content." They restored to him all his income and rights and the property that had been confiscated by Bobadilla. "But never did they allow that he would have a role in governing."[2] Within a year, the sovereigns appointed Nicolás de Ovando as governor of the Indies, making it clear that Columbus's title of Viceroy and Governor, as granted in the Capitulations of Santa Fe, was now essentially meaningless.

With no role in governing and no plans yet for another voyage, Columbus turned his attention to two projects. The first was to carefully document and record all the promises and agreements given him by the monarchs. He endeavored to document all that was due him and his heirs and to do so clearly and plainly as a reminder to the sovereigns, to his heirs, and to anyone else who might be interested that he was not receiving the promised benefits of his great life work, the Enterprise of the Indies. His son Diego was now a young man of twenty; Fernando, a youth of twelve. Columbus was in his fiftieth year in an era when the average life span was about fifty years: he was clearly concerned for the future of his sons. After assembling copies of all the pertinent documents, Columbus had at least four copies made of what is known as the Book of Privileges. He sent one copy to Nicoló Oderigo, the former Genoese ambassador to Castile and Aragon. Another copy went to the Bank of St. George in Genoa. A third copy was sent to Hispaniola in the care of his representative, Alonso Sanchez de Carvajal, and a fourth was deposited at the monastery of Santa María de las Cuevas with Friar Gaspar de Gorricio (to whom Columbus had also entrusted his *majorat,* or will). The four copies, though not identical, have thirty-seven documents in common and constitute a remarkable summary of many of the important historical documents of the day, including a copy of the papal bull *Inter caetera,* which divided the New World between Portugal and Spain. The book would become a valuable resource to Columbus's heirs in their lengthy legal battles with the crown over the next several decades. It is an even more valuable resource to historians.

The second great project undertaken by Columbus after his return to Spain was an extensive compilation of scriptural and authoritative citations, together with his own commentaries and explanations, all of which were designed to support his assertion that his discoveries were a part, an important part, of the Divine plan. He was aided in this effort by his friend Friar Gorricio at Las Cuevas, who provided some suggestions and editing.

Gorricio described the document as a book, or collection, of authoritative writings, sayings, opinions, and prophecies concerning the need to recover the Holy City and Mount Zion and the finding and conversion of the islands of the Indies and of all peoples and nations.[3] It is generally known today as the *Libro de las profecías,* the "Book of Prophecies." A less confusing and more descriptive title might be Notebook of Prophetic Statements and Scriptures.

The *Libro de las profecías* consists of 84 folios yielding 168 pages bound together to form a single manuscript. Nine pages are blank, and three contain only a single sentence; nine and one half sheets have been cut and removed from the document. It appears that most of the document was compiled between early 1501 and March 1502, with a few later additions to the text, including a note regarding the eclipse of the moon on 29 February 1504.

The handwriting includes that of Columbus's then-thirteen-year-old son, Fernando, with extensive passages written by the hand of Gorricio, some small sections by an unidentified hand, and some passages in Columbus's own distinctive handwriting. Columbus's health was continuing to fail, and it was difficult for him to write. One medical scholar posits that he suffered from Reiter's syndrome, a severe form of arthritis that often affects the joints as well as causing painful inflammation of the eyes, both symptoms described by Columbus. As a result, both the Book of Privileges and the *Libro de las profecías* are largely in handwriting other than his own, and while accompanying correspondence indicates that Columbus sought the advice and input of Gorricio on the *Libro,* it is clear that Columbus was the ultimate author of both documents. As Fernandez-Armesto notes, "Columbus's collection of prophecies shows the influence of no hand other than Columbus's own."[4]

The *Libro de las profecías* is an unfinished work. In a letter to Friar Gorricio dated 13 September 1501, Columbus states his intention to revise the materials and turn them into poetic form, but there is no evidence that he ever achieved this monumental goal. A reference to the bound manuscript is found in the inventory of Diego Columbus's property, and it was then cataloged as item number 2091 in the library of Diego's brother, Fernando. Both Fernando and Las Casas mention it as a source they used in writing their histories. It ultimately found its way to the *Biblioteca Colombina* in Seville, along with other items from Fernando's library, and was described and recatalogued in the library's catalogue of 1888.

The document was seen and mentioned by several early Columbus biographers, including Washington Irving, but none of them included material from the *Libro* in their works. Not until 1892 was the full text transcribed and printed. In that year it was included in the *Raccolta di documenti e studi pubblicati dalla R. Commissione Colombiana,* a collection of documents published as part of the quadricentennial celebration of Columbus's First Voyage. Only 560 copies of this collection were printed, so access was limited—a scholar would first have to find one of the volumes, and then he or she would need an extensive knowledge of both Latin and Spanish in order to read it.[5]

Those scholars who did have access to the *Libro* either ignored it (as did Irving) or found it an embarrassment to its author. William H. Prescott, the great historian of the conquest of Peru and Mexico, describes the *Libro* as "dark and mysterious annunciations of sacred prophecy" and "visionary fancies." French historian Henri Harisse expressed his hope that it "will never be published." Filson Young, whose four-volume biography of Columbus was published in 1906, decries the deep state of Columbus's mental health reflected in this collection of scriptures and prophecies: "Good Heavens! In what an entirely dark and sordid stupor has our Christopher now sunk—a veritable slough and quag of stupor out of which, if he does not manage to flounder himself, no human hand can pull him."[6] Both Morison and Fernandez-Armesto see the document largely as a ploy by Columbus to place himself back in the good graces of the sovereigns by convincing them that he was a man of divine destiny.

The publication of the first English translation of the *Libro* by Delno C. West and August Kling in 1991 opened an essentially new era of scholarship by making this important document accessible to a broader audience. West and Kling placed the *Libro* in "the larger body of apocalyptic literature from the late middle ages in Europe" and see the book as neither radical nor the ravings of a psychotic man nor of a man in a theological stupor but as a well-thought-out collection of biblical and scholarly sources that support Columbus's frequent and unwavering assertion that he was led by God to open the gates of the Ocean Sea as part of the great plan of history.

More than any other document he wrote, the *Libro de las profecías* gives the student of Columbus direct insight into the Discoverer's mind and heart. The ideas and concepts set forth in his collection of statements and biblical prophecies were not developed at age fifty—the fundamental ideas can be seen in his writings at least as early as 1481, when he was thirty years old and his great idea was still taking form.

[margin handwritten note: We should understand it as divine inspiration.]

It shows him as a serious and dedicated student, not just of the Bible but of ancient and medieval authors. His sources include writers from Christian, Jewish, and Muslim backgrounds. Columbus was remarkably well read.

The key themes of the *Libro de las profecías* are clear and simple. They are that God had called Columbus and qualified him to open the gates of the Ocean Sea for the purposes of preaching the gospel to all nations and obtaining the gold necessary to finance a new crusade, retake Jerusalem, and rebuild the temple in preparation for the return of the Savior.

Like many of his age, Columbus believed that the end of the world was not far distant and that while his discoveries were key, there was still much to be done to fulfill all the prophecies: "Much of the prophecies remained to be fulfilled, and I believe that these are great events for the world. I believe that there is evidence that our Lord is hastening these things. This evidence is the fact that the Gospel must now be proclaimed to so many lands in such a short time."[7] And time was short. In 1481, Columbus had calculated that 1,759 years remained until the end of the world. Now, thirty years later, using what he apparently viewed as more reliable sources, he calculated that only 155 "years are lacking for the completion of the seven thousand years which would be the end of the world according to the learned opinions that I have cited above."[8] Columbus felt a great urgency about his work.

The idea for the Enterprise of the Indies came to him as inspiration, "with a hand that could be felt" (*con mano palpable*), and his mind was enlightened "with a radiance of marvelous illumination from his sacred Holy Scriptures." The scriptures, together with the fire of the Holy Ghost, urged him "to press forward with great haste." The bulk of the *Libro de las profecías* consists of the scriptures that illuminated his mind and kept him pressing forward with his great enterprise.

The book begins with a lengthy introduction in which Columbus

sets forth his themes and establishes his credentials. Aware that a doc-
trinal dissertation written by a layman with little or no formal education was likely to be received with skepticism, he explains his method
of scriptural exegesis. He draws upon St. Thomas Aquinas's statement
that "the Holy Scripture is expounded by four methods. The first
is as history . . . The second is allegory . . . The third is tropology
[which Columbus explains as teaching us how we should act] . . . The
fourth is analogy."[9] He gives several examples of the application of this
methodology, using it to analyze selected verses from Psalms and from
1 Corinthians.

He readily admits that his observations will be open to criticism
based on the fact that "I am unlearned in literature, a layman, a mariner, a common worldly man." But he responds by quoting Matthew:
"O Lord, because thou has hid these things from the wise and prudent and hast revealed them to little ones."[10] He notes that the ancient
apostles lacked formal education yet made "exalted statements." Like
the ancient apostles, Columbus declares that he has been enlightened
by the fire of the Holy Ghost and his mind illuminated by the Holy
Scriptures. He adds this remarkable and, at the time, almost heretical
declaration: "I believe that the Holy Spirit works among Christians,
Jews and Moslems, and among all men of every faith, not merely
among the learned, but also among the uneducated." This was a particularly bold statement in the days of the Spanish Inquisition.

Having thus established his credentials, Columbus turns to citing
the scriptures and other authorities to show with clarity and certainty
that all he had undertaken "turned out just as our redeemer Jesus Christ
had said, and as he had spoken earlier by the mouth of his holy prophets." He quotes Matthew 24:14, "This gospel of the kingdom shall be
preached in all the world for a witness unto all nations, and then shall
the end come." He also quotes Mark 13:10, "The gospel must first be
published among all nations," and explains that by "first" Mark means

"before the end comes." He highlights a statement from Nicolas of Lyra, "that there is another preaching of the gospel that is yet to take place, with such effectiveness that all the Gentiles will accept the faith of Christ." From the writings of St. Augustine he notes that "the God of Israel . . . will be worshiped not only in the single nation known as Israel, but he will be worshiped in all the nations."[11] With these and other citations, Columbus builds his case that before the Savior returns to establish his kingdom on the earth, all nations must hear the gospel message and that his Voyage of Discovery was an essential element in fulfilling these prophecies. How could the gospel be preached to the inhabitants of the New World if Columbus had not opened the way?

In his discussion of the prophesied spread of the gospel, Columbus cites John 10:14, 16: "I am the good shepherd: and I know mine, and mine know me etc. And other sheep I have that are not of this fold: them also I must bring. And they shall hear my voice: and there shall be one fold and one shepherd."[12] He devotes six paragraphs to this particular verse and includes references to the metaphor of one flock in citations from Augustine, St. John Chrysostom, and St. Gregory. He concludes that these other sheep "are the remnant people, of whom it is elsewhere prophesied [he here refers to Isaiah 10:22] . . . Indeed these are the remnants of that nation, who shall have believed in Christ."[13]

Though he sees events through a medieval lens, Columbus creates a compelling argument that in the last days the gospel will go to all the world, that it will go with clarity and power, and that the faithful Gentiles who accept the gospel will come into the fold of Christ. He provides in the *Libro* the supporting evidence for the prophetic statement he had made three years earlier off the coast of Venezuela that in this New World, Christianity would find new life and vigor.

He draws upon Psalms and Isaiah to establish the necessity of re-building the temple and the Holy City and urges the monarchs in no uncertain terms to move forward boldly to obtain control of the Holy

City and use the wealth that would flow from the Indies to rebuild the temple with all the opulence of Solomon's Temple. Bringing Jerusalem into Christian hands and rebuilding the temple was a theme that motivated Columbus throughout the many years since the Enterprise of the Indies had begun to take shape in his mind.

The *Libro de las profecías* is a remarkable and substantial work. It shows Columbus as a serious student with a keen and disciplined mind. To give a sense of its scope, the document cites from 247 chapters of the Bible (including 84 chapters from Psalms and 61 from Isaiah). Citations also come from the Koran and fifty-three different authors, ranging from Aristotle to Roger Bacon.[14] It consists of four major sections: an introduction, a section dealing with the past ("*De Preterito*"), a section dealing with the near future ("*De Presenti et Futuro*"), and a section dealing with the last days ("*De Futuro. In Novissimis*"). Notes at the end of the manuscript include a list of eighty-three additional scriptures that Columbus apparently hoped to include in a more finished manuscript and also a lengthy poem. The poem is written in an unidentified hand but may have been composed by Columbus.

The *Libro de las profecías* reinforces Columbus's frequently stated belief that he had been chosen, or called, of God before he was born to play a significant role in the opening of a new age that would culminate with the end of the world. He paraphrases a favorite passage from Seneca's *Medea:* "In the latter years of the world will come certain times in which the Ocean Sea will relax the bonds of things, and a great land will open up, and a new mariner like the one who was the guide of Jason, whose name was Typhis, will discover a new world."[15] Years later, Columbus's son Fernando wrote a note in the margin next to this passage in his own copy of *Medea:* "This prophecy was fulfilled by my father . . . the Admiral in the year 1492."[16]

At the conclusion of the section dealing with the near future, Columbus inserts a short poem entitled "Joy in the birth of Saint

John the Baptist." Fernandez-Armesto observed, "He saw himself, like that other hero of his, John the Baptist, as 'a man sent from God.'"[17] Columbus had a particular affinity for John the Baptist and saw himself in a similar role as the forerunner of a new dispensation, the final dispensation before the second coming of Christ. West observed, "John the Baptist was . . . the messenger of the New Testament. He paved the way for Christ's mission during the First Advent as Columbus would pave the way for the Second Advent."[18] Washington Irving, in his landmark biography of the Admiral, observed that Columbus "considered his great discovery but as a preparatory dispensation of Providence."[19]

The *Libro de profecías* opens a window into the scholarly and religious mind of Columbus, and it opens a window into his heart and spirit. Columbus firmly believed that as John the Baptist was the forerunner and messenger of Christ in the meridian of time, so he himself was the messenger of the new heaven and new earth in the last days. As John the Baptist carried the Savior out of the waters of baptism and declared to the people His divine Sonship, so Christopher Columbus, *Xpo Ferens,* carried the message of Christ across the uncrossable waters and presented the Savior to a new world in a new age.

Chapter 14

NATURE'S WRATH
AND GOD'S INFINITE MERCY

By God's will and good seamanship.[1]

SAMUEL ELIOT MORISON

ccupied as he was with the Book of Privileges and the *Libro de las profecías,* Columbus was nevertheless anxious to sail again to the New World. Early in 1501, he wrote to Friar Gorricio, "In the business of the Indies, nothing has been heard or is heard, not for our ill but for our good."[2] Ever the optimist, for Columbus no news was good news. But, as was often the case, the sovereigns had other things on their minds, and outfitting a new expedition for the man whose tenure in Hispaniola had been the cause of so much contention was a low priority. Ferdinand, who seemed always to have a hand in the ever-shifting political landscape of Europe, was occupied in dealing with the French and Italians, and he had also arranged yet another strategic marriage, this time of his youngest daughter.

In May, Columbus wrote again to Gorricio from the court, "Here there is always something going on which puts all other matters in the background. The Lady Princess departed in the name of our Lord, and it is believed that now something will be done about the Indies."[3] The "Lady Princess" was young Catherine of Aragon, and she had departed on 21 May for England to marry Arthur, Prince of Wales. The prince and princess had been betrothed for eighteen months, but not until Arthur turned fifteen were they considered old enough to marry. Catherine and the prince met on 4 November and were married ten days later. Within five months of the marriage, Arthur died from an illness and Catherine found herself a widow at age sixteen. Seven years would pass before she married Arthur's brother, Henry VIII, when she was twenty-three and he was eighteen. It was a marriage that would change the history of England and much of the world.

In the meantime, others were sailing the Ocean Sea, which Columbus had opened, and gaining both fame and fortune. Pedro Álvares Cabral discovered Brazil and claimed it for Portugal. Columbus's friend Amerigo Vespucci was venturing down the coast of South America. Juan de Escalante, an officer on Columbus's Third Voyage, was given permission to travel to the Caribbean. Even the infamous Alonso de Hojeda was allowed to take four ships to the Indies for his own account. And on 3 September 1501, Nicolás de Ovando was officially appointed by the sovereigns as governor of the Indies. The only concession the monarchs made to Columbus was to allow him to send a representative to Hispaniola to collect his personal property that had been confiscated by Bobadilla. The crown appointed Alonso Sanchez de Carvajal to represent Columbus and issued a detailed order regarding the return of Columbus's papers, books, and personal possessions.

Ovando sailed from Cádiz on 13 February 1502 with a fleet of thirty ships carrying twenty-five hundred men, including the young Bartolomé de Las Casas. Another month passed before Columbus was finally granted permission to prepare for a fourth voyage. In contrast to the great fleet captained by Ovando, Columbus was authorized four vessels.

Still, Columbus seemed pleased. He was always happier at sea than when he was trying to manage unmanageable colonists, and there was still much to explore. This fourth voyage was to be dedicated solely to exploration. Hoping to avoid trouble, the sovereigns expressly prohibited Columbus from stopping at Hispaniola on the outward voyage, although they did grant him permission to put in at Santo Domingo before returning home if he deemed it necessary to resupply his ships and men for the homeward crossing.

Columbus's hope was not to return across the Atlantic at all but to find a strait that would lead to the Indian Ocean. Knowing that Vasco de Gama was sailing to India via Africa, Columbus held out the possibility of finding his way to the Indian Ocean, meeting up with de Gama, and returning home around the Cape of Good Hope, thus circumnavigating the globe. The sovereigns provided Columbus with a letter of introduction carrying greetings to de Gama and instructed that they "should deal with one another as friends, as captains and subjects of Kings bound together by love and kinship."[4]

The four ships were procured and readied for the expedition at Seville in a matter of weeks. The ships were small, about the size of the Admiral's favorite *Niña,* well suited for exploration among the islands and along the coasts, yet sturdy enough for an ocean crossing. They carried a total crew of 135 in addition to Columbus and a few others; Fernando reports a total of 140 personnel, but not all of them were included on the official roster.

Many of the crew were old friends and had sailed with Columbus on previous voyages, testimony to the high esteem in which he was still held by seamen. Pedro de Terreros, who had been with Columbus on each of the three previous voyages, captained *La Gallega.* The *Vizcaína* was captained by Bartolomeo Fieschi, a Genoese mariner whose family had been friends of the Colombus family from before Christopher's birth. The *Santiago* was captained by Francisco de Porras, whose brother accompanied him as auditor and representative of the crown. The Porras brothers were not Columbus's choice but were on the voyage at the insistence of the treasurer of Castile (who kept their sister as a mistress). They would prove to be both incompetent and disloyal, and their actions would result in the deaths of several men. But Columbus's brother Bartholomew sailed aboard the *Santiago* and acted as virtual captain.

Also accompanying Columbus on this voyage was his son Fernando, a boy of thirteen. Fernando's recollections of the voyage add an important eyewitness account to the adventure that was about to begin.

Columbus was fifty-one, an aged man for the era, and he was in ill health. He and Fernando sailed on the flagship *La Capitana,* but he gave command of the vessel to a former shipmate and faithful friend, Diego Tristán.

Columbus referred to this voyage as *El Alto Viaje,* "the High Voyage," probably because he had high hopes for discovery of the elusive strait and the first circumnavigation of the earth. Those hopes would not be realized, but the voyage would be an adventure of epic proportions: a hurricane, battling the elements, leaky ships, heroism, loyalty, mutiny, shipwreck, courage, and endurance. Of the four ships, which seemed so seaworthy as they were being loaded at the port of Seville, not one would make it back to Spain. Of the 135 men and boys on the official payroll, a quarter of them would never return.

The adventure began as they left Cádiz in early May. Word had come that the Moors were attacking the Portuguese fortress of Arzila on the coast of Morocco. Manuel I of Portugal was now the son-in-law of Isabella and Ferdinand, and it is likely that the sovereigns asked Columbus to sail that way in hopes of providing a show of force. But by the time Columbus's little fleet of four unarmed caravels arrived on 13 May, the Moors had retreated. Columbus remained on his ship, where he greeted a delegation sent by the governor that included cousins of Doña Felipa, Columbus's deceased wife. The stopover was apparently brief, as the fleet arrived at the Grand Canary on 20 May. The ships departed for the ocean crossing on 25 May and made landfall at Martinique on 15 June. At just twenty-one days, it was the fastest crossing that Columbus had made. It was one of the last things that would go well on this voyage.

Columbus was unhappy with the *Santiago:* he was concerned about its suitability for exploration along the coast (he referred to it as *"el navio sospechoso,"* which translates as "the dubious ship") and hoped to exchange it for a more suitable ship at Santo Domingo, where a large fleet was preparing to return to Spain. He arrived at the harbor of Santo Domingo, but in accordance with his instructions from the sovereigns, he stayed aboard his ship, which was anchored at sea. He requested permission to enter the harbor to investigate the possibility of acquiring a better ship to replace the *Santiago* as well as to protect his little fleet from a storm that he sensed was brewing.

Columbus had witnessed two hurricanes before, one in August 1494 and another in October 1495, and he recognized the signs: an oily swell rolling from the southeast, thin cirrus clouds racing across the sky with only light gusts at the surface, an unusually high tide, an oppressive feeling in the air. He advised Governor Ovando to detain the homeward-bound fleet in port until the storm had passed. But the weather seemed fair, and Ovando was not inclined to take any advice from the Viceroy, whom he was effectively replacing. He declined Columbus's request for shelter in the harbor and sent the fleet on its way, mocking Columbus as a prophet and soothsayer for attempting to forecast bad weather on such a beautiful summer day.

Denied shelter in the harbor, Columbus quickly moved his little fleet to the west and anchored close to shore where the island provided some protection from the northwest winds. The wind increased throughout the day of 30 June, and by nightfall the full force of the storm was unleashed. Only the *Capitana* remained anchored; the cables snapped on the other three ships, and they were driven out to sea. "The storm was terrible," wrote Columbus,

> and on that night my fleet was broken up. Everyone lost hope and was quite certain that all the rest were lost. What mortal man, even Job himself, would not have died of despair? Even for the safety of myself, my son, brother and friends, I was forbidden in such weather to put into land or enter harbors that I, by the grace of God, had obtained for Spain by my own blood and sweat."[5]

The *Santiago,* under the command of Porras, was nearly lost, but the *Adelantado,* whom Fernando described as the best seaman on the voyage, took control and brought the ship safely through. By prior arrangement, the ships met at a small harbor to the west, all surprised to see the other ships afloat and their shipmates alive. Columbus gave credit first to God (as always) and second to his brother Bartholomew, whose seamanship saved the *Santiago* and her crew.

God was less merciful with the homeward-bound fleet. The thirty ships sent by Ovando after disregarding Columbus's warning met the full force of the hurricane as they neared the northeastern tip of Hispaniola. Some were swamped and sunk at sea, and others were driven to shore and smashed to pieces on the rocks. More than five hundred men died, including Bobadilla and Roldán, both of whom had caused so much trouble for Columbus and created such turmoil in the new colony.[6] Only a single ship, the *Aguja,* made it to Spain, and she was carrying payments to Columbus that the sovereigns had ordered Ovando to disgorge. Back in Spain, Columbus's son Diego received for his father 4,000 pesos of gold from aboard the *Aguja.* If Columbus saw some poetic justice in these events, he never made note of it. His enemies, frustrated by the good fortune of the man they hated, claimed that Columbus had conjured up the hurricane with magic arts.

Having survived the hurricane, Columbus and his crew did what they could to repair the storm-battered ships and then set a south-westerly course into a previously unexplored section of the western Caribbean, hoping to find passage through the continent to the Indian Ocean. On 30 July they reached the island of Bonacca, just off the northern coast of modern-day Honduras, where they spent a few days trading with the natives. Columbus was impressed that these natives were wearing cotton clothing, with the women even covering their faces like the Moors in Granada, and he was convinced he was nearing a more highly civilized land. From Bonacca they sailed to the coast of Honduras, about 30 miles distant, and again encountered well-dressed Indians, some with thick quilted clothing that protected them against arrows. On 14 August, Columbus took possession of the land in a for-mal ceremony that was attended by hundreds of Indians, and all cele-brated the event with a feast.

By now Nature had had time to regroup after the hurricane of July, and the fleet found itself bucking against fierce headwinds and unre-lenting foul weather for twenty-eight days while attempting to sail east along the northern coast of Honduras. Sails were torn, anchors lost, and supplies destroyed as the storm raged day and night. "Other storms have I seen," reported Columbus, "but none has ever lasted so long or been so terrifying. Many whom we thought very brave were reduced to terror on more than one occasion."[7] Columbus fell ill and "was many times at the point of death"; the men built him a small shelter on the deck where he could have some protection from the tempest. As the storm raged on, Columbus worried about his brother Bartholomew on the unseaworthy *Santiago.* He worried also about thirteen-year-old Fernando but expressed pride in his son who stepped up and worked like "he had been sailing for fifty years." He worried about his son Diego back in Spain, fearing that he would become an orphan and be "stripped of the honors and estates that should have been mine."[8] But ultimately, Nature tired of her torment, the storm wore itself out, and good weather returned. As the fleet reached the cape where the coast turns south, fair winds and smooth sailing returned. The Admiral named the cape *Gracias a Dios* ("Thanks Be to God").

With good wind and fair weather, the fleet covered more distance in two days than they had traveled in the previous four weeks. On 16 September they anchored at the mouth of a wide and deep river, and Columbus sent several men in boats upriver to obtain wood and water. As they were returning, the wind picked up and sent such a swell across the bar that one of the boats was overturned and two men drowned. Columbus named the river *Río de los Desastres* ("River of Disasters").

The fleet continued south along the coast, passing from present-day Nicaragua to Costa Rica. On 25 September, the Admiral stopped at a wooded island which he named *La Huerta* ("the Garden"), where they spent ten days resting, repairing and resupplying the ships, trading with the Indians, and trying to learn what they could of the land and the coast that lay ahead. On 5 October they sailed on, reaching a channel that led into a large bay. Hoping this was the long-sought strait, the ships entered the channel and were disappointed to find only a large, island-studded bay. They did find, however, an Indian wearing a large gold ornament on his breast, the first sign of gold they had seen along the coast.

They also understood the natives to say that a great sea lay just to the south. Following the directions of the Indians, they sailed into what is now called Chirique Lagoon, thinking that this was the passage to the Indian Ocean. But again they were disappointed. The scenery, however, provided some compensation: the lagoon is an immense spread of blue water surrounded by green peaks that rise 11,000 feet above sea

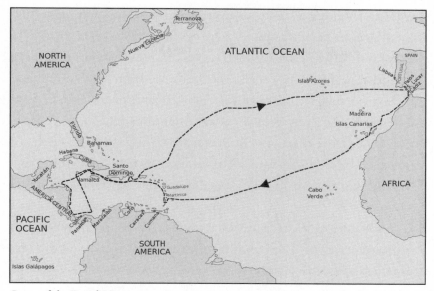

Route of the Fourth Voyage.

level. The fleet spent ten days fishing, trading, and exploring. Still try-ing to learn from the Indians about the location of a strait, Columbus learned instead that he was on an isthmus between two seas and that a province known as Ciguare was located on the ocean nine days' travel across the *cordillera* ("mountain ranges"). The Indians assured him that in the province of Ciguare there was a vast quantity of gold. He also understood the Indians to say that in Ciguare the people had horses and also ships with cannon, swords, and shields and "wear rich clothing and have good houses. They say also that Ciguare is surrounded by wa-ter and that ten days' journey away is the river Ganges."⁹ The challenges of communicating largely through gestures and drawings is evident in the report of this exchange.

Columbus must have reasoned that if the Indians considered this land an isthmus with a width of a nine days' journey, then the long sought for strait did not exist. In any event, he made no further mention of seeking a strait but continued his explorations along the coast of present-day Panama.

Nature's fury was not yet totally spent, however, and in December the weather again turned rough. The fleet was hammered by wind and rain, "a great violence of sea and storm."[10] Unable to continually fight the elements, the ships went where the wind drove them, often back-tracking along the coast. The little vessels were showing the effects of so much bad weather, and the crews were exhausted. They took refuge in a small bay and tried to wait out the storm. After fifteen days, the weather seemed to improve, and they put out to sea again. "When I had gone four leagues," Columbus reported, "the storm returned and so exhausted me that I did not know what to do." There was little he could do as the storm raged on. "For nine days I was lost with no hope of life. Eyes never saw the sea so rough, so ugly or so seething with foam." So fierce was the tempest that they could make little headway, nor could they find shelter from the storm under any headland. "There I was held in those seas turned to blood, boiling like a cauldron on a mighty fire. The skies had never looked more threatening. For a day and a night they blazed like a furnace and the lightning burnt in such flashes that every moment I looked to see whether my masts and sails had not been struck."[11]

And through it all, the crews were continually drenched by unrelenting rain. "One cannot say that it rained, for it was like a repetition of the deluge. The crews were now so ground down that they longed for death to release them from their martyrdom."[12] Adding to their terror, on 13 December an enormous waterspout, a swirling column of water that seemed to reach into the clouds, passed between two ships. Fernando reports that were it not for imploring Divine protection by reciting from the Gospel of John, the ships would have been overwhelmed and sunk.

A two-day break in the storm brought some welcome relief, but in the calmer weather the little fleet was encircled by a great school of sharks. The men saw it as an ill omen. Using chains and hooks, they killed several of the sharks, and though some considered it bad luck to eat shark meat, all ate due to the scarcity of food. Fernando reports that after eight months at sea in the heat, humidity, and rain, all the biscuits were filled with worms. "I saw many who waited until the arrival of darkness to eat the biscuit porridge so they would not have to see the worms in it; others were so accustomed to eating it that they didn't even bother to pick them out, fearing that in doing so they would lose their dinner."[13]

The rough weather continued. From 26 December to 3 January they took refuge in a small harbor that Fernando said "was like a great canal."[14] His description was prescient: they were anchored within sight of the current entrance to the Panama Canal. Had Columbus taken dugout canoes up the Chagres River, he would have been within 12 miles of the Pacific. But neither he nor his crew was fit for such exploration; that inland journey would first be accomplished by Vasco Nuñez de Balboa in 1513. Balboa's expedition would include more than a thousand men and take twenty-three difficult days to reach the summit from which they would become the first Europeans to view the Pacific Ocean.[15]

The crew spent most of the Christmas season replenishing the ships with wood, water, and local grain and did what they could to repair the storm-battered vessels. With good weather on 3 January, Columbus ordered anchors raised and directed the captains to exit the harbor and sail west along the coast with the intent of going back to Veragua, near the present-day border of Panama and Costa Rica, where they had heard reports of substantial amounts of gold. No sooner had they entered open sea than a new storm hit, and they beat their way with difficulty up the coast, taking three days to cover 60 miles.

On Epiphany, 6 January 1503, they dropped anchor at the mouth of a river that Columbus christened *Belén* ("Bethlehem"). After determining that there were about seven feet of water on the Belén bar, the ships crossed the bar in the high tide and anchored safely inside the sheltered river. Columbus determined to stay put until the rainy season was over, and it continued to rain without stopping for another month. Columbus entertained the local *cacique,* Quibián, on board the *Capitana,* and the men began to explore the immediate area. As soon as the weather permitted, Bartholomew led an expedition up the neighboring Veragua River and, following instructions from Quibián, found an area where they easily retrieved a small amount of gold from the soil. Columbus determined to build a small settlement, the beginning of a *factoría,* and leave his brother in charge while he returned to Spain for additional men and supplies. They built ten or twelve small buildings with palm thatch roofs and moved most of the remaining supplies to the *Gallega,* which would be left with Bartholomew, the *Adelantado.*

Columbus was ready to return to Spain now that the rains had stopped, but the lack of rain resulted in a precipitous drop in the water level, leaving only two feet of water over the bar: the ships were trapped in the river. With great irony, Fernando records that they now had no recourse "but to pray to God that He would send us rain, as we had formerly pleaded that He would send us fair weather."[16]

The Indians, seeing that the Spaniards were making plans for a permanent settlement, turned hostile. They began appearing in small groups arrayed for battle, perhaps hoping to frighten the Christians into leaving. Concerned, Diego Méndez volunteered to investigate. He took a few men in a small boat and rowed a mile or two down the coast where he saw a thousand warriors encamped. "With that amazing coolness of the Spaniard which came from his overweening sense of superiority to all heathen, [he] stepped ashore alone to speak with them."[17] Returning to his boat, he stayed just offshore throughout the night where he could see any movement of the Indians and quickly row back and alert his comrades. Under his watch, the Indians made no move, and Diego reported back at dawn.

Still unsure of the Indians' intent, Columbus wanted to contact Quibián. Méndez volunteered again. He made his way up the Veragua River to the chief's village, where he found the war party encamped. He made his way boldly to the chief's hut. Upon his approach the women and children began to shriek and howl, and the chief's son rushed out of the hut screaming at Méndez and nearly pushed him over. Méndez kept his composure, however, and staged a little scene that he had planned. He had brought with him a mirror, a comb, and a pair of scissors, and calmly sat down on the ground where his companion, Rodrigo de Escobar, gave him a haircut in view of all. It was surely one of the strangest episodes in the long history of the European conquest of America, but it worked. He presented his barber kit to the curious chief, was fed, entertained, and released to return to his shipmates.

Méndez returned with the intelligence that the Indians were massed and well armed, undoubtedly with the intent to annihilate the Christians. Méndez recommended to Columbus that they capture Quibián and his chiefs and hold them as hostages. The *Adelantado* was given that assignment, which he executed perfectly. He captured the chief and nearly thirty members of his household, bound them, and put them under the charge of Juan Sanchez, chief pilot of the fleet. Sanchez put the prisoners in a small boat to deliver them back to the ships where they could be confined in the hold, but the wily chief complained that the ropes were so tight that they were hurting his wrists. His captor loosened the knot, the chief quickly slipped his hands free, jumped into the river, and swam away in the dark.

With Quibián free, an attack was imminent. Mercifully, the sailors' prayers for rain were answered, and Columbus quickly took advantage of the higher water to get the ships out of the river to the open sea. Three of the ships were successfully floated over the bar; the *Gallega* and about twenty men under the command of Bartholomew and the intrepid Diego Méndez stayed behind to guard the compound. With the three ships gone and only a few men left behind, the Indians saw their chance. About four hundred of them rushed into the little village. One of the Spaniards was killed and several were wounded, including the *Adelantado,* who suffered a wound to the chest. But the Spaniards, though few in number, were better armed, and after three hours of intense fighting, the Indians finally retreated.

In the meantime, Diego Tristán, captain of the *Capitana,* had been sent by Columbus to obtain fresh water. Tristán witnessed the fight from his boat but could do nothing. When the conflict ended, his men advised him to quickly get back to the safety of the ships, but Tristan responded that he had been ordered by the Admiral to obtain water, and he would do so. They rowed a short distance up the river to a point where the water was clear but were quickly ambushed. Tristán was killed by a spear that pierced his eye. All his men were killed with the exception of one who was able to swim underwater long enough to escape and take the sad news back to the Admiral.

While all this was taking place, Columbus was alone on board the *Capitana* anchored some distance offshore. He was suffering with a high fever.[18] The Admiral heard the sound of gunshots and realized that his men, including his brother, were under attack. Knowing the overwhelming number of Indians, he could only assume, when the sound of the muskets died down, that all had been killed. Adding to his weak physical condition was the distress of fearing that his men and his brother were dead. What followed was one of the seminal experiences of the Admiral's life:

> I was completely alone outside on this dangerous coast in a
> high fever and a state of great exhaustion. All hope of escape was
> dead. I struggled up to the highest point of the ship, weeping and
> calling in a trembling voice to your Highnesses' Lord of Hosts in

every direction for comfort, but there was no reply. Exhausted and groaning, I fell as if asleep and heard a very compassionate voice saying: "O fool, slow to believe and serve thy God, the God of all! What more did he do for Moses or David his servant than he has done for thee? Since thou wast born, ever has He had thee in His watchful care. When He saw thee at an age that pleased Him, He caused thy name to sound marvelously in the land. The Indies, which were so rich a part of the world, He gave thee for thine own; thou hast divided them as it pleased thee, and He enabled thee to do this. Of the barriers of the Ocean Sea, which were closed with such mighty chains, He gave thee the key; and thou wast obeyed in many lands, and among Christians thou hast gained an honorable fame. What did He do more for the people of Israel when He brought them out of Egypt? Or for David, who from a shepherd He made to be King of Judea? Turn thyself to Him, and know now thine error; His mercy is infinite; thine old age shall not prevent thee from achieving all great things; He has many inheritances very great. Abraham was over a hundred years old when he begat Isaac, and Sarah was not a young girl. Thou criest for help, doubting. Answer, who has afflicted thee so greatly and so often, God or the world? The privileges, letters and promises that God gives are all fully kept, and after receiving service his favors increase and He grants his servants paradise. I have spoken of that which thy Creator has done for thee and does for all men. Now in part He shows thee the reward for the anguish and danger which thou hast endured in the service of others."

I heard all of this as if I were only partially conscious, and I had no answer to give to words so true, but could only weep for my errors. He, whoever he was who spoke to me, ended by saying: "Fear not; have trust; all these tribulations are written upon marble and are not without cause."[19]

The date was 6 April 1503.

Chapter 15

SHIPWRECKED

Alone in my trouble, sick, in daily expectation of death, and encompassed about by a million savages . . . my soul will be forgotten if it here leaves my body. Weep for me, whoever has charity, virtue, truth, and justice.[1]

CHRISTOPHER COLUMBUS

olumbus seemed buoyed by his experience with the Celestial voice, and with his faith and confidence renewed, he was anxious to get his men out of danger. Although strong breakers made it impossible to get a boat across the bar and into the river, one of the sailors volunteered to swim through the surf with a message for the *Adelantado* and the other men on shore to abandon the besieged settlement and make their way as best they could to the three ships anchored at sea.

The resourceful Diego Méndez engineered the evacuation of the men and supplies. The men took refuge in the *Gallega*, where Méndez had them wrap provisions in cloth from the sails. Then latching two canoes together, they ferried the provisions and the men across the bar and out to the ships. It required numerous trips to ferry all of the supplies, but they would be needed for the voyage home.

And home was where Columbus desired to go. But after nearly a year at sea with little or no opportunity to scrape and caulk the hulls, the ships were so worm-eaten that it was clear they would never survive the 7,000-mile crossing from Panama to Spain. Columbus appointed Méndez as captain of the *Capitana* in place of Diego Tristán, who had died in his efforts to obtain fresh water on the night of the battle, and the three leaky ships left Veragua and headed for Santo Domingo in Hispaniola, hoping that from there they could purchase or charter more seaworthy vessels for the Atlantic crossing.

"I left in the name of the Holy Trinity on Easter evening, with the ships rotten, all eaten by worms and full of holes." The decision to abandon Veragua was not an easy one, as the Admiral had hoped to establish a trading post in what was certainly the richest gold-producing area he had seen. Anticipating that armchair analysts at home would criticize his decision, he wrote preemptively to the sovereigns: "Let those who are accustomed to find fault and to censure, asking there, where they are in safety, 'Why did you not do this or that?' make answer now. I wish they were on this voyage; I verily believe that another voyage of another kind awaits them, or our Faith is vain." [2]

They had traveled only a week when they could no longer keep the *Vizcaína* afloat, and she was abandoned in Porto Bello, from whence they followed the Panamanian coast further east, all of the men crowded onto the two remaining ships. They continued their eastward course beyond the Gulf of San Blas, and Columbus would have continued further east before turning north to Hispaniola, but his officers and crew were concerned that to continue would put them too far east and they would miss Hispaniola altogether. He ultimately acquiesced to the desires of the crew, and the fleet turned north. Had they followed the Admiral's advice, they might have avoided the difficulties that awaited them.

The fact was that they did not know where they were, having been blown about by the storms of winter, nor did they know how to get back to Hispaniola. As always, Columbus's instincts were right, but he may have been too old and too ill to argue with the pilots. On 12 May, four weeks out from Belén, they reached the shore of Cuba, 200 miles west of the nearest harbor on the island of Hispaniola and over 500 miles from their desired landfall at Santo Domingo. Inching their way eastward along the coast, they were hampered by storms, contrary winds, and the strong westward current. Every day the condition of the ships worsened. Knowing they could not beat against the wind and current in such ships, Columbus determined to swing southward towards Jamaica in the hopes that the sinking ships could make their way to Hispaniola from there, taking advantage of the relative shelter provided by the island.

"The hulls of the ships were so full of holes that we had to work day and night pumping water from the holds."[3] Each ship had three pumps working continuously, and if a pump broke some would use pots to bail out the ship while others worked feverishly to repair the pump. But it was a losing battle. On 25 June they entered into the bay of St. Ann on Jamaica with the water almost up to the deck of the *Capitana*. No longer able to keep the ships afloat, they ran them ashore as far as they could, grounding them next to each other. For the third time in his life, Columbus was shipwrecked, but this time he had little hope of rescue.[4]

St. Ann's Bay is a deep lagoon, well protected by coral reefs that shelter it from the rough seas. The crews grounded the ships "board to board"[5] facing a wide, flat beach of white sand with an expansive view of the ocean. On the forecastle and aftcastle, which remained above water, they built small wooden shelters that provided some protection from the weather as well as from potentially hostile Indians.

The Admiral determined to keep the men on the ships rather than construct a small settlement on the island, knowing from his previous experience at Navidad, La Isabela, and Santo Domingo that his people were "by nature disrespectful" and that no command or punishment would be sufficient, as Fernando noted, to prevent them from "entering the villages and huts of the people and taking whatever they could, offending their women and children, and creating thereby fights and quarrels that would have made us enemies. . . . But this did not happen because the men were confined to the ships, from which they could not leave without receiving permission and signing out. This so pleased the Indians that for very little cost they brought us all we needed."[6]

With the ships securely grounded, the last of the rations were distributed to the men, and Columbus sent Diego Méndez with three others on a diplomatic mission to contact the local chiefs and barter for food. A satisfactory arrangement was made whereby the locals supplied the Christians with food at established rates, paid by the Spaniards in beads, combs, hawk's bells, fishhooks, and similar trinkets.

The question now confronting Columbus was how to get home. No one in Hispaniola or Spain knew where they were, and it was unlikely that any ship would arrive in Jamaica because it was already known that there was no gold on the island. The last remaining boat had been lost in the storm shortly before they had arrived at Jamaica, and the men had no tools with which to build a new one. The only solution that seemed to be available was to send a few men in a dugout canoe across 100 miles of open ocean and thence another 350 miles along the coast of Hispaniola to Santo Domingo.

The indomitable Diego Méndez volunteered for the task. As Méndez readied supplies for the undertaking, Columbus penned a series of letters for him to deliver, including a lengthy letter to the sovereigns that included a detailed description of the entire voyage. Known as *Lettera Rarissima,* it provides poignant insight into Columbus's feelings at this time, deprived of his rights and marooned with little chance of rescue:

I came to serve at the age of twenty-eight years, and now I have not a hair on my body that is not grey, and my body is infirm, and whatever remained to me from those years of service has been spent and taken away from me and sold, and from my brothers, down to my very coat, without my being heard or seen, to my great dishonour. . . . The pure devotion which I have ever borne to the service of your highnesses and the unmerited wrong that I have suffered will not permit me to remain silent, although I would fain do so; I pray your highnesses to pardon me. I am so ruined as I have said; hitherto I have wept for others; now, Heaven have mercy upon me, and may the earth weep for me.[7]

With one other Spaniard and six Indians, Méndez set off from St. Ann's Bay and made his way along the coast of Jamaica to the point where it is nearest Hispaniola. There, while ashore alone, he was surrounded by Indians who seemed intent on killing him and seizing the canoe and its cargo. While the Indians were drawing lots to see who would have the privilege of killing him, Méndez slipped away and escaped with his men and canoe back to the relative safety of St. Ann's.

A second attempt was made shortly thereafter, but this time with an armed escort led by Bartholomew Columbus. On this second attempt, Méndez was accompanied by a second canoe under the command of Bartolomeo Fieschi, the Genoese captain of the recently abandoned *Vizcaína*. Each canoe carried six Spaniards and ten Indians. At the northeast point of Jamaica, the Spaniards assigned to the rescue mission bade a tearful farewell to Bartholomew—the men in the canoes with Mendez and Fieschi not knowing if they would survive the unprecedented crossing and Bartholomew knowing that his life and the lives of those waiting for him back at St. Ann's depended on their success.

The men needed to cross more than 100 miles of open water. Under the July sun, heat and thirst became their enemies. On the second night out, with the fresh water gone, one Indian died of thirst, and others were so weak they could only lie in the bottom of the canoes. The men rinsed their dry mouths with saltwater. As the moon rose on the third night, the men could make out the profile of a low island on the horizon. It was the little rock of Navassa, and there they found some pools of water in the hollows of the rocks. Some of the Indians drank too much too quickly and died, and others became sick. Méndez succeeded in starting a little fire with flint and steel and cooked some shellfish for dinner. In the light of the next morning the men could see the shore of Hispaniola, some thirty miles distant, and in the cool of the evening resumed their journey and arrived at Cape Tiburon before dawn.

The plan was that Fiesche would return with his canoe to Jamaica to inform the castaways that the crossing had been successful, thus giving them hope for a rescue. But the Indians, who had suffered so much, refused to get back in the canoe, and the Spaniards, who felt that, like Jonah, they had been delivered out of the belly of the whale after three days of suffering, feared it would be tempting God to try the crossing again. No word of the successful crossing was sent back to Columbus on Jamaica.

Méndez made his way along the coast of Hispaniola as far as Azua, where the fleet had put in after the hurricane more than a year earlier. There he learned that Governor Ovando was in Xaragua subduing a native rebellion. Méndez set out overland to meet Ovando at the governor's field headquarters.

The news that Columbus was marooned on Jamaica was not displeasing to Ovando. Columbus still technically held the title Viceroy and Governor of the Indies, and as such remained a potential threat to Ovando's power and prestige. Méndez reported that Ovando "kept me with him for seven months, during which time he burnt or hanged eighty-four ruling *caciques,* among them the lady Nacaona, the greatest chieftain in the island."[8] Having completed his bloody and brutal pacification of the region and no doubt with the expectation that by now Columbus and his men had perished, Ovando allowed Méndez to proceed to Santo Domingo.

"I left on foot for Santo Domingo," recalled Méndez, "and waited there for ships to come from Castile. None had come for more than a year, but thanks be to God three arrived during my stay, one of which I bought and loaded with provisions: bread, wine, meat, hogs, sheep and fruit. I then sent it to the place where the Admiral was, so that he and all his men might come in it to Santo Domingo and from there return to Castile."[9] Méndez does not mention that Ovando retained a ship at Santo Domingo for his own use but refused to send it to rescue Columbus. By the time Méndez was able to send a ship back to his marooned shipmates, he had been gone from Jamaica for nine months.

Meanwhile, Columbus and his men were waiting. Weeks passed, and Fiesche did not return as hoped with the news that the canoes had reached Hispaniola. The men on Jamaica were left to assume that Méndez and Fiesche had been lost at sea and that no rescue ship would come.

As summer turned to autumn, the situation in Jamaica slowly deteriorated. Some of the men became sick, and all had been living under strict confinement for months without the beneficial distraction of being engaged in the daily challenges of sailing or building a permanent colony. As the men began to murmur, the Porras brothers plotted a mutiny. They convinced many of the men that the Admiral had no intention of returning to Spain, that he had in fact been banished from Castile, and that he had intentionally journeyed to Jamaica to die. Promising to lead an escape and return home, the Porras brothers convinced forty-eight of the men to join them in their mutiny. Believing that Columbus would inflict severe punishment on them for their rebellion, they determined to kill him first.

At the predetermined moment, Francisco de Porras barged into the little cabin where the Admiral was confined to his bed with arthritis. "Sir," demanded Porras, "why is it that you do not wish to return to Castile and prefer to keep us here, abandoned?"

"The Admiral," reported Fernando, "upon hearing such arrogant words spoken in such an unusual tone, realized what was happening. Exuding calm, he responded that he saw no way to make the journey until those that had left in the canoes returned with a ship sufficient to make the voyage; that he was as desirous as anyone to leave, both for his personal welfare and the welfare of all, for he was responsible for all the men."[10] Columbus offered to convene a council of the officers to discuss their situation, but Porras responded that this was no time for words. Drawing his sword, he exclaimed, "I am going to Castile with all who wish to follow me!" This was the signal for the mutineers to join in the chant, "We want to go with him! We want to go with him!" Two or three men faithful to the Admiral rushed into the room and prevented Porras from killing him in his bed, but Porras and the other mutineers escaped by using ten canoes that Columbus had purchased from the Indians.

The rebels made their way to the northeastern coast of the island from where Méndez and Fiesche had departed some months earlier. Their plan was to follow the path of Méndez and Fiesche to Hispaniola, and with the aid of some Indians who agreed to accompany them, they set off into the channel. But the sea was so rough that it appeared the canoes would be swamped. To lighten the load, the mutineers killed some of the Indians and threw them overboard. Other Indians, hoping to save their own lives, jumped overboard, but as the Indians clung to the sides of the canoes to keep from drowning, the mutineers hacked off their hands. Eighteen Indians were killed; the rebels kept alive only enough to maneuver the canoes, as the Spaniards could not manage the boats by themselves. "Had it not been for this," reported Fernando, "they would have accomplished the most imaginable cruelty in leaving not one alive. Such was the reward [of the Indians] for having believed their lies and deceit."[11] The mutineers returned to shore and set up camp.

No sooner had the Porras brothers and their gang left St. Ann's Bay than Columbus was surprised by the sight of a Spanish ship approaching the harbor. To the Admiral's dismay, however, it was captained by Diego Escobar, one of the principal leaders of Roldán's rebellion in 1495. He may have been sent by Ovando as a way of adding insult to Columbus's injured status or perhaps just to determine if Columbus had perished. If the latter, he was disappointed. Though not well, the Admiral was very much alive. Escobar refused to take any men with him or even any letters, but he did disclose the welcome news that Méndez had reached Hispaniola.

The news undoubtedly cheered the fifty or so men who remained at St. Ann's Bay, and Columbus focused, with good success, on improving the health of his sick comrades. But after a few weeks the supplies being provided by the Indians began to dwindle. Fernando observed that the Tainos did little farming but lived off the land, and they complained that a Spaniard ate more in a day than an Indian did in twenty. The barter had been going on so long that most of the Indians had all the trinkets they desired.

Columbus, who had with him his Nuremburg almanac, took advantage of a lunar eclipse that would take place on the night of 29 February 1504. He assembled the chiefs for a conference during the day of the 29th and informed them that the great God of Heaven was displeased with the negligence of the Indians in providing for the Spaniards. If they did not change their ways, the great God would chastise them with famine and pestilence. Columbus then advised them to watch the moon that night, and they would see a sign of God's displeasure. That night, as the shadow fell across the moon, Indians came running from all directions to the ships, "pleading with the Admiral to intercede for them before God, promising that in the future they would be diligent in bringing all that was needed."[12] The Indians were true to their promise, and the men never again lacked for food.

Meanwhile, Columbus sent word to the rebels of the success of Méndez, assured them that another ship would undoubtedly soon arrive, and offered pardons to all if they would come and rejoin the group. His patience and magnanimity in offering amnesty to these rebels is truly remarkable. He had done the same with Roldán on Hispaniola. But like Roldán, Porras was unrepentant. He convinced his band of rebels that Columbus had simply conjured up the passing caravel with his magic arts, an accusation to which Columbus's enemies seemed to retreat whenever the facts were against them. The rebels responded to the offer of amnesty by planning an attack on Columbus and his men.

As the mutineers approached St. Ann's Bay, Columbus sent a small force under the leadership of his brother to sue for peace and convince the rebels to return and join the other men. The mutineers refused the offer and charged at Bartholomew and his men. In the fighting that followed, several of the mutineers were killed, but the men loyal to Columbus prevailed and Francisco de Porras was taken captive. Shortly thereafter, the remaining rebels sent a message to Columbus, pleading for mercy and saying "they had repented for what they had done and desired to return to his service."[13] The Admiral issued a general pardon to all but Porras, whom he kept in confinement, and the remaining rebels returned. The rebellion of the Porras brothers had resulted in the death of numerous Indians and ten or twelve Spaniards, including the faithful Pedro de Terreros, captain of the *Gallega,* who died of wounds he incurred in the battle with the mutineers.

Within a month of the return of the surviving mutineers, the ship chartered by Méndez arrived in the harbor, just as Columbus had assured his men it would. On 29 June 1504, the unnamed ship weighed anchor and all the men, loyal sailors and mutineers alike, sailed out of St. Ann's Bay. A year and five days after running their sinking ships into the sand, they were again on their way home.

But the ill fortune that had shadowed this long and tiring expedition was not yet fully expended. The rescue ship was in poor shape, her sails rotten, her mainmast sprung, and she leaked so badly that it was only with great effort that the crew kept her afloat. They fought against the wind and the current. Foul weather forced them to seek shelter along the coast of Hispaniola. The 500-mile voyage to Santo Domingo took them six and a half weeks, longer than most of Columbus's ocean crossings. They had avoided drowning at sea by grounding their ships in a forlorn bay, averted starvation and potentially hostile Indians, and survived murderous mutineers. Diego de Porras, in his official report as *escribano* of the expedition, simply reported, "We were in Jamaica doing no service. The reason for our going to Jamaica, no one knows, except for sheer caprice."[14]

The refugees arrived in Santo Domingo on 13 August 1504, where Ovando made a pretense of welcoming the Admiral and invited him to stay in the governor's mansion, a house that Columbus probably considered rightfully his own. But his welcome was, as Fernando characterized it, *la paz del escorpión* ("a scorpion's kiss"): the governor's first official act upon Columbus's arrival was to set the murderous Porras free.

Columbus spent a month in Santo Domingo before he was able to charter a ship to take him home. Together with his brother, his son Fernando, Fieschi, and twenty-two of the survivors, he set sail for Castile on 12 September 1504. Bedridden, the Admiral hired Diego Rodriquez to captain the ship. A few others, including the Porras brothers, sailed on the caravel that had rescued them in Jamaica.

It was still the hurricane season, and the ships soon encountered a fierce storm. The ship carrying the Porras brothers returned to Santo

Domingo to repair the damage to it. Even though the storm broke the main mast of Columbus's ship, he was determined to sail on. The ingenious Columbus brothers engineered a new mast using a cross-yard, some bits of plank, and rope. Their crossing took fifty-six days and ended with the arrival of their battered little ship at Sanlúcar at the mouth of Guadalquivir River on 7 November 1504. They had been gone for two and a half years. Fernando, a boy of thirteen when they left, was now a young man of sixteen. Columbus was fifty-three and feeling the effects of advancing age. In Jamaica he had suffered such "anxieties and [was] at such an end, that it is a wonder that I am still alive . . . My sufferings could not be written in a thousand pages."[15] He had failed to find the strait leading to the Indian Ocean, had failed to meet up with Vasco de Gama, and had failed to ensure his fame by circumnavigating the globe. He was tired and sick. The last voyage of the Admiral of the Ocean Sea had, after so much tribulation, come to its inglorious end.

Chapter 16
DEATH COMES FOR THE ADMIRAL

I have served your Highnesses with such diligence and
love as I would expend to obtain Paradise.[1]

CHRISTOPHER COLUMBUS

pon reaching the mouth of the Guadalquivir at Sanlúcar, Columbus's ship waited for the tide to carry it upriver to Seville. Once docked at Seville, the captain and passengers would have registered at the *Casa de Contratación*, and a record would have been made of all gold and other valuables brought from the Indies. The very existence of the Casa must have been a surprise to Columbus, and an unpleasant one. An agency of the crown, the Casa was established by a royal decree issued in January 1503 while Columbus was waiting out the rainy season at the mouth of the Río Belén. Under rules issued by the sovereigns, the Casa was empowered to regulate and administer all trade with the Indies—it maintained a ship registry, a registry of captains, and a customs house—and beginning in February of 1503, all trade with the New World passed through the Casa. The ship that brought Columbus back to Seville had been

192

one of the first ships to sail from Spain under this new administrative system. For Columbus, who had been granted in the Capitulations of Santa Fe the lead role in all trade with the lands and islands he discovered, the existence of the Casa represented a further gutting of the rights he felt he had been granted and which he had worked so hard to reestablish before leaving on his Fourth Voyage in 1502.

From Jamaica, Columbus had written that his body was ill and infirm; a year later, arriving back in Spain, he had to be carried on a litter. He settled into a house in Seville, informed the sovereigns that he was back, and awaited an invitation to make a personal report. He began an active correspondence with his son Diego, who was still living at the court, where he was now a member of the queen's bodyguard. The letters nearly all begin with the salutation "Very dear son" and conclude with the valediction "Your father who loves you more than himself," followed by the Admiral's pyramidal signature.

Of the ten letters to Diego that survive, the first is dated 21 November 1504. Though Columbus did not yet know it, Queen Isabella was days from death. During the months that Columbus was stranded on Jamaica, the queen's health had declined visibly. She suffered from pain and fever, and shortly before her death her attendants noticed the appearance of a large tumor. On 12 October 1504, twelve years to the day from Columbus's first landing in the New World, she made out her will. At the time, the Admiral was still at sea making his weary way home on his final voyage.

On the evening of 26 November a crowd assembled in the square of the Medina del Campo, the small town where the court was in residence, and King Ferdinand emerged from the royal quarters to announce that the queen of Castile was dead. The next day, in accordance with her wishes, the queen's body was wrapped in a coarse Franciscan robe, and the sad cortege began its slow journey from Medina del Campo to Granada. The journey required three weeks, passing through each town and village along the way to allow mourners to view the coffin. Rain fell constantly during the entire time: rivers overflowed, bridges were washed away, and the roads turned to mud. It seemed as if all heaven was mourning.

On the day of the queen's death, Peter Martyr wrote to inform Talavera, "My hand falls to my side for sorrow . . . The world has lost its noblest ornament."[2] Certainly, Columbus had lost his noblest friend and supporter. His own illness prevented him from attending the royal funeral in Granada, the same city to which a young and vigorous Isabella had summoned Columbus to inform him that she had changed her mind and would approve his proposed voyage to seek the East by sailing west.

Diego was to represent his father at the funeral, and Columbus instructed him "to affectionately and with great devotion commend the soul of the Queen, our Lady, to God. Her life was always Catholic and Holy and ready for all the things of His holy service, and for this reason it must be believed that she is in His holy glory and beyond the desires of the rough and wearisome world."[3]

Though his queen had gone to a better place, Columbus was still in this rough and wearisome world. For many months he would engage in a futile effort to right what he saw as grievous wrongs. His titles had been made meaningless, and he was not receiving the full income due him under the Capitulations. He worried about the future of his sons, their status, and their well-being.

He was also concerned that the men who had accompanied him on the Fourth Voyage had not been paid their wages. On 28 November, Columbus wrote to Diego and repeated his "wish that their Highnesses would provide for the payment of these poor people who have passed through incredible hardships."[4] A few days later he wrote again: "We must strive to obtain a reply to my letter from their Highnesses, and to have them order that these people be paid. I wrote in regard to this subject four days ago."[5] Nothing happened. On 29 December, Columbus wrote again: "The payment of the people who went with me has been delayed. I have provided for them here what I have been able. They are poor and are obliged to go in order to earn a living."[6] Several of the men eventually went to the court to present their case in person but to no avail. Years would pass before they received any payment.

Through all this, Columbus's own health remained poor. He confided to Diego that he could write only at night, as his hands had no strength in the day. He would have gone to court himself, but his condition was so painful and so aggravated by the cold that he feared he would not survive the journey.

Bartholomew and young Fernando joined Diego at court in December to help draw attention to Columbus's petitions. Diego Deza, now the archbishop of Seville, also joined in the cause. Juan de Coloma, who had negotiated the Capitulations in 1492, was enlisted to help, along with Columbus's friend Amerigo Vespucci. The ever-faithful Diego Méndez made an appearance at court on behalf of Columbus.

King Ferdinand, just as he had in the past, spoke encouragingly but did nothing. As always, other affairs at court took priority. The death of Isabella raised the prospect of a significant shift in power; Ferdinand ruled Aragon, but the heir to the crown of Castile was his eldest daughter, Juana, who was married to Philip of France. Juana was considered mentally unstable, and Philip and Ferdinand had a less than amicable relationship. Philip had presumptuously declared that Naples was a French possession, and Ferdinand had sent an army to secure Naples as an Aragonese territory. No sooner had Ferdinand finally taken firm control of Naples than Isabella died and their daughter and son-in-law became the apparent monarchs of Castile. Juana and Philip were living in Flanders at the time of Isabella's death, however, and in their absence, Ferdinand declared himself regent and governor until their arrival in Castile.

But succession to a throne in medieval Europe was never simple. Even before Isabella's death, Peter Martyr had reported that the nobles of Castile "sharpen their teeth like frothing boars in the hope and expectation of a great change . . . convinced that there is always something to be gained when discord is at hand."[7] Ferdinand found his considerable diplomatic skills fully occupied in keeping Castile and his own power stable after Isabella's death.

Furthermore, Ferdinand had never fully shared Isabella's zeal for the New World. The de facto capital of Ferdinand's Aragon was Barcelona, and like the city's, Ferdinand's view was always to the Mediterranean. The Indies belonged not to Aragon but to Castile, and Ferdinand seemed much more interested in Naples and Sardinia than in Hispaniola or Paria. So Columbus found himself again waiting while Ferdinand attended to other matters he regarded as being of greater interest and concern.

Through his proxies at the court and through his letters, the Admiral continued to wage his campaign for justice for his family and for a new crusade. He even wrote to Pope Julius II in Rome to plead his case. But all with no result. In a letter to Archbishop Deza, Columbus was candid and realistic about his expectations: "Since it seems that his Highness is not willing to comply with what he has promised with his word and in writing jointly with the Queen—God rest her soul—I feel that for a simple ploughman like me to battle on with him against me would be like beating against the wind."[8]

Columbus's letters from this period convey a profound sense of loneliness. "I wish you would write me more often," he said to Diego. "I would like to see a letter from you every hour." He concludes the same letter by reminding his son "to write me very often. . . . There is a messenger from there to here every day."[9] Two days later he says, "I am surprised to have not received a letter from you or others. . . . Everyone here has letters."[10] Bartholomew and Fernando left Seville for the court on 5 December 1504; eight days later Columbus writes Diego that he "has not heard from them since they left."[11] On 21 December he writes, "Very dear son: the Adelantado and your brother and Carvajal left here sixteen days ago. They have not written me since leaving."[12] In spite of his arthritis, Columbus sent off a flurry of letters. "Tell the others," he wrote Diego, "that I have not written to them individually because it is very painful for me to write. They should not be like me, but each of them should write me very often. My great sorrow is that everyone here receives letters every day [from their friends at court] and I, who have so many [friends] there, receive none."[13]

His last letter to Diego was written on 25 February 1505 and carried to court by his friend Amerigo Vespucci. The letter is written in support of two men who were being prosecuted and for whom Columbus desired that pardons be granted. He asked Diego to have Méndez present the petition to the king during Holy Week. He begins the letter, as always, "Very dear son," and signs it simply "Your father, Xpo Ferens."[14]

As spring brought warmer weather to Andalusia and better health to Columbus, he determined to go to court himself and requested royal permission to ride a mule from Seville to Segovia. The use of sure-footed mules, whose gait was much gentler than that of a horse, had become so popular that Andalusian horse breeders had used their influence to limit the use of mules only to those authorized by royal decree. "I would be glad for the license to ride a mule, if it is not too much trouble to obtain it, and of a good mule."[15] The king granted Columbus's request on 23 February. It was, asserted Morison, "the only favor that King Ferdinand ever granted to the Discoverer of America."[16]

The arthritic Columbus traveled by mule from Seville to Segovia, a distance of nearly 400 miles. Ferdinand granted him an audience, received him graciously, spoke kind and encouraging words, but did nothing. Las Casas commented:

> I do not know why he [Ferdinand] was not only ungrateful in words and deeds but actually harmed Columbus whenever possible, although his words belied his actions . . . I have never been able to ascertain the reason for this dislike and unkingly conduct toward one whose unparalleled services no other monarch ever received. Perhaps he was unduly impressed by the arguments and false testimonies of the Admiral's enemies and rivals.[17]

In October the court moved to Salamanca, then to Valladolid in March, and Columbus followed, even as his health worsened. In Valladolid he rented a small house, now a museum known as the *Casa de Colón,* where he was confined to bed most of the time. In the spring of 1506, Juana and Philip finally arrived in Spain to assume their roles as rulers of Castile, too late to be of any assistance to Columbus. Unable to travel to greet the new monarchs personally, Columbus sent his brother to declare his loyalty.

His health failing rapidly, Columbus affirmed his will and added a codicil on 19 May 1506. The document confirms Diego as his heir and instructs Diego to "make a provision for Beatriz Enriquez, mother of Don Fernando, my son, so that she may be able to live honestly, being a person to whom I am under very great obligation."[18] In the hope that ultimately his privileges would be restored, he made generous grants, including two that he hoped would fulfill his cherished dreams: he set aside one fund to teach the principles of Christianity to the Indians of Hispaniola and another fund to finance a crusade to recapture Jerusalem so the temple could be rebuilt.[19]

He would not live to see his dream of a great Christian realm in the New World. Instead, what he saw was cruelty and greed rapidly destroying the peoples he had encountered on his voyages. "I never think of Hispaniola or Paria or these other countries without tears in my eyes," he had written from Jamaica. "I thought that our settlements there would be an example to others. But on the contrary they are in a state of exhaustion."[20] A few days after Isabella's death but before Columbus had received news of it, he urged Diego, who was then in court, to inform her that "the Indies are being lost, they are in a thousand flames."[21] He was tired, he was discouraged, he was deeply disappointed, but his faith was unwavering. In a letter to Deza he expressed the firm assurance that "I have done what I can; and now let it be left to the Lord our God to do it, Whom I have always found very favorable and a very present help in trouble."[22]

Knowing there was little time left, family and friends gathered around Columbus's bed in the little rented house in which he lived. Both of his sons were there, along with his brother Diego, but Bartholomew was on his errand to salute the new monarchs of Castile. Méndez and Fieschi, who had risked their lives for him during those desperate months in Jamaica, were in the room. A priest was called, who administered the last rites. Then, according to those present, Columbus whispered the words, "*In manus tuas, Domine, commendo spiritum meum*" ("Into thy hands, Lord, I commend my spirit"). The date was 20 May 1506, the Feast of the Ascension.

Neither the municipal records of Valladolid nor the records of the royal court make any mention of the death of the first Admiral of the Ocean Sea. The only record of his passing is found in the Carthusian monastery, which noted his death and burial in its registry. No official from the court attended the simple funeral; no bishop or dignitary was present. The Admiral of the Ocean Sea, Viceroy and Governor of the Indies, whose assurance in his own divine mission propelled him to undertake a voyage that would change the world like no voyage before or since, who over the centuries would become perhaps the most widely recognized historical figure on earth, died as he was born: unnoticed.

Crowded into the margins of the last leaf of the *Libro de las profecías* is a poem, written in an unidentified hand but apparently authored by Columbus and added to his collection of prophecies shortly before his death. The final stanza reads:

> *Think well, as far as in thee lie,*
> *Upon the just, released at last*
> *From travails suffered in the past*
> *Into the light eternally.* [23]

Chapter 17

WHY COLUMBUS MATTERS

And it shall come to pass in that day, that the Lord shall set his hand the second time to possess the remnant of his people.[1]

ISAIAH 11:11

olumbus's great achievement was not just that he discovered America but that he discovered the route there and back and by so doing launched a process that was irreversible. Others may have preceded him—almost certainly the Vikings and perhaps the Chinese—but no one before Columbus knew how to replicate and institutionalize the round-trip journey. Part of Columbus's great genius was his discovery and use of the Atlantic wind patterns that allowed him not just to reach the New World but to return to the Old and then repeat the round-trip voyage again and again and again. Plans for a second voyage began within days of his return, and the route he developed on that voyage was followed by sailing ships until the age of steam. Even today, yachts crossing from Europe to the Caribbean follow his route. He didn't just stumble across the ocean and bump into a new world; he built the highway.

If others did, in fact, reach the Americas before Columbus, they failed to inform the rest of the world, and a discovery that is unknown is no discovery at all: informing others is an essential element of discovery. While there is solid evidence that at least the Vikings reached the shores of America long before Columbus, their voyages had no effect on history partly because there was no contemporary record telling the world of their accomplishment. "Only with Columbus's undertaking," wrote Taviani, "did Europe, Islam, India, China, and Japan learn of the existence of a New World. And that changed the course of human history profoundly."[2] Any voyage prior to Columbus is relegated to a footnote in history.

Columbus not only replicated his voyage but published it to the world so others could replicate it. His historic voyages marked a turning point in world history. Prior to 1492, the world was highly fragmented and diverse. Plant and animal life had developed independently: some plants, like sweet potatoes and corn, grew only in the Western Hemisphere, whereas others were unique to Asia. In fact, it was the presence of unique but highly desirable spices in Asia and their absence from Europe that was one of the drivers of fifteenth-century exploration. "The world was divided among sundered cultures and divergent ecosystems," observed Fernandez-Armesto:

> Every continent had its peculiar repertoire of plants and animals. Life-forms grew apart, even more spectacularly than the differences that grew between peoples, whose cultural variety multiplied, and whose appearance and behavior diverged so much that when they began to reestablish contact, they at first had difficulty recognizing each other as belonging to the same species or sharing the same moral community.
>
> With extraordinary suddenness, in 1492 this long-standing pattern went into reverse. The aeons-old history of divergence virtually came to an end, and a new, convergent era of the history of the planet begin.[3]

With the First Voyage of Columbus, the world began to be connected in ways not seen since the days of Noah. In our modern age, the same crops and species are found in similar climates on every continent. Even people and races have become intermixed in a way never before known.[4] In the post-Columbian world, tomatoes, which originated in Mexico, became a staple of Italian cuisine; chocolate, another Aztec food, became a signature product of Belgium and Switzerland; chili peppers became an integral part of Thai dishes; and potatoes became the principal crop of Ireland. Air travel and electronic communications have been layered onto Columbus's achievement such that fashions and fads spread with the speed of light around the globe. The fact that one can purchase a Coca-Cola or a Big Mac in almost every country of the world is, in certain respects, a legacy of Columbus. Of greater significance, the presence of Latter-day Saint congregations on every continent is made possible, in part, by events set in motion with Columbus's world-changing voyage of 1492.

The Western European world into which Columbus was born was, by many measures, a world in decline. Two years after his birth, the great city of Constantinople fell to the Ottoman Turks, making trade with the Indies difficult and dangerous and isolating Europe from the Levant. Morison observed that "at the end of 1492 most men in Western Europe felt exceedingly gloomy about the future."[5] The great empires of China and Islam were the most advanced and dominant civilizations on the planet. Europe was, by contrast, a cultural backwater. The rise of Islam in the East was shrinking both the territory and the influence of the Christian nations. Continued efforts to recover control of the Holy Sepulcher in Jerusalem had failed, and successive calls by the popes for a new crusade were seen as opportunistic devices to raise money.

No country or empire in Europe was comparable to the empires of the ancient world. Europe consisted largely of a number of city-states vying with each other for power and were constantly at war. The Holy

Roman Empire was a distant memory. The relatively wealthy city-states of Genoa and Venice competed for the remaining trade in the Mediterranean and North Atlantic, capturing each other's ships and confiscating cargos. Spain did not exist as a nation. Its two largest kingdoms, Castile and Aragon, remained separate and distinct kingdoms even though their monarchs were married to each other, and a large portion of modern Spain was wrested from the Moors in 1492 only after a long and costly war. Castile and Aragon would continue to be ruled separately, with separate laws, finances, and bureaucracies, for many years.

But when Columbus's little storm-battered ship floated into Lisbon in March 1493, it was as if someone had struck a match in dry tinder. The news spread across Europe with remarkable speed, and as old ideas faded, a new landscape—not just geographical but intellectual, artistic, and spiritual—emerged. Within a relatively few years, Spain would rule a new empire that extended across the sea to Latin America and to the Philippines, a breadth of dominion eclipsing anything in history. France and England, jealous and fearful of Spain's new wealth, would soon challenge Spain both in the New World and in Europe.

The Catholic Church was the ostensible source of unity among the factions of Europe, but the decline and corruption of the Church reached what some consider its peak with the ascension to the papacy of Rodrigo Borgia in 1492. A native of Xátiva in Valencia, the new pope Alexander VI had already fathered at least three illegitimate children during his tenure as a cardinal and would father at least four more while he was pope.

On other fronts, too, Europe was in decline. No significant advances in science or technology had been made in a century. University enrollment was in decline across the continent. Not a single new institution of higher learning was founded in Spain in the fifteenth century. The best highways in Europe were those that had been built by the Roman Empire centuries earlier. The basic technologies that would ultimately change the world were developed first in China, not Europe.

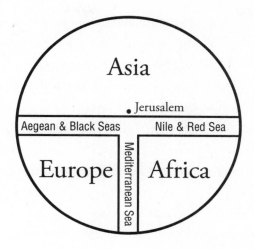

Paper and printing, gunpowder, steel—inventions that would define the modern world—all originated in China. But the expansive opportunity of a new continent enabled Europe to refine and employ these technologies in a way that gave shape to a new world era in much the same way that an expanding American frontier in the eighteenth and nineteenth century would expand and inspire the spirit of America.

For Europeans in 1492, the world consisted of three continents: Europe, Africa, and Asia, each believed to have been settled by one of the sons of Noah. This was often depicted in what is now called a T-O map. The "O" represented the world, which was divided by the "T" into the three parts, separated by bodies of water: the Mediterranean between Europe and Africa, the Nile and Red Sea between Africa and Asia, and the Aegean and Black Seas between Europe and Asia. Jerusalem was at the center where the three land masses joined. The idea of a fourth continent had no place in this theo-geography. The Book of Mormon explains "that after the waters had receded from off the face of this land it became a choice land above all other lands, a chosen land of the Lord."[6] It was a land that was "preserved"[7] from the days of Noah and hidden from all except those whom the Lord led there. Lehi explained that "there shall none come unto this land save they shall be brought by the hand of the Lord." The land would be "kept . . . from the knowledge of other nations; for behold, many nations would overrun the land."[8] Scholars West and Kling wrote, "The secret of the Ocean Sea had not been penetrated earlier because God wanted it hidden until He was ready."[9] George Q. Cannon stated that "for centuries [America] was hidden from all the nations of the earth. It was not until the fifteenth century that God inspired Columbus to go forth and seek a passage across the Atlantic."[10] Orson Hyde, in declaring that Moroni guided Columbus's three ships across the sea, indicates "an important reason why the discovery should be made: The history and record of a fallen people, containing light . . . and truth from heaven, were buried in the soil of the Western Continent; and although engraven on golden leaves in a strange and unknown tongue, still they must come forth."[11]

The existence of the Americas had been so well hidden over the millennia that the idea of a three-continent world was deeply engrained in the medieval mind. It took years for Columbus and his contemporaries to comprehend the geographic implications of his discovery. When Peter Martyr, in a letter dated 1 November 1493, referred to *"Colonus ille Novi Orbis repertory"* ("that famous Columbus, the discoverer of a New World") it is clear that by "new world" he meant new portions of Asia. Columbus himself used the term *"otro mundo"* ("another world") when writing about his First Voyage, but, again, it is clear that by this he meant simply a new part of Asia. Not until the Third Voyage, when Columbus encountered the coast of the mainland, did he realize that he had come upon a different and new continent, and not until the Fourth Voyage did he realize that this continent, as a practical matter, blocked access to the Orient. The existence of a previously unknown and unimagined continent shattered the existing conceptions of world geography. Magellan's circumnavigation of the globe from 1519 to 1522 finally cemented this new geography in the minds of Europeans.

Columbus's initial discovery spawned a proliferation of new

voyages. As early as 1494, others began making voyages to the New World, and within a very few years additional settlements were established. In 1521, when Hernán Cortés was thirty-six years old, he conquered the great Aztec empire of central Mexico, a flourishing civilization on a continent that was unknown at his birth. Within forty-two years of Columbus's return from the Voyage of Discovery, men had sailed around the world, the empires of the Aztecs and Incas had been discovered and conquered, and great new cities had been established in Peru and Mexico. Spain had emerged from a war-weary and nearly bankrupt amalgamation of medieval kingdoms into the wealthiest and most powerful empire on earth. Over the span of a single generation, the world had been transformed, and events had been set in motion that ultimately shaped the world in which we now live.

Bartolomé de Las Casas, who as a boy had gazed in wonder upon the first Indians to appear in Europe, recognized the momentous import of Columbus's First Voyage: "Is there anything in the world comparable to the opening of the tightly shut doors of an ocean that no one dared enter before?"[12]

Not only did Columbus unlock the gates of the Ocean Sea but his accomplishments were a decisive factor in unlocking the intellectual and spiritual darkness that had encompassed Europe for centuries and was just beginning to fade. An awakening of the human spirit would be felt across Europe and manifest in many ways. In 1517, Martin Luther would publish his ninety-five theses, daring to speak out against corruption in Rome and forcing reforms in the Church. Luther would later translate the Bible into German, a work that would have an enormous effect on German culture.

Luther's work would be followed by William Tyndale's translation of the Bible into English in 1525, the publication of which would change not only English history but the English language. Henry VIII, as a result of his desire to divorce Catherine of Aragon, the daughter of

Isabella and Ferdinand, would break with Rome in 1534 and create the Church of England. With new protestant churches in Germany and England, the Reformation would become the Protestant revolution.

Additional English editions of the Bible, notably the Geneva Bible, would take the Bible to a wider audience, including many English citizens who separated themselves from the Church of England. Some of those Separatists, as they called themselves, carried copies of the Geneva Bible with them across the Ocean Sea, as foreseen by Nephi.[13] Strangers in a strange land, they founded a small colony on Cape Cod and would be known by successive generations not just as pilgrims but as the Pilgrims. Their literal and spiritual descendants would ultimately break from England, declaring themselves a free and independent nation, a declaration that would be defended by a long and difficult war against what was by then the most powerful nation on earth. Improbably and miraculously, they would prevail and create a new nation.

In the early days of that new nation, a family descended from one of the early immigrants to Cape Cod would, through a series of seemingly unremarkable circumstances, relocate to a rural area near a hill known anciently as the Hill Cumorah. And from that hill, the young Joseph Smith would take the record written by Nephi, translate it, and publish it to the world. With the publication of the Book of Mormon, Nephi's prophecy, which Columbus never read but which he so clearly understood and so faithfully fulfilled, would be published to the world, and the fulness of the gospel would begin to flood the earth.

Not just Columbus's voyage but what it led to caused Francisco López de Gómara to proclaim that it was "the greatest event since the creation of the world, save the incarnation and death of Him who created it."[14] Columbus turned the key given him by the Almighty and opened a new age. Perhaps no other single individual did more to prepare the way for the last dispensation of the gospel of Jesus Christ than did Christopher Columbus, *Xpo Ferens*.

Chapter 18

COLUMBUS, THE MAN

The chief concern of Christopher Columbus was not what men would think of him but what God would think of him.[1]

WEST AND KLING

 here is little agreement regarding the nature and character of the man Columbus. Over the course of five centuries, he has been reviled by some and proposed for sainthood by others.[2] The vast diversity of opinions regarding the man is evidence of his complexity. He was a man of contradiction and paradox—devout in his religious duties but heretical in his ideas, a brilliant navigator who had trouble making an accurate reading of the North Star, an uneducated man who spoke four languages and wrote extensively in two of them.

The inability to categorize Columbus into a neat, consistent portrait results in part from the age in which he lived. He was born into a world that was still dominated by medieval thought and institutions. But it was a world that was changing, and he would become one of the primary agents of change. By the time of his death, the Renaissance was

Strange man.

well under way. Columbus lived his life with one foot firmly planted in the Middle Ages and the other in the modern world. Much of his thinking and learning was medieval in nature, but he built on that medieval knowledge a lifetime of observation and experience in a genuinely modern way. He was a man of both the Old World and the New World in space, time, and thought.

Two events that took place shortly after Columbus's birth had a significant effect on his life, his accomplishments, and his legacy. The fall of Constantinople to the Ottoman Turks in 1453 resulted in a closing of the traditional trade routes that supplied Europe with highly desired Oriental spices and spurred the search for new trade routes. Without the loss of Constantinople, it is doubtful that Columbus would have found support for his Enterprise of the Indies. The fall of Constantinople also resulted in an exodus of Greek scholars from the former Byzantine capital. Many of those scholars settled in Italy and brought with them knowledge and ideas that would stimulate new thinking in Europe.

Three or four years after Columbus's birth, Johan Gutenberg published his Latin Vulgate edition of the Bible using movable type. Though not the first book Gutenberg had printed, it was the largest. Fewer than two hundred copies were printed, but it demonstrated the feasibility of using the printing technology perfected by Gutenberg. By 1480, there were 110 printing presses in Europe using Gutenberg's technology, 50 of which were in Italy. By the end of the century, more than twenty million volumes had been produced. Columbus owned several of those books, and there is evidence he read many others. Perhaps equally important, the success of the printing industry enabled reports of Columbus's voyages to spread rapidly throughout Europe.

The fall of Constantinople to the Turks and the rise of printing set the medieval world of southern Europe into commotion, and it was into this world that was trying to find its new equilibrium that

Setting the stage

Columbus stepped. He was as complex and as contradictory as the age in which he lived. Still, as one reads his words and reviews his actions, a portrait of the man begins to emerge.

If there is any one thing about Columbus on which historians agree, it is that "he was an exceptionally gifted sailor."[3] Of the great Columbus scholars over the past two centuries, perhaps only Henry Vignaud, an American who emigrated from the United States to France during the Civil War, was disparaging in his assessment of Columbus's skills as a mariner. But as Paulo Taviani wryly noted, Vignaud's "experiences on a body of water were limited to sight-seeing tours on the river Seine."[4]

Columbus did what no predecessor had been able to do, something that, until it was done, seemed impossible to achieve with the technology of the day. Time and time again, when his pilots and fellow captains disagreed with his navigation, the Admiral was proven to be correct. His confidence in his seafaring abilities enabled him to initiate the era of open sea navigation—he was the first who was willing and capable of sailing purposefully with no sight of the coastline or a predetermined landfall. He was, by all accounts, the greatest mariner of his age. It was his gift.

Columbus was a voracious reader and a remarkable student. He had a knack for learning, and he took full advantage of the new opportunities to acquire and read books. Writing to the monarchs of Castile and Aragon late in his life, he noted, "Mine is a calling that inclines those who pursue it to desire to understand the world's secrets. Such has been my interest for forty years."[5] He may have learned to read and write basic Latin as a boy in Genoa, but he learned Spanish as an adult, probably while living in Portugal. Spanish became the language which he used in daily life and in which he wrote nearly all of his notes and manuscripts. He was very well versed in the Bible—by today's standards he would be considered a serious lay biblical scholar—and he read and studied geography, history, astronomy, geology, and philosophy. He was conversant with Ptolemy, Aristotle, Seneca, Plato, Augustine, Thomas Aquinas, and scores of other classical authors. He was also a keen observer of nature. Not only did he decode the Atlantic trade winds but he gave detailed descriptions of the flora, fauna, and inhabitants of the Indies. He had a remarkable ability to grasp complex ideas and to develop reasoned explanations for unfamiliar phenomena. For all this, Columbus referred to himself as "an uneducated man" and an "uninformed sailor" and simply states that God gave him the "spirit of intelligence."[6] That spirit of intelligence enabled him to become educated. West and Kling observed, "He was an unlettered man with superior intellect and genius."[7] Taviani put it more succinctly: "The man was a genius."[8]

Columbus was also a devout Christian. In the fifteenth century that meant he was a devout Catholic, because Christianity and Catholicism were one and the same. He faithfully attended to his daily religious duties. Fernando said of his father, "In matters of religion he was so strict that for fasting and saying all the canonical offices he might have been taken for a member of a religious order. And he was so great an enemy to swearing and blasphemy, that I swear I never heard him utter any other oath than 'By San Fernando!'"[9] Las Casas said, "He observed the fasts of the Church most faithfully, confessed and made communion often, read the canonical offices like a churchman or member of a religious order, hated blasphemy and profane swearing."[10] Indeed, Columbus expressed one of his great concerns in a letter written while marooned on Jamaica: "Here in the Indies I am cut off from the prescribed forms of religion, alone in my troubles, sick, in daily expectation of death . . . and so far from the Holy Sacraments of the Blessed Church that my soul will be forgotten if it leaves my body."[11]

His Christianity was not just an outward demonstration. As Las Casas observed, "He was a man of courageous spirit and lofty thoughts

. . . patient and long-suffering, a forgiver of injuries, and wished nothing more than that those who offended against him should recognize their errors, and that the delinquents be reconciled with him."[12] Las Casas noted also that "he was a man of great devotion . . . sober and moderate in food, drink, and dress."[13]

Columbus had an unshakable sense of mission. Throughout his writings one sees the consistent theme that the Lord put into his mind that it would be possible to sail to the Indies and gave him the will and the skill to do it. Even though "all who found out about my project denounced it with laughter and ridiculed me,"[14] he was undeterred. When he was denied funding by King João II of Portugal, he moved to Castile. When he was denied money by Ferdinand and Isabella, he sent his brother to England and France while he continued to persist in Spain. When his men mutinied in the Atlantic, he pressed on, saying that it was "useless to complain since he had come to find the Indies and thus had to continue the voyage until he found them."[15]

Such certainty and steadfastness does not always wear well with others, and it was so with Columbus. As Morison observed, "Columbus was a Man with a Mission, and such men are apt to be unreasonable and even disagreeable to those who cannot see the mission."[16] Columbus simply knew, without any doubt, that God had entrusted him with the key to unlock the Ocean Sea, and although "the leading persons in all the learned arts" concluded that his ambition and objective "was in vain,"[17] he was unmoved. God had made him the messenger of the new heaven and new earth. He was a man with a mission, unshakable and unstoppable.

Finally, what emerges from Columbus's words as we have them in his letters, journals, and other documents is a man of deep and abiding faith. His piety was not a hollow set of daily rituals or outward appearances; his faith in God was the foundation of all he did, it was the driver of his life, and it sustained him through disappointment, rejection, and deep discouragement. He was "longsuffering in the challenges and adversity that always beset him, which were incredible and infinite, always with great faith in the divine Providence."[18] His faith begat hope that enabled him to do what others deemed impossible. He prayed with faith and received answers through faith: "I prayed to the most merciful Lord concerning my desire, and he gave me the spirit and the intelligence for it."[19] Sick and alone at Belén, he received comfort from a Celestial voice assuring him that "mercy is infinite," that the promises "God gives are fully kept," and admonishing him, "Fear not, have trust."[20]

His sense of mission was unshakable because his faith removed all doubt: "Who can doubt that this fire was not merely mine, but also of the Holy Spirit?"[21] When all was said and done, everything "turned out just as our redeemer Jesus Christ had said, and as he had spoken by the mouth of his holy prophets."[22]

Columbus was a man who was far from perfect, and he seems to have been willing to admit it. Perhaps that is why he was so lenient and forgiving of the treachery of Roldán and the mutiny of the Porras brothers. "I am only a most unworthy sinner," he wrote, "but ever since I have cried out for grace and mercy from the Lord, they have covered me completely. I have found the most delightful comfort in making it my whole aim in life to enjoy his marvelous presence."[23]

In the end, Columbus's achievements and his universal fame are a reflection of his personal faith. "Peter stepped out upon the water," he wrote, "and to the extent that his faith remained firm, he walked upon it. Whoever finds so much faith as a grain of mustard seed will be obeyed by the mountains. Knock and it must be opened unto you. No one should be afraid to undertake any project in the name of our Savior, if it is a just cause and if he has the pure intention of his holy service."[24] Columbus's faith remained sufficiently firm to enable him, like Peter, to step out upon the water.

EPILOGUE

It has pleased Him to reward me for these toils and dangers. He has truly poured out victory, and may it please God to diminish those who malign my honor, and with such dishonesty and malice have ridiculed me and defamed my undertaking without knowledge of my desire to be of service.[1]

CHRISTOPHER COLUMBUS

he last years of Queen Isabella's life were marked by sorrow. When Prince Juan, her only son, died in 1497, Peter Martyr wrote, "The light of all Spain has been extinguished."[2] It was both a personal and public tragedy, but Isabella accepted his death stoically and with great faith. Soon after Juan's death, his widow gave birth to a stillborn daughter. The following year, the queen's eldest daughter, Isabella, wife of King Manuel I of Portugal, also died. In 1502, Catherine, her youngest child, was widowed at age sixteen. Of Isabella and Ferdinand's five children, two were dead and one was a young widow in a foreign land. Two years later, Isabella herself died after a long and painful illness.

Nearly four hundred years after her death, in 1893 Queen Isabella of Castile became the first woman to be featured on a United States postage stamp: her image appeared on three commemorative stamps issued to mark the World Columbian Exposition held in Chicago. In 1958 a process was initiated in the Roman Catholic Church to have Isabella canonized, and in 1974 the Vatican gave her the title "Servant of God."

Upon the death of Queen Isabella in 1504, Ferdinand was no longer king of Castile—the union of the two kingdoms had been a personal union defined by the marriage between their respective monarchs. Prince Juan, the heir to the throne of both Castile and Aragon, had died in 1497, moving Peter Martyr to remark, "There lies buried the hope of all Spain."[3] Juan had certainly been the hope of Ferdinand. At the time of Isabella's death, Ferdinand and Isabella's oldest surviving child, Juana, was heir to the throne of Castile and was living in the Netherlands where her husband, Philip of Hapsburg, ruled as archduke. Ferdinand was suspicious of his son-in-law Philip and was determined that the kingdom of Aragon not go to Philip or to Philip's son Charles. Among other things, he did not want the kingdom ruled by the house of Hapsburg. When Isabella died, Ferdinand attempted to have himself named as permanent regent of Castile but was unable to obtain the support of the Castilian nobility. Ferdinand determined that the only way to prevent his grandson from becoming king of Aragon was to marry a younger woman in hopes of producing a son who would become his heir. Less than two years after the death of Isabella, he married Germain de Foix, a niece of Louis XII of France. She was eighteen; Ferdinand, fifty-four. Germain bore him a son, who died within hours of birth. Philip had died six months after Ferdinand's marriage, and Philip and Juana's son Charles became the Hapsburg king of Castile and Aragon after Ferdinand's death in 1515. Ferdinand was buried next to Isabella in Granada.

Ferdinand and Isabella's granddaughter Mary, the child of Catherine of Aragon and Henry VIII, became Queen Mary I of England upon the death of her half brother, Edward. Mary, a devout

Catholic, imprisoned her half sister, Elizabeth, for suspected support of the Protestant movement, but upon Mary's death Elizabeth became Queen Elizabeth I. It was Queen Elizabeth's navy that defeated the Spanish Armada in 1588, effectively ending Spain's control of the Ocean Sea.

Three years after Ferdinand's death, his Hapsburg grandson Charles was named Holy Roman Emperor. During Charles's reign, the newly united Spain became the largest empire in the world, extending across the globe. The conquest of Mexico and Peru took place under his rule as well as the opening of the legendary silver mines of Potosí (in present-day Bolivia). Vast amounts of wealth began pouring into Spain from the New World, just as Columbus had predicted, but rather than using that wealth to fund a new crusade, it was used to finance a series of costly European wars. The abundance of gold and silver led to severe inflation. Spain ultimately defaulted on its debts and declared bankruptcy. Still, the vestiges of empire persisted for centuries. The first significant loss of territory did not come until 1763 when Spain ceded to France the vast Louisiana Territory in North America. Forty years later the French sold the territory to a young United States of America, who commissioned two explorers, Meriwether Lewis and William Clark, to explore the new acquisition.

Columbus's brother Bartholomew, who had worked so closely with the Discoverer in developing and executing the Enterprise of the Indies, died in 1514 or 1515 in Santo Domingo, where he served under his nephew Diego. He was interred with Columbus at the monastery of Las Cuevas in Seville.

Columbus's younger brother Diego, who returned to Spain as a prisoner with Columbus and Bartholomew, remained in Spain and devoted himself to religious matters. He died about 1515.

Diego, Columbus's eldest son, spent most of his early life in the court of Ferdinand and Isabella, where he made a favorable impression on King Ferdinand. Not long after Columbus's death, Ferdinand granted him the titles that had belonged to his father. Diego married the king's cousin María de Toledo, and they had seven children. As the second Admiral of the Ocean Sea and Viceroy of the Indies, Diego was sent to Santo Domingo in 1509 as governor, replacing Nicolás de Ovando. Diego returned to Spain in 1514 and six years later went back to Hispaniola. In 1523 he again returned to Spain, where he died in 1526. His body was interred with those of his father and uncle at Las Cuevas until his remains were later transferred to Santo Domingo.

Diego's elder son, Luis, became the third Admiral of the Ocean Sea and Viceroy of the Indies. He was a gambler, a spendthrift, and a womanizer. His mother arranged for him to exchange his titles for the duchy of Veragua and a perpetual annuity, bringing to an end the lengthy series of lawsuits between Columbus's heirs and the crown. As part of this arrangement Luis was also named marquess of Jamaica. Thereafter, the hereditary title of the Columbus family was duke of Veragua. Luis was convicted of bigamy when his second wife accused him of marrying another woman while he was still married to her. He was eventually exiled to Oran in North Africa, where he died. His descendant Cristóbal Colón de Carvajal y Gorosábel is the eighteenth duke of Veragua.

Fernando wrote a history of his father that was printed in Italian in 1571 and is an important source on the life of the Columbus. Fernando's account of the Fourth Voyage, in which he participated as a young boy, is particularly informative. He became a scholar and a bibliophile, amassing a library of more than fifteen thousand volumes, including books and manuscripts that had been in the possession of his father. It was one of the finest libraries in Europe, and he maintained a full-time staff to catalogue and care for his collection. Upon his death in 1539, he left the library to his nephew Luis, but Luis was in Santo Domingo at the time. As a result, the library was neglected for many years, and most of the books were lost. About two thousand of the volumes did survive, however; they now compose the *Biblioteca Colombina* in Seville. Those volumes include many of the primary source materials regarding Christopher Columbus, including the nine books known to have been owned by the Admiral. In the *Biblioteca* is Fernando's copy of Seneca's *Medea*. Next to the prophetic passage that had meant so much to Columbus, Fernando wrote: "This prophecy was fulfilled by my father . . . the Admiral, in the year 1492."

Diego Méndez, whose loyalty and courage resulted in the rescue of Columbus and his men from Jamaica, remained a loyal friend. He assisted Diego with legal issues after Columbus's death and accompanied him to Santo Domingo when Diego was appointed governor. In his will he gave these instructions for his epitaph:

> "Here lies the Honorable Gentleman Diego Méndez, who greatly served the Royal Crown of Spain in the Discovery and Conquest of the Indies with the Admiral Don Cristóbal Colón of Glorious Memory, who discovered them, and afterwards with his own Ships and at his own Cost. He died _____. He begs for Charity's sake a Pater Noster and an Ave María."
>
> In the middle of the said stone let there be carved a canoe, which is a dug-out tree in which the Indians navigate, for in such a one I navigated three hundred leagues; and above it let them set the letters that say CANOA.[4]

Bartolomé de Las Casas, who was eight years old when he witnessed the return of Columbus in 1493, traveled to the Indies with his father in 1502. He received his own *encomienda* and owned Indian slaves, even after being ordained a priest in 1510, the first priest ordained in the New World. After witnessing atrocities committed in the conquest of Cuba, he began to change his views regarding the treatment of Indians, although his first solution was to use slaves from Africa to do the hard labor that the Indians seemed constitutionally incapable of performing. He later regretted that solution, opposed slavery, and became an advocate for the Indians. In 1561 he completed *Historia general de las Indias,* a remarkable history of the early decades of Spanish discovery and colonization. He is critical of Columbus's actions as governor but adamant about the Discoverer's providential role, writing that "the divine and great Master chose, among all the sons of Adam that in our times were upon the earth, that illustrious and great Columbus"[5] for the task of unlocking the gates of the Ocean Sea.

As for Christopher Columbus, not even death would stop his travels. His remains would continue to be moved back and forth across the Ocean Sea and around the Caribbean long after he died, and considerable debate continues about the current location of his bones. Immediately after his death, he was interred at the Franciscan monastery of San Francisco in Valladolid, but his remains were transferred in 1509 to a family mausoleum that his son established at Las Cuevas in Seville. Diego later specified in his will that both he and his father be buried in Santo Domingo, and the Admiral's bones were moved there in about 1541. When Santo Domingo came under the control of France in 1795, the bodies of both Columbus and Diego were moved to Cuba, a Spanish possession, although some have speculated that only the bones of Diego were removed. Following Cuban independence in 1898, the remains were again moved, this time to the Cathedral of Seville, where they were placed in the large and impressive monument that attracts visitors today. But during construction in 1877 at the church in Santo Domingo, builders uncovered a small lead box containing bones, dust, and a single lead bullet. Inscribed on the box was the name Cristóbal Colón. This box was later transferred to the *Faro a Colon,* a large museum in Santo Domingo built in 1992 as part of the quincentenary celebrations of the First Voyage. DNA tests have proved inconclusive: whether the Admiral is buried in the Old World or the New World is still in dispute.

From the time he first proposed his Enterprise of the Indies to

King João II of Portugal, Columbus has had both supporters and detractors. His reputation in Spain was at a low point at the time of his death, and it did not recover quickly. Over the next several decades, the great conquistadores delivered the gold that Columbus had only promised, and they were generally held in much higher esteem than the Admiral. The lengthy legal battle between Columbus's heirs and the crown produced a great deal of testimony, much of it clearly false but which nevertheless cast Columbus in a negative light.

In recent decades, Columbus has had his share of detractors who blame him for every misfortune that has occurred in the world he opened. A respected modern historian (not a Columbus expert) summarized the popular notion by writing, "Now we know that Columbus was not the first to come here and was actually more the despoiler than the discoverer, for he laid waste a country full of people living harmoniously in a highly developed culture."[6] This idea was popularized by Kirkpatrick Sale, who characterizes Columbus as "swarmy."[7] But such sweeping generalizations ignore the facts: there is little evidence that Columbus himself was a "despoiler" or "laid waste to a country" (though there is ample evidence that many of the early explorers and colonists, including Roldán, Hojeda, Bobadilla, and Ovando, brutally destroyed the native population). And it is far from accurate to describe Native Americans as a "people living harmoniously in a highly developed culture." Such a view of the "noble savage" was never factual. In the Caribbean, the natives encountered by Columbus wore little or no clothing and warred among themselves, with some of them practicing cannibalism.[8]

The early British settlers in North America, however, began to view Columbus as part of their peculiarly American heritage, and after the Revolutionary War, Columbus became an iconic figure in the new nation. The nation's capital, the District of Columbia, was named for him, as were two state capitals, Columbus, Ohio, and Columbia, South

Carolina. The term *Columbia* became a poetic name for the United States, and Columbia was often depicted as a woman in statues and paintings. In late 1825, the minister plenipotentiary of the United States in Madrid invited Washington Irving, the American author, to visit Madrid and translate "a work then in the press, edited by Don Martin Fernandez de Navarette . . . containing a collection of documents relative to the voyages of Columbus, among which were many of a highly important nature, recently discovered."[9] Irving never did produce a translation of Navarette's *Colección* but instead wrote *The Life and Voyages of Christopher Columbus,* which was published in 1828. Despite extending to nearly two thousand pages, the laudatory biography was enormously popular and went through 175 printings by the end of the nineteenth century.

Following instructions received from the resurrected Moroni, Orson Hyde's "Prince of America," on 22 September 1823, Joseph Smith first uncovered the plates containing Nephi's prophecy regarding Columbus.[10] The Book of Mormon was published in 1830, and The Church of Jesus Christ of Latter-day Saints was formally organized on 6 April of that year, 317 years after Columbus had heard a Celestial voice while anchored near the mouth of the Río Belén.

Columbus's two great dreams would ultimately become reality as a result of the Restoration. During his lifetime he had failed to see the evangelization of the New World—his dream of taking the gospel of Christ to the "other sheep" and creating one fold and one shepherd seemed to have died in the struggles and depredations of Hispaniola. He never saw the realization of the great Christian community he had envisioned in the New World. But in recent decades the restored gospel has found root among the peoples and lands discovered by Columbus, with more than twelve million Latter-day Saints living in the New World, nearly half of those in Latin America and the islands of the Caribbean.[11]

No crusade was ever launched by Spain, despite the constant urging of Columbus. He never realized his dream of seeing the Holy Land back in Christian hands and the great temple of Solomon being rebuilt. But on 3 August 1831, Joseph Smith dedicated land for a temple in Jackson County, Missouri. There, at some point yet in the future, a new temple will be built as part of a New Jerusalem, fulfilling Columbus's dream in a way he could not fully foresee.

On 17 September 2000, a temple of The Church of Jesus Christ of Latter-day Saints was dedicated in Santo Domingo, the city founded on Hispaniola by Columbus and his brother where he experienced such disappointment, turmoil, and heartache. In the dedicatory prayer, that house was blessed to "be a house of peace, and a refuge from the noise and confusion of the world."[12] In that sacred building visitors can experience the peace and refuge that Columbus dreamed of but never found in Hispaniola.

In the early years of the Restoration, divine truth was revealed at a remarkable pace, culminating with the restoration of the sealing power and proxy work for the deceased. The Saints were forced to abandon the Nauvoo Temple not many months following the death of Joseph Smith, and a new temple was not completed for more than thirty years. In 1877, a few months after the dedication of the St. George Temple, Wilford Woodruff, then a member of the Quorum of the Twelve Apostles, experienced a remarkable manifestation while in the St. George Temple:

> The spirits of the dead gathered around me, wanting to know why we did not redeem them. Said they, "You have had the use of the Endowment House for a number of years, and yet nothing has ever been done for us. We laid the foundation of the government you now enjoy, and we never apostatized from it, but we remained true to it and were faithful to God." . . . They waited on me for two days and two nights. I thought it very singular, that

notwithstanding so much work had been done, and yet nothing had been done for them . . . I straightway went into the baptismal font and called upon brother McCallister [J. D. T. McCallister, first counselor in the temple presidency] to baptize me for the signers of the Declaration of Independence, and fifty other eminent men, making one hundred in all, including John Wesley, Columbus, and others."[13]

Three days later, on 24 August 1877, Christopher Columbus was ordained a high priest by Wilford Woodruff. Of the one hundred eminent men who had been baptized in the preceding days, only four were ordained to that priesthood office.[14] President Woodruff never explained why he ordained Columbus to the office of high priest, yet for Columbus it seems a singular and appropriate honor. He had striven throughout his life to serve both his sovereigns and his God. His service had often been flawed and imperfect, and except for a few brief moments and a few faithful friends, he had been rebuffed by earthly kings and ridiculed by the wise and powerful men of his age. But he had succeeded in accomplishing what God had foreordained him to do and what Nephi had foreseen: wrought upon by the Spirit of God, this "man among the Gentiles" had gone forth upon the many waters to the promised land.[15] With these sacred ordinances, administered in the new dispensation of which he had been a forerunner, Christopher Columbus was honored and recognized for what he had always believed he was: the man who bore Christ across the uncrossable waters, the messenger of the new heaven and the new earth.

Of the new heaven and the new earth,
of which our Lord spoke in the Revelation of John
and earlier by the mouth of Isaiah, he made me
the messenger and showed me where to go.

CHRISTOPHER COLUMBUS

TIME LINE

Events in the life of Christopher Columbus are in bold type.

1451   Amerigo Vespucci born in Florence.
Isabella, future queen of Castile, born in Ávila.
Christopher Columbus born in or near Genoa.

1452   Ferdinand, future king of Aragon, born.
Leonardo da Vinci born near Florence.

1453   Constantinople falls to Ottoman army, which then
moves west to Belgrade.

1455   Johan Gutenberg prints the Bible using movable type.

1459   Serbia falls to the Ottoman Empire.

1460   Southern Greece falls to the Ottoman Empire.
Construction of Machu Pichu begins.

1463   The Ottomans conquer Bosnia.

c. 1465   **Columbus goes to sea.**

c. 1466   Moctezuma II, future Aztec king, born.

1469   Prince Ferdinand and Princess Isabella marry at
Valladolid.

1471   Albrecht Dürer, German artist, born.

1473   Copernicus born in Poland.
        Golf first played on the Old Course at St. Andrews.

1474   Bartolomé de Las Casas born.
        Isabella crowned queen of Castile.

1476   **Shipwrecked off the coast of Portugal.**

1477?   **Voyage to Iceland.**

1478   **Voyage to Madeira to buy sugar.**

1479   **Marries Felipa Perestrello e Moniz.**

1479/80 **Diego Columbus born in Porto Santo.**

1480   Ferdinand Magellan born.

1481   João II becomes king of Portugal.
        Portuguese build fortress at São Jorge da Mina in
        Africa.

1482?   **Sails to São Jorge da Mina.**

1483   Martin Luther born.

1484   **Proposes the Enterprise of the Indies to King João II**
        of Portugal.

1485   **Felipa Perestrello e Moniz, Columbus's wife, dies.**
        His plan rejected by João II, Columbus and his son,
        Diego, move to Castile.
        Henry Tudor defeats Richard III and becomes Henry
        VII of England.

1486   **Meets for the first time with Ferdinand and Isabella**
        to propose his Enterprise of the Indies.

1488   **Beatriz de Harana gives birth to Columbus's second**
        son, Fernando.
        Bartholomew Dias rounds the Cape of Good Hope.
        Columbus visits Portugal.

1492   Granada falls to the armies of Castile and Aragon.
        Ferdinand and Isabella expel Jews from Spain.

3 August 1492 **Columbus embarks on First Voyage.**

6 September 1492   **Departs San Sebastian in the Canary Islands.**

12 October 1492   **Landfall, probably at San Salvador Island.**

24 December 1492   *Santa María* **grounded in Hispaniola.**

16 January 1493   **Departs from Hispaniola to return to Spain.**

14 February 1493   **Receives revelation from a Celestial voice.**

4 March 1493   **Arrives in Lisbon.**

15 March 1493   **Arrives in Palos, completing First Voyage.**

April 1493   **Meets with Ferdinand and Isabella in Barcelona.**

25 September 1493   **Embarks on Second Voyage.**

3 November 1493   **Landfall at Dominica.**

27 November 1493   **Arrives at Navidad to find the men of the garrison dead.**

2 January 1494   **Founds La Isabela on Hispaniola.**

March 1494   **Leads first "model" Spanish expedition into the interior.**

24 April–
September 1494   **Explores Cuba and Jamaica.**

29 September 1494   **Returns to Hispaniola to find the colony in disarray.**

March 1495   **Begins a series of campaigns to explore and pacify the interior of Hispaniola.**

10 March 1496   **Departs for Spain.**

Spring/Summer 1496   **At the instruction of Columbus, Bartholomew Columbus founds Santo Domingo.**

11 June 1496   **Columbus arrives at Cádiz.**

1497   John Cabot, a Genoese mariner, sails from England to Newfoundland.

Vasco da Gama embarks on successful voyage to India via the Cape of Good Hope.

Atahualpa, last emperor of the Inca, born in Quito.

6 October 1497   Prince Juan, son of Ferdinand and Isabella, dies.

30 May 1498   **Columbus embarks on his Third Voyage.**

31 July 1498   **Landfall at Trinidad.**

5 August 1498   **First documented landing on American mainland.**

14 or 15 August 1498   **Records in journal the discovery of "a very great continent, which until today has been unknown."**

19 August 1498   **Arrives at Hispaniola to find Roldán's rebellion.**

25 December 1499   **Again hears a Celestial voice.**

August 1500   **Francisco de Bobadilla begins official investigation.**

September 1500   **Columbus and his brothers arrested and put in chains.**

October 1500   **Columbus and his brothers sent back to Spain.**

16 December 1500   **Received by Ferdinand and Isabella.**

1501   **Begins work on *Libro de las profecías*.**

13 September 1501   Nicolás de Ovando appointed governor of Hispaniola.

11 May 1502   **Departs Cádiz on Fourth Voyage.**

15 June 1502   **Makes landfall at Martinique.**

29 June 1502   **Denied shelter in harbor of Santo Domingo.**

30 June 1502   Hurricane destroys all but one ship of homeward-bound Spanish fleet; Bobadilla dies in storm. **Columbus's ships survive, as does the one ship carrying his belongings back to Spain.**

30 July 1502   **Arrives at Bonacca and begins exploration of the coast of the Isthmus of Panama.**

November–   **Severe weather continues to plague the fleet.**
December 1502

6 January 1503   **Anchors in mouth of Río Belén.**

6 April 1503   **Receives revelation.**

16 April 1503   **Escapes from Río Belén.**

April 1503   **Abandons the worm-eaten *Vizcaína* on the coast of Panama.**

25 June 1503   **Unable to reach Hispaniola, runs ships aground in St. Ann's Bay, Jamaica, where he and his crew remain for 370 days.**

July–August 1503   **Diego Méndez reaches Hispaniola by canoe. Porras brothers lead mutiny on Jamaica.**
Leonardo da Vinci begins painting Mona Lisa.

29 February 1504   **Uses knowledge of eclipse to convince Indians to continue providing food to his men.**

3 August 1504   **Rescue ship arranged by Méndez arrives in Jamaica.**

12 September 1504   **Departs Santo Domingo for Spain.**

7 November 1504   **Arrives at Sanlúcar, Andalusia.**

26 November 1504   Queen Isabella dies.

May 1505   **Recovered slightly from his poor health, travels to court by mule.**

20 May 1506   **Columbus dies at Valladolid.**

1507   The first recorded epidemic of smallpox in the New World decimates the Tainos in Hispaniola.

1512   Polish mathematician and astronomer Copernicus writes a brief treatise asserting the earth revolves around the sun.

1513 Vasco Nuñez de Balboa crosses the Isthmus of Panama and views the Pacific Ocean.

1517 Martin Luther posts his Ninety-Five Theses in Saxony.

1519 Charles I of Spain, grandson of Ferdinand and Isabella, becomes Charles V of the Holy Roman Empire.
Magellan begins his globe-circling expedition.
Hernán (or Hernando or Fernando) Cortés begins the conquest of Mexico.

1521 Magellan's ships return to Europe, completing first successful circumnavigation of the globe.

1523 Hernán Cortés introduces the cacao bean to Spain.

1531 Henry VIII breaks with Rome, and the Church of England separates from the pope.

1532 Francisco Pizarro conquers the empire of the Inca.

1536 Buenos Aires founded by Pedro de Mendoza.

1537 William Tyndale publishes his English translation of the Bible.

1539 Fernando de Soto explores North America.

1554 Portuguese missionaries found São Paulo.
Shakespeare and Cervantes born.

1564 Galileo born.

1571 American Indians kill Spanish missionaries at future site of Jamestown, ending Spain's efforts to push northward along the Atlantic coast.

1585 Colony of Roanoke founded by the English in North America.

1588 Spanish Armada defeated by England.

1607 Jamestown, Virginia, founded by the English.

1620 Pilgrims arrive at Cape Cod on the *Mayflower*.

1621 King James Version of the Bible published.

1636 Harvard University founded.

1643   Isaac Newton born.

1689   John Locke publishes his first "Letter Concerning Toleration."

1729–1735   John and Charles Wesley create Methodist Church.

22 February 1732   George Washington born.

1775   War breaks out between England and the American colonies.

2 July 1776   Declaration of Independence approved by Continental Congress.

1783   America defeats Great Britain to gain independence.

1787   Constitution of the United States finalized by Constitutional Convention in Philadelphia.

9 September 1791   New federal district of the United States officially named the District of Columbia.

1805   Joseph Smith Jr. born in Vermont.
Smith family moves to an area near the Hill Cumorah in New York State.

Spring 1820   Joseph Smith's First Vision.

21–21 September 1823   Moroni appears to Joseph Smith and shows him where to find the plates on which a record had been kept of ancient American peoples.

1827   Joseph Smith removes the plates from the Hill Cumorah to translate them "by the gift and power of God" (Introduction, Book of Mormon).

March 1830   Book of Mormon published.

6 April 1830   The Church of Jesus Christ of Latter-day Saints organized at Fayette, New York.

1877   St. George Temple dedicated in Utah.

21 August 1877   **Columbus baptized by proxy in the St. George Temple** as part of a group of one hundred eminent

men, including all the signers of the Declaration of Independence, most of the past presidents of the United States, and John Wesley.

24 August 1877 **Columbus ordained a high priest by proxy,** along with George Washington, John Wesley, and Benjamin Franklin.

1991–1992 Ordinances for members of the crew of the First Voyage performed in the Provo Utah Temple.

Appendix 2

TEMPLE ORDINANCES FOR COLUMBUS AND CREW OF THE FIRST VOYAGE

The St. George Temple was dedicated in the spring of 1877, the first temple in Utah and the first to be completed after the departure of the Latter-day Saints from Nauvoo in 1845. Wilford Woodruff, who was ordained an apostle in 1839 at the age of thirty-two, became the first president of the St. George Temple in 1877. He was an extensive and faithful journal writer; a typescript copy of his journals fills several volumes in the Harold B. Lee Library at Brigham Young University. His journal entries for 21 and 24 August 1877 read as follows:

> Aug 21, 1877 I Wilford Woodruff went to the Temple of the Lord this morning and was Baptized for 100 persons who were dead including the signers of the Declaration of Independence all except John Hancock [who had been baptized earlier in the Endowment House] and [William Floyd]. I was Baptized for the following names:
>
> [He then lists 54 names, including Benjamin Franklin, Thomas Jefferson, and John and Samuel Adams.]
>
> Baptized for the following Eminent men:
>
> [He then lists 44 names, including Washington Irving, Amerigo Vespucci, Christopher Columbus, and John Wesley.]

When Br McAllister had Baptized me for the 100 Names I Baptized him for 21, including Gen Washington and his forefathers and all the Presidents of the United States that were not in my list Except Buchannan Van Buren & Grant.

It was a very interesting day. I felt thankful that we had the privilege and the power to administer for the worthy dead especially for the signers of the declaration of Independence, that inasmuch as they had laid the foundation of our Government that we could do as much for them as they had done for us. . . .

24 [Aug] We gave Endowments to 130. W Woodruff Ordained 2 High Priests. One for Christopher Columbus.[1]

Prior to a major remodeling of the St. George Temple, Ezra Taft Benson, then president of the Quorum of the Twelve Apostles, was asked by Church President Spencer W. Kimball to visit the St. George Temple and see if he could locate the records of the ordinances mentioned by Wilford Woodruff. He reported the following:

> In the archives of the temple, I saw in a book, in bold handwriting, the names of the Founding Fathers and others, including Columbus and other great Americans, for whom the work had been done in the house of the Lord. This is all one great program on both sides of the veil. We are fortunate to be engaged in it on this side of the veil. I think the Lord expects us to take an active part in preserving the Constitution and our freedom.[2]

Wilford Woodruff spoke publicly of his experiences relating to the ordinance work for these "eminent men" on at least three occasions, including the dedication of the Salt Lake Temple and his final address in general conference. Additional details of these events are given in Blaine M. Yorgason et al., *All That Was Promised: The St. George Temple and the Unfolding of the Restoration,* and Vicki Jo Anderson, *The Other Eminent Men of Wilford Woodruff.*

In preparation for the quincentenary celebration at Brigham Young

University in 1992, De Lamar Jenson, who served as chair of the university's quincentenary committee, compiled a list of eighty-seven verified members of Columbus's crew from the First Voyage, based on the research done by Alice Bache Gould. Ordinances for all eighty-seven crew members, as well as an additional twenty-one possible members of the crew, were performed in the Provo Utah Temple in 1990 and 1991.

NOTES

INTRODUCTION

1. Fernandez-Armesto, *Columbus on Himself,* 17.
2. 1 Nephi 13:12. Modern prophets have repeatedly affirmed that the "man among the Gentiles" in this scripture refers to Columbus. See Garr, *Christopher Columbus,* 73–79.
3. Bernáldez, *Historia de los reyes Católicos,* 357.
4. The revelation that Columbus records in his account of the Fourth Voyage has remarkable similarities to parts of Doctrine and Covenants 121 and 122. See chapter 14 of this work.
5. 1 Nephi 13:12.
6. Fernandez-Armesto, *Columbus on Himself,* ix.
7. Madriaga, *Christopher Columbus,* 16.
8. Provost, "Seven Years in Spain Prior to 1492," in Gerace, *Columbus and His World,* 66.
9. Delaney provides an excellent summary of the treatment of Columbus's spirituality in "Columbus's Ultimate Goal," 260–92.
10. Humboldt, *Examen,* 1:110. The translation is from Watts, "Prophecy and Discovery," 79.
11. Fernandez-Armesto, *Columbus on Himself,* ix.
12. Fernandez-Armesto, *Columbus on Himself,* viii.
13. Bown, *1494,* 131.
14. Delaney, "Columbus's Ultimate Goal," 279.
15. Fernandez-Armesto, *Columbus on Himself,* x–xi.
16. Nibley, *Prophetic Book of Mormon,* 50.
17. West and Kling, *Libro,* 107; emphasis added.

PROLOGUE

1. Morison, *Admiral of the Ocean Sea,* 223.
2. Dunn and Kelley, *Diario,* 59.
3. Morison, *Admiral of the Ocean Sea,* 226.

CHAPTER 1: THE PROPHECY OF NEPHI

1. 1 Nephi 2:6.
2. 2 Kings 17:6.
3. Isaiah 3:1, 4, 5, 8.
4. See 2 Nephi 5:28–33.
5. 1 Nephi 1:4.
6. 1 Nephi 2:16.
7. 1 Nephi 11:1.
8. 1 Nephi 13:12.
9. See Garr, *Christopher Columbus,* 73–79, for several statements by modern-day prophets and apostles regarding Columbus as the man spoken of by Nephi.
10. West and Kling, *Libro,* 105.

CHAPTER 2: FROM WEAVER'S SON TO MARINER

1. Varela and Gil, *Textos,* 492.
2. See Morison, *Admiral of the Ocean Sea,* 8.
3. See, for example, the work of Estelle Irizarry. Irizarry substantiates her claim that Columbus was Catalan Jew by citing the frequent use of the "/" in Columbus's writings, an orthographic practice common in Ladino, the Judeo-Spanish language used in Iberia in the fifteenth century. Although these arguments are interesting, Columbus had significant contacts with *converso* (Christianized) Jews in Spain and, as an immigrant, might have picked up some practices and ideas from them as he assimilated a new culture and language in Portugal and Spain. What is certain is that Columbus was a devout Christian. None of the arguments regarding Columbus's alleged Jewish Catalan origins preclude his own frequent assertion that he was Genoese, an assertion well supported by contemporary documents.
4. Varela and Gil, *Textos,* 356.
5. See Delaney, *Quest for Jerusalem,* 219.
6. See "St. Christopher," *Original Catholic Encyclopedia,* online edition. Christopher is a combination of *Christo* ("Christ") and the verb *fero* ("to bear or to carry").
7. Colón, *Historia del almirante,* 42.
8. Columbus's son Fernando states that his father "studied in Pavia" ("*estudió en Pavia*"); (Colón, *Historia del almirante,* 49) apparently referring to the University of Pavia, located about 75 miles north of Genoa; however, the

matriculation records of the University of Pavia, which have been well pre-served, do not show that Columbus ever attended. Some scholars have sug-gested that Fernando's statement may derive from the fact that the primary school operated by the weavers guild in Genoa was located on Vicolo ("al-ley") Pavia. This argument was first made in 1894 by Cornelio Desimoni, a historian who studied law at the University of Genoa. Fernando's comment may actually give credence to the supposition that Columbus attended pri-mary school in Genoa. See Watts, "Prophecy and Discovery," 74–75. Las Casas stated that Columbus "studied the basics [*los primeros rudimentos*] of writing, primarily grammar, in Pavia, and became skilled in Latin" (*Historia*, 1:46), which seems to support Desimoni's argument.

9. Farina and Tolf, *Columbus Documents*, 29–30.
10. Varela and Gil, *Textos*, 360.
11. West and Kling, *Libro*, 105.
12. Colón, *Historia del almirante*, 54.
13. Varela and Gil, *Textos*, 492. The words as recorded by Columbus are "*De los atamientos de la mar Océana, que estavan cerrados con cadenas tan fuertres, te dio la llave.*"
14. Matthew 16:19.
15. West asserts that Columbus received the key by heavenly manifestation while "in his youth." See *Libro*, 48, 53–54; West, in "Stupor or Faith," in Gerace, *Columbus and His World*, 46. Nevertheless, I have been unable to find any basis for this claim in the citations given by West. I believe this assertion may have come from a misreading of the texts, although his con-clusion may well be correct.
16. Las Casas, *Historia*, 1:471.
17. Colón, *Historia del almirante*, 56.
18. When Constantinople fell in 1453 to Mehmet the Conqueror, the cessa-tion of trade, which had been dominated by Genoa and Venice, meant that many Genoese mariners were out of work. This situation resulted in a dis-persion of experienced seamen across the Mediterranean, and many of them eventually settled in Portugal. In 1481, the councilors of King João II ad-vised that he expel the Genoese, who were both numerous and prosperous, but João declined, recognizing that in a country of two million inhabitants, these skilled mariners were a valuable resource. Columbus and his brother Bartholomew became part of that valued expatriate community.
19. Morison, *Admiral of the Ocean Sea*, 27.

CHAPTER 3: IN PORTUGAL
1. Hierro and Pereda, *Atlas ilustrado*, 29.
2. Colón, *Historia del almirante*, 53.
3. Varela and Gil, *Textos*, 89.

4. Some historians suggest that Bartholomew preceded his brother to Lisbon; others, that Bartholomew joined his brother later. All that is known is that both Christopher and Bartholomew were in Lisbon together for some time.

5. Morison, *Admiral of the Ocean Sea*, 60. The incidents that follow are also reported by Morison.

6. Morison, *Admiral of the Ocean Sea*, 60–61.

7. Colón, *Historia del almirante*, 56.

8. Colón, *Historia del almirante*, 56–57.

9. Varela and Gil, *Textos*, 90.

10. Varela and Gil, *Textos*, 90.

11. Varela and Gil, *Textos*, 90–91. The postil is written in Latin, and Varela and Gill render a Spanish translation in *Textos*: "*Nota que navegando con frecuencia desde Lisboa al Sur, a Guinea, observé con diligencia la derrota.*" Morison claims that the postil should be read to say that Columbus made frequent observations during a single voyage, but in Varela and Gil's Spanish rendering, it is clear that "frequency" refers to sailing, not to taking observations or readings. The transcript of the original Latin reads, "*Nota quod sepe nauigando ex Ulixbona ad austrum in Guinea notaui cum diligentia uiam, ut solent naucleres et malinerios . . .*"

12. Colón, *Historia del almirante*, 57.

13. Colón, *Historia del almirante*, 57.

14. Morison, *Admiral of the Ocean Sea*, 68

15. West and Kling, *Libro*, 105.

16. Las Casas, *Historia*, 1:106.

17. The Peruvian historian Luis Ulloa argues that Columbus reached the New World in a Norwegian-Portuguese expedition in 1477. The supporting evidence is dubious, however. The Spanish historian Juan Manzano argues that Columbus had knowledge of the islands of the Caribbean from a sailor-pilot who had been blown across the Atlantic by a storm, returned to Madeira where Columbus cared for him briefly before the old mariner died, and left Columbus his charts and data. Las Casas says he heard the story of the old mariner in Hispaniola, and it has been reported in various forms across the centuries, but the evidence is scant and the arguments all circumstantial (Las Casas, *Historia*, 1:103–6). There is no evidence that any ship has ever been blown across the Atlantic by a storm, and current knowledge of wind and storm patterns suggests that such an event would be virtually impossible, although Davidson disputes this (Davidson, *Columbus Then and Now*, 106–8). See Manzano, *Colón y su secreto*; Perez, *Mirabilis in altis*; and Morison, *Admiral of the Ocean Sea*, 61–63. Orson Hyde suggests a different reason for Columbus's certainty: "This same angel [Moroni] was with Columbus, and gave him deep impressions, by dreams and by visions, respecting this New World" (in *Journal of Discourses*, 6:368).

18. Taviani, *Christopher Columbus,* 185.
19. Colón, *Historia del almirante,* 65–67. The original letter has never been found, but Fernando copied the correspondence into his *Historia.* Columbus copied Toscanelli's original letter (in Latin) onto a blank page in his copy of Sylvius's *Historia rerum.*
20. Varela and Gil, *Textos,* 479.
21. Colón, *Historia del almirante,* 67–68.
22. The English translation of the quotations is from West and Kling, *Libro,* 87. The original postils are written in Latin.
23. Varela and Gil, *Textos,* 94.
24. West and Kling, *Libro,* 109.
25. Morison, *Admiral of the Ocean Sea,* 42.
26. The date of Felipa's death is not known, although most historians assume it was about 1484. Columbus makes no mention of her death in any of his extant writings. She is buried with members of her family in the Carmo Convent in Lisbon.
27. Taviani, *Christopher Columbus,* 167.

CHAPTER 4: TAKING THE QUEST TO CASTILE

1. Fernandez-Armesto, *Columbus on Himself,* 47.
2. It is difficult to date or even place in chronological order many of the events in Columbus's life during the seven years after his arrival in Castile. Two basic, and conflicting, chronologies exist. The first was developed by Vignaud and published in his *Historie* in 1911. Morison generally follows that chronology, and as a result, it is the best known and most commonly accepted; Delany likewise follows essentially the same chronology. Nonetheless, a different sequence of events was proposed by Manzano in *Cristóbal Colón* in 1964. Manzano tracked the well-documented movements of the Spanish court during those years and used that data to determine where and when Columbus might have met with members of the court. This analysis highlighted several inconsistencies in the Vignaud chronology. I have, for the most part, followed the Manzano sequence in this chapter, but note that the sequence and location of many of these events cannot be verified. For a detailed discussion of this issue, see Provost, "Seven Years in Spain Prior to 1492," in Gerace, *Columbus and His World,* 57–68.
3. Varela and Gil, *Textos,* 407.
4. Taviani, *Christopher Columbus,* 171.
5. West and Kling, *Libro,* 225–26.
6. Some historians posit that he was poisoned, but the evidence is slim.
7. Catherine became the first wife of Henry VIII of England, who divorced her so he could marry his mistress Anne Boleyn.
8. As noted earlier, even the date and place of the meeting are uncertain.

9. Morison, *Admiral of the Ocean Sea,* 86.
10. This citation and those immediately following are from Morison, *Journals,* 22–23.
11. West and Kling, *Libro,* 105.
12. Morison, following the more traditional chronology, has the Talavera commission giving their report in Seville in late 1490. His explanation for the long delay is summarized in a single phrase, "Simply the custom of the country" (*Admiral of the Ocean Sea,* 98).
13. Las Casas, *Historia,* 1:230.
14. Las Casas, *Historia,* 1:230–31.
15. Varela and Gil, *Textos,* 535.
16. Morison, *Journals,* 21.
17. Varela and Gil, *Textos,* 92.
18. The seventh duke of Medina Sidonia, Guzman's great-grandson, was appointed Admiral of the Ocean Sea and commanded the great Spanish Armada that was defeated by the British in 1588. That defeat shifted control of the Atlantic from Spain to England.
19. Las Casas, *Historia,* 1:237.
20. Taviani, *Christopher Columbus,* 192.
21. Las Casas, *Historia,* 1:227.
22. Dunn and Kelley, *Diario,* 17.
23. Of Diego Deza, Columbus later wrote, "He was the cause of . . . my remaining in Castile when I was about to leave the country" (Varela and Gil, *Textos,* 518).

CHAPTER 5: PREPARATIONS

1. Oviedo, *La historia general,* 20.
2. A *maravedis* was a copper coin in common use, but its value varied over time. At the time of the First Voyage, 1,000 *maravedis* were worth about .3529 ounces of gold. Using a modern value of $700 per ounce for gold (a typical price before 2008), 2 million *maravedis* would be valued at just under $500,000. By comparison, at the time of the First Voyage, a cow in Spain might be valued at about 2,000 *maravedis*. Amerigo Vespucci rented a home in Seville for 7,000 *maravedis* per month. In 1502, Nicolas Ovando received a salary of 360,000 *maravedis* as governor of Hispaniola.
3. Funding sources per Fernandez-Armesto, *Columbus on Himself,* 62–63. Morison gives a slightly different accounting (*Admiral of the Ocean Sea,* 103–4). A citizen of Palos had robbed some Portuguese ships, and Castile had made reparations with the understanding that Palos would repay the crown.
4. Morison, *Journals,* 30–31.
5. A summary of various estimates is given in Phillips, "Sizes and Configurations of Spanish Ships," in Gerace, *Columbus and His World,* 69–98.

6. Dunn and Kelley, *Diario,* 291.

7. Morison, *Admiral of the Ocean Sea,* 114.

8. Dunn and Kelley, *Diario,* 18.

9. *Pleitos Colombianos,* ed. Antonio Muro Orejon et al. (Seville, 1964), 8:332, as quoted in Jensen, "Christopher Columbus and the Pinzóns of Palos," 22. Testimony in the *Pleitos* indicates that Pinzón was encouraged by Father Marchena to participate in the voyage, suggesting again the significance of the role of Marchena in Columbus's enterprise.

10. See Gould, *Nueva lista documentada.* Alice Gould, a native of Boston, spent forty years in Spain researching and documenting the names of the crew. Gould's maternal grandfather, Josiah Quincy, visited Joseph Smith in Nauvoo in 1844 and later served as mayor of Boston.

11. One of the myths surrounding the First Voyage is that the crew consisted largely of criminals who were offered pardons if they would sail with Columbus. In fact, only four of the crew members had been prisoners. One of them, Bartolomé de Torres, had been imprisoned for killing a man in a brawl; the other three were imprisoned for helping de Torres escape from prison.

12. West and Kling, *Libro,* 239.

CHAPTER 6: THE FIRST CROSSING

1. Morison, *Admiral of the Ocean Sea,* 215.

2. Dunn and Kelley, *Diario,* 21.

3. Columbus referred to the journal as the *Diurnal,* a contemporary form of the Latin *diurnalis,* "daily journal" (Varela and Gil, *Textos,* 247n).

4. Fernandez-Armesto, *Columbus on Himself,* 68–69.

5. Dunn and Kelley, *Diario,* 17–21.

6. Columbus recorded using the quadrant to determine latitude on three occasions in the Caribbean during the First Voyage. On 21 November 1492 he took a reading from on board the *Santa María,* which suggested he was at 42 degrees of latitude (roughly the latitude of Boston and Barcelona). The figure was so obviously and wildly wrong that Columbus stated he no longer intended to use the quadrant until they reached land where it could be repaired! See *Diario,* 163. Readings made during the Second and Third Voyages were also unreliable. During the year he spent on Jamaica during the Fourth Voyage, however, he made several readings over an extended period of time and determined the latitude of Jamaica within half a degree (Peck, *Cristoforo Colombo,* 27–28).

7. Morison, *Admiral of the Ocean Sea,* 195.

8. Peck, "History of Early Dead Reckoning and Celestial Navigation," 5, http://www.newworldexplorersinc.org/EarlyNavigation.pdf, accessed 14 August 2013. Peck replicated Columbus's voyage from Gomera to San

Salvador in his deep-water sailing ship, *Gooney Bird*, in 1987 and again in 1991. His carefully controlled and monitored voyages were the first scientific attempts to accurately re-create this key segment of Columbus's First Voyage. See Peck, *Cristoforo Colombo.*

9. Taviani, "Columbus the Man," in Gerace, *Columbus and His World*, 5.

10. Quoted in Taviani in "Columbus the Man," in Gerace, *Columbus and His World*, 5. The earliest transcription is found in *Raccolta*, part 3, vol. 2, "Lettera a Gerolano Annavi," 107.

11. Quoted in Taviani in "Columbus the Man," in Gerace, *Columbus and His World*, 5. Charcot led two expeditions to the Antarctic.

12. Orson Hyde, in *Journal of Discourses*, 6:368.

13. West and Kling, *Libro*, 105.

14. Dunn and Kelley, *Diario*, 41.

15. Dunn and Kelley, *Diario*, 43.

16. Dunn and Kelley, *Diario*, 45.

17. Dunn and Kelley, *Diario*, 55.

18. See Dunn and Kelley, *Diario*, 29n; Kelley, "Navigation of Columbus," in Gerace, *Columbus and His World*, 121–40; Peck, "History of Early Dead Reckoning," 7, available at http://www.newworldexplorersinc.org /EarlyNavigation.pdf, accessed 14 August 2013.

19. Dunn and Kelley, *Diario*, 57.

20. Dunn and Kelley, *Diario*, 369.

21. See Morison, *Admiral of the Ocean Sea*, 220–21.

22. Dunn and Kelley, *Diario*, 57.

23. Oviedo, *La historia general*, 12.

24. Morison, *Admiral of the Ocean Sea*, 215.

25. Dunn and Kelley, *Diario*, 57–59.

26. Dunn and Kelley, *Diario*, 63.

27. Dunn and Kelley, *Diario*, 65. The issue of Columbus taking possession of this and subsequent islands has been debated by historians. If Columbus believed he had reached the outskirts of the great empires of the Orient, already inhabited and governed by strong monarchs, why did he claim that the Indies were now Spanish possessions? Hindsight, of course, is what makes writing history possible—with the perspective of decades and centuries, the historian can make sense (or try to make sense) of past events. Making history, on the other hand, is much messier—participants rarely understand with any degree of clarity the nature of the events in which they participate. Columbus carried with him both a letter of introduction to the Great Khan and an expedition banner with the symbols of Castile and Aragon. I suspect he was ready to use either one, depending on what he found upon landing. With no sign of the Great Khan, Columbus did what

the Spaniards had done in the Canaries and the Portuguese in the Azores: claimed the territory for their sovereign.

CHAPTER 7: IN THE NEW WORLD

1. Varela and Gil, *Textos*, 223.
2. Dunn and Kelley, *Diario*, 65.
3. Dunn and Kelley, *Diario*, 69.
4. Dunn and Kelley, *Diario*, 69.
5. Dunn and Kelley, *Diario*, 113.
6. Dunn and Kelley, *Diario*, 137.
7. Dunn and Kelley, *Diario*, 141.
8. Dunn and Kelley, *Diario*, 167.
9. Dunn and Kelley, *Diario*, 235.
10. Dunn and Kelley, *Diario*, 243.
11. Dunn and Kelley, *Diario*, 261.
12. Dunn and Kelley, *Diario*, 273.
13. Dunn and Kelley, *Diario*, 277.
14. Dunn and Kelley, *Diario*, 269.
15. Dunn and Kelley, *Diario*, 287.
16. Dunn and Kelley, *Diario*, 291.
17. Dunn and Kelley, *Diario*, 317.
18. Dunn and Kelley, *Diario*, 313.
19. Dunn and Kelley, *Diario*, 323.

CHAPTER 8: THE RETURN VOYAGE

1. Varela and Gil, *Textos*, 225.
2. The term *árbol seco* is an example of Columbus's frequent use of Portuguese phrases in his writings. The more typical Spanish sailing term is *navegar con las velas recogidas*, "to navigate with the sails furled," while the Portuguese use *árvore seca*. Historian Juan Gil has identified several such examples of Portuguese construction as well as numerous *Italianismos* in the writings of Columbus (*Columbiana*, 168–213). Although Columbus left a wealth of written materials, his writings pose several textual challenges for scholars. First, in some important instances the originals are not available and scholars are left to rely on copies and extracts (such as the *Diario*) with their inherent errors of transmission. Second, although Columbus wrote primarily in Spanish, it was not his primary language, and his writings contain constructs and syntax indicative of a person writing in a second language (as noted above). Third, it is not always possible to read the handwriting due to deterioration in the documents, and in some cases different meanings can be construed based on how one interprets the marks on the page or what assumptions one makes for words that are missing from the text. And fourth, the Spanish language of 1500 has changed and evolved over the centuries;

the creation of the *Real Academia* (with its magnificent motto, *Limpia, fija y da splendor),* which brought uniformity in spelling and usage to the language, did not come about until 1713.

3. Dunn and Kelley, *Diario,* 363.

4. Dunn and Kelley, *Diario,* 363–64.

5. Dunn and Kelley, *Diario,* 365.

6. Colón, *Historia del almirante,* 164–65. All the quotations in the following two paragraphs are from this source.

7. Colón, *Historia del almirante,* 164.

8. Fernandez-Armesto, *Columbus on Himself,* 92.

9. Dunn and Kelley, *Diario,* 365. The barrel and its contents have never been found, but that did not prevent a German publishing company from printing in 1890—just in time for the quadricentennial celebrations—what it claimed to be a facsimile edition of Columbus's long-lost parchment.

10. Dunn and Kelley, *Diario,* 373.

11. Dunn and Kelley, *Diario,* 375.

12. Dunn and Kelley, *Diario,* 377.

13. Dunn and Kelley, *Diario,* 379.

14. Dunn and Kelley, *Diario,* 383.

15. Dunn and Kelley, *Diario,* 389.

16. Dunn and Kelley, *Diario,* 391.

17. The letter may have been retrieved by Columbus and sent by him from Lisbon to the monarchs. This letter, together with several other documents, surfaced in 1985 when a Catalan bookseller claimed to have purchased them from an estate on Majorca. The documents were published in 1989 by Antonio Rumeu de Armas under the title *Libro copiador de Cristóbal Colón.*

18. Dunn and Kelley, *Diario,* 391.

19. Dunn and Kelley, *Diario,* 391.

20. Dunn and Kelley, *Diario,* 391.

21. Dunn and Kelley, *Diario,* 391–93.

22. Varela and Gil, *Textos,* 226.

23. Dunn and Kelley, *Diario,* 395.

24. Dunn and Kelley, *Diario,* 401–3.

CHAPTER 9: THE WORD SPREADS

1. *Documentos inéditos para la historia de España,* 9:242. Letter 133 from Peter Martyr to Count Tendilla and the Archbishop of Granada dated 13 September 1493.

2. Las Casas, *Historia,* 1:469.

3. Las Casas, *Historia,* 1:477.

4. Morison, *Admiral of the Ocean Sea,* 355.

5. Colón, *Historia del almirante,* 179.

6. It appears that at least three letters describing the First Voyage were written by Columbus to representatives of the crown: one addressed to Santángel, the *escribano de ración* of Aragon (dated 15 February 1493 with a postscript dated 14 March 1493), one to Gabriel Sánchez, treasurer of Aragon (dated 29 April 1493), and one addressed to the monarchs (dated 4 March 1493). The letter to Santángel was printed in Barcelona by Pedro Possa in late March or early April 1493. Only a single copy of this letter is known to exist.

7. Quoted in Delaney, *Quest for Jerusalem,* 120.

8. Thacher, *Christopher Columbus,* 1:343, letter to Gabriel Sánchez dated 29 April 1493.

CHAPTER 10: TRIUMPH AND TRAGEDY

1. Quoted in Jane, *Four Voyages,* 26.

2. It seems a quaint notion that two European kingdoms would divide ownership of the entire unknown world and its oceans without concern for any other nation or country, yet this is exactly what happened, and it shaped international relations for centuries. The Treaty of Tordesillas established the concept that the open seas could be viewed as the territory of a specific nation. This premise would be the focus of international dispute and argument for centuries. Not until 1994 was an international treaty approved by the United Nations firmly establishing that open seas were, in fact, open to ships of any nation. In the late twentieth century, Argentina cited the Treaty of Tordesillas in its legal arguments claiming rightful possession of the Falkland Islands—the Falklands, argued Argentina, lie west of the line of demarcation and hence legally belonged to Spain, whose rights in the area were inherited by Argentina.

3. Morison, *Journals,* 203. See also Dunn and Kelley, *Diario,* 69.

4. 1 Nephi 15:13.

5. Morison, *Journals,* 204.

6. Morison, *Journals,* 204.

7. Fonseca proved to be an able administrator and would oversee the organization of fleets sailing to the Indies for the next several years. However, Fonseca and Columbus were often at odds, and Fonseca made no secret of his dislike for Columbus, whom he saw as a poor administrator.

8. Morison, *Admiral of the Ocean Sea,* 402.

9. The cannon, or lombards, as they were known, were a relatively new innovation that had played a decisive role in the defeat of the Moors in Spain. They were typically 12 feet long and made of iron or bronze 2 inches thick. They could throw a stone ball weighing as much as 175 pounds.

10. Jane, *Four Voyages,* 48.

11. Varela and Gil, *Textos,* 244.

12. Morison, *Admiral of the Ocean Sea,* 428–29.

13. Las Casas, *Historia,* 1:500. Las Casas was particularly harsh in his characterization of Hojeda, writing, "Had he not been born, the world would have lost nothing" (*Historia,* 2:406).

14. Las Casas, *Historia,* 2:46.

15. Colón, *Historia del almirante,* 230.

16. Morison, *Admiral of the Ocean Sea,* 483.

17. Although Columbus himself never owned slaves, in 1495 and again in 1496 he sent enslaved Indians back to Spain (500 in 1495 and 300 in 1496). There is no report of any other shipments of slaves by Columbus, but he did grant 300 slaves to Francisco Roldán and his followers to take back to Spain with them. The enslavement of non-Christian people who had fought against Christians was a common practice: far more natives were enslaved by the Spaniards in the Canary Islands than in Hispaniola. When Málaga fell to Castile in 1487, many of the captured Muslim defenders were enslaved: 683 slaves were given to prelates or knights, Cardinal Mendoza received 70 slaves, and a few were sent to the Pope (Thomas, *Rivers of Gold,* 7n18). In 1490, there were an estimated 100,000 slaves in Spain, many of them Muslims captured during the Reconquista. Columbus's friend Amerigo Vespucci was active in the slave trade in Seville. Queen Isabella was angered by the shipment of slaves to Spain by Columbus but not particularly for moral reasons; she was upset because she felt that Columbus was usurping her authority by shipping slaves to Spain without her express permission (Davidson, *Columbus Then and Now,* 445). As the first governor and viceroy of Spain's newly discovered territories, Columbus can accurately be named as the man who introduced slavery to the New World, but it is also true that had someone other than Columbus established the link between the Old and the New Worlds, the result would likely have been the same.

18. 1 Nephi 13:14; see also 1 Nephi 1:11 and 2 Nephi 1:11–12. The verses in 2 Nephi, in particular, seem to foreshadow the early colonization of Latin America: "Yea, he will bring other nations unto them, and he will give unto them power, and he will take away from them the lands of their possessions, and he will cause them to be scattered and smitten. Yea, as one generation passeth to another there shall be bloodsheds, and great visitations among them." In the course of a single generation, most of the great tribes and civilizations of the Americas were indeed "scattered and smitten."

19. Quoted in Morison, *Southern Voyages,* 119. See also Brigham, *Christopher Columbus,* 31.

20. Quoted in Morison, *Southern Voyages,* 135.

21. West and Kling, *Libro,* 105.

22. Las Casas, *Historia,* 2:114–15.

23. Colón, *Historia del almirante,* 266.

CHAPTER 11: A NEW WORLD, THE GARDEN OF EDEN, AND THE FUTURE OF
CHRISTIANITY

1. Quoted in West and Kling, *Libro,* 153.
2. Colón, *Historia del almirante,* 259.
3. Morison, *Admiral of the Ocean Sea,* 506.
4. A letter from Pedro de Ayala, the Spanish emissary to the Court of St. James, refers to Cabot as "another Genoese like Columbus," in Biggar, *Precursors,* 28, available online at http://www.bris.ac.uk/Depts/History/Maritime /Sources/1498ayala.htm. Cabot became a citizen of Venice; he later fled to Valencia to avoid creditors.
5. Cabot sailed again with five ships in May of 1498, and the passengers and crew included Friar Buil, the priest who had been so troublesome on Columbus's Second Voyage. The ship carrying Buil was forced by a storm to land in Ireland; the other four ships and Cabot were never heard from again.
6. Columbus noted that the islands were anything but *verde* (green): they were "falsely named, for they are so dry that I saw nothing green on them" (Varela and Gil, *Textos,* 369).
7. The maritime term *doldrums* came into use in the eighteenth century to describe the areas near the equator in both the Atlantic and Pacific Oceans. The equatorial heat causes low air pressure as the heated air rises from the ocean. The rising air results in frequent calms but can also result in severe squalls when the rising air is rapidly replaced.
8. Las Casas, *Historia,* 2:220; emphasis added.
9. Varela and Gil, *Textos,* 372. Morison suggests that this wave may have been caused by a volcanic disturbance (*Admiral of the Ocean Sea,* 537).
10. Fernandez-Armesto, *Columbus on Himself,* 128.
11. Las Casas, *Historia,* 2:264.
12. Varela and Gil, *Textos,* 377.
13. See West and Kling, *Libro,* 18.
14. John Mandeville, *Travels,* 184–85, as quoted by Delaney, *Quest for Jerusalem,* 173.
15. Varela and Gil, *Textos,* 380. The Orinoco discharges at its mouth a volume of water many times greater than that of the Nile or of any river in Europe.
16. Varela and Gil, *Textos,* 380. Latter-day revelation confirms the biblical account of the Garden of Eden. It adds the important information that the garden was located on what is now the North American continent. See Doctrine and Covenants 116; 117:8.
17. Varela and Gil, *Textos,* 383–84.
18. Las Casas, *Historia,* 2:255.
19. Morison, *Admiral of the Ocean Sea,* 548.

CHAPTER 12: EAST OF EDEN

1. Morison, *Admiral of the Ocean Sea,* 558–59.
2. Las Casas, *Historia,* 2:316.
3. The title *Adelantado* was originally a quasimilitary title given to the governor of a newly conquered territory. The term is translated into English literally as "Advanced," referring to the forward territory in a campaign.
4. Hojeda successfully found the pearl fisheries, discovered several new islands, and found the Gulf of Maracaibo, to which he gave the name *Venezuela* ("Little Venice"). Hojeda's crew included one of the pilots from Columbus's First Voyage, Juan de la Cosa (who may or may not have been the same Juan de la Cosa who sailed with Columbus on the Second Voyage), and a Florentine sailor and friend of Columbus living in Seville named Amerigo Vespucci. Vespucci wrote an account of Hojeda's 1499 voyage. Another letter attributed to Vespucci recounts that voyage and a voyage supposedly made by Vespucci down the coast of South America, as well as additional voyages in 1497 and 1503. The 1497 and 1503 voyages were never made, but on the basis of this letter, German mapmaker Martin Waldseemüller applied the name America to the new continent. The letter was ultimately determined to be a forgery.
5. Colón, *Historia del almirante,* 320.
6. A document purporting to be a copy of testimony taken by Bobadilla was recently found by Isabel Aguirre in the archives at Simancas (the national archives of Spain were moved to the citadel in Simancas in 1563, and the archives of the Indies were transferred there in 1784 from Seville). A transcript of the newly discovered document was published in 2006 as *La caída de Cristóbal Colón: El juicio de Bobadilla* (The fall of Christopher Columbus: The judgment of Bobadilla). The testimony was taken in late September 1500, apparently after Columbus was imprisoned. It contains no indication that Columbus was ever questioned or given an opportunity to respond to the accusations. See Varela, *La caída de Cristóbal Colón.*
7. Varela and Gil, *Textos,* 430–31.
8. Varela and Gil, *Textos,* 430.
9. Varela and Gil, *Textos,* 430. See Isaiah 66:22; Revelation 21:1.

CHAPTER 13: THE MIND AND HEART OF COLUMBUS

1. Quoted by Columbus in *Libro de las profecías* (West and Kling, *Libro,* 141).
2. Oviedo, *La historia general,* 4:70–71.
3. Rusconi, *Book of Prophecies,* 5.
4. Fernandez-Armesto, *Columbus on Himself,* 157.
5. For a more detailed history of the manuscript, see Rusconi, *Book of Prophecies,* 8–17.

6. This and subsequent citations are from West, "Enterprise to the Indies," in Gerace, *Columbus and His World,* 49–51.

7. West and Kling, *Libro,* 110.

8. West and Kling, *Libro,* 109.

9. West and Kling, *Libro,* 101.

10. West and Kling, *Libro,* 107.

11. West and Kling, *Libro,* 143.

12. West and Kling, *Libro,* 229.

13. West and Kling, *Libro,* 233.

14. For a list of authors quoted, see West and Kling, *Libro,* 23.

15. Rusconi, *Book of Prophecies,* 227.

16. See Morison, *Admiral of the Ocean Sea,* 50.

17. Fernandez-Armesto, *Columbus on Himself,* 156.

18. West and Kling, *Libro,* 73.

19. Irving, *Life and Voyages of Christopher Columbus,* 57.

CHAPTER 14: NATURE'S WRATH AND GOD'S INFINITE MERCY

1. Morison, *Admiral of the Ocean Sea,* 591.

2. Varela and Gil, *Textos,* 449.

3. Varela and Gil, *Textos,* 450–51.

4. Morison, *Journals,* 313.

5. Varela and Gil, *Textos,* 485–86.

6. Bobadilla governed Hispaniola for two years. He was, according to the assessment of Hugh Thomas, "effective even if he was ruthless" (*Rivers of Gold,* 197).

7. Varela and Gil, *Textos,* 486.

8. Varela and Gil, *Textos,* 487.

9. Varela and Gil, *Textos,* 488.

10. Varela and Gil, *Textos,* 489.

11. Varela and Gil, *Textos,* 489.

12. Varela and Gil, *Textos,* 489–90.

13. Colón, *Historia del almirante,* 350.

14. Colón, *Historia del almirante,* 350.

15. For a brief history of the Panama Canal, see the author's "A Night Visit to the Panama Canal," http://raciones.wordpress.com/2013/04/12/a-night-visit-to-the-panama-canal/.

16. Colón, *Historia del almirante,* 361.

17. Morison, *Admiral of the Ocean Sea,* 626–27.

18. This coast was later known as the Mosquito Coast or the Malaria Coast, and it was malaria and yellow fever that proved the greatest impediment to building a canal across the isthmus more than three centuries later.

19. Varela and Gil, *Textos,* 491–92. The account is included in Columbus's

account of the Fourth Voyage, and translations can be found in Jane (*Four Voyages*) and elsewhere. I have used here the recently discovered copy of the letter, which is also included in the *Libro copiador* as it is believed to be a more reliable text.

CHAPTER 15: SHIPWRECKED

1. Varela and Gil, *Textos*, 502.
2. Varela and Gil, *Textos*, 493.
3. Colón, *Historia del almirante*, 372.
4. He was shipwrecked off the coast of Portugal in 1476 and later at Navidad with the *Santa María* on Christmas Eve of 1492.
5. Colón, *Historia del almirante*, 372.
6. Colón, *Historia del almirante*, 373.
7. Jane, *Four Voyages*, 110; Varela and Gil, *Textos*, 501.
8. Cohen, *Four Voyages*, 315. Nacaona, usually referred to as Anacaona, was the widow of Canoabá, the *cacique* who had killed the men left at Navidad. Anacoana, however, had established a working peace with the Spaniards. She entertained Ovando and his armed escort for three days in Xaragua, at the conclusion of which Ovando ordered his men to attack the Indians and set the hall on fire. The massacre at Xaragua brought the area under Ovando's undisputed control. Ovando served as governor of Hispaniola for seven years, formalized the *encomienda* system under which the Indians were forced to work for the Spaniards, and introduced African slaves to the Caribbean because he found them more physically capable than the natives. It is estimated that by the time Ovando was removed as governor, the native population had declined to 60,000 or less from at least 250,000 in 1492.
9. Cohen, *Four Voyages*, 315–16.
10. Colón, *Historia del almirante*, 378.
11. Colón, *Historia del almirante*, 379.
12. Colón, *Historia del almirante*, 382.
13. Colón, *Historia del almirante*, 394.
14. Fernandez-Armesto, *Columbus on Himself*, 175.
15. Varela and Gil, *Textos*, 502.

CHAPTER 16: DEATH COMES FOR THE ADMIRAL

1. Varela and Gil, *Textos*, 508–9.
2. *Documentos inéditos para la historia de España*, 10:90, Peter Martyr letter 279.
3. Varela and Gil, *Textos*, 314, letter to Diego, undated.
4. Varela and Gil, *Textos*, 510, letter to Diego from Seville, 28 November 1504.
5. Varela and Gil, *Textos*, 513, letter to Diego from Seville, 1 December 1504.
6. Varela and Gil, *Textos*, 522, letter to Diego from Seville, 29 December 1504.

7. *Documentos inéditos para la historia de España,* 10:89, Peter Martyr letter 277.
8. Varela and Gil, *Textos,* 531, letter to Diego Deza, undated.
9. Varela and Gil, *Textos,* 511, 513, letter to Diego from Seville, 1 December 1504.
10. Varela and Gil, *Textos,* 514, letter to Diego from Seville, 3 December 1504.
11. Varela and Gil, *Textos,* 517, letter to Diego from Seville, 13 December 1504.
12. Varela and Gil, *Textos,* 518, letter to Diego from Seville, 21 December 1504.
13. Varela and Gil, *Textos,* 523, letter to Diego from Seville, 29 December 1504.
14. Varela and Gil, *Textos,* 527, letter to Diego from Seville, 25 February 1505.
15. Varela and Gil, *Textos,* 523, letter to Diego from Seville, 29 December 1504.
16. Morison, *Admiral of the Ocean Sea,* 664.
17. Las Casas, *History of the Indies,* trans. Collard, 138–39.
18. Varela and Gil, *Textos,* 535.
19. Although Columbus was not wealthy, he was certainly not destitute. Through the good offices of Alonso Sanchez de Carvajal, who had been appointed to handle his financial affairs in the Indies, Columbus had begun to receive a share of the income that was beginning to flow from the Indies into Spain. Much of Columbus's dispute with the crown had to do with the proper determination of the Admiral's share of that wealth.
20. Varela and Gil, *Textos,* 499.
21. Varela and Gil, *Textos,* 512, letter to Diego from Seville, 1 December 1504.
22. Varela and Gil, *Textos,* 531.
23. West and Kling, *Libro,* 258. English translation by Fernandez-Armesto, *Columbus on Himself,* 182.

CHAPTER 17: WHY COLUMBUS MATTERS

1. Quoted by Columbus in *Libro de las profecias* (West and Kling, *Libro,* 249).
2. Taviani, *Columbus,* 262.
3. Fernandez-Armesto, *1492,* 2.
4. One of the signs of the last days is that "the whole earth shall be in commotion" (D&C 45:26). An interesting manifestation of this commotion is the movement of peoples around the globe. Walking the streets of nearly any large city (and many smaller towns) in North America or Europe, one can easily identify people from a variety of nationalities and races. This mixing of peoples is an important element in the spreading of the restored gospel. For example, a young missionary serving in the Spain Barcelona Mission during the first decade of the 2000s spoke with natives of eighty-seven different countries during less than twenty-four months in Spain. Convert baptisms in that mission came from such diverse nations as Egypt, China, Equatorial Guinea, and Burkina Faso (Data in possession of the author).
5. Morison, *Admiral of the Ocean Sea,* 3.

6. Ether 13:2.

7. Ether 2:7.

8. 2 Nephi 1:6–7.

9. West and Kling, *Libro*, 63.

10. George Q. Cannon, in *Journal of Discourses*, 23:103.

11. Orson Hyde, in *Journal of Discourses*, 7:108. The remarks are contained in a speech delivered on 4 July 1853 in which Hyde does not mention Moroni by name but refers to "the Spirit Angel"; however, it is clear from his remarks on 4 July 1854 (in *Journal of Discourses*, 6:368) that he is referring to Moroni. Elder Hyde's assertion about Moroni's role in guiding Columbus and others is consistent with the declaration in Doctrine and Covenants 27:5 that Moroni was sent to Joseph Smith "to reveal the Book of Mormon, containing the fulness of my everlasting gospel," and that Moroni held "the keys of the record of the stick of Ephraim." Elder Russell M. Nelson declared, "One specific angel held keys of responsibility for the Book of Mormon. That angel was Moroni!" (*Ensign*, November 2007, 45).

12. Las Casas, *Historia*, 1:47.

13. See 1 Nephi 13:20–25.

14. López de Gómara, *La historia general de las Indias*, 1:4. See also Jane, *Four Voyages*, xv.

CHAPTER 18: COLUMBUS, THE MAN

1. West and Kling, *Libro*, 74.

2. Columbus was first proposed for sainthood in the Catholic Church in 1866 and again in 1909.

3. Taviani, "Columbus the Man," in Gerace, *Columbus and His World*, 5.

4. Taviani, "Columbus the Man," in Gerace, *Columbus and His World*, 5. Taviani's statement is clever but not entirely accurate. Vignaud was born in New Orleans and captured during the Civil War by Union forces in 1862. He escaped and fled to Paris, where he spent the remainder of his life. He served as first secretary in the American Legation in Paris for many years.

5. West and Kling, *Libro*, 105.

6. West and Kling, *Libro*, 104.

7. West and Kling, *Libro*, 21.

8. Taviani, "Columbus the Man," in Gerace, *Columbus and His World*, 7.

9. Colón, *Historia del almirante*, 49.

10. Las Casas, *Historia*, 1:44.

11. Varela and Gil, *Textos*, 501–2.

12. Las Casas, *Historia*, 1:45.

13. Las Casas, *Historia*, 1:44.

14. West and Kling, *Libro*, 105.

15. Dunn and Kelley, *Diario*, 57.

16. Morison, *Admiral of the Ocean Sea,* 46.
17. West and Kling, *Libro,* 107.
18. Las Casas, *Historia,* 1:44.
19. West and Kling, *Libro,* 105.
20. Varela and Gil, *Textos,* 492.
21. West and Kling, *Libro,* 105.
22. West and Kling, *Libro,* 107.
23. West and Kling, *Libro,* 111.
24. West and Kling, *Libro,* 111.

EPILOGUE

1. Varela and Gil, *Textos,* 218.
2. *Documentos inéditos para la historia de España,* 9:347. Letter 183 from Peter Martyr to the Archbishop of Granada.
3. *Documentos inéditos para la historia de España,* 9:346. Letter 182 from Peter Martyr to the Cardinal of Santa Cruz.
4. Jane, *Four Voyages,* 140.
5. Las Casas, *Historia,* 1:41.
6. Bushman, *America Discovers Columbus,* 8.
7. Sale, *Conquest of Paradise,* 18.
8. Hugh Thomas observed, "Had it not been for the Spanish invasions, it is likely that the Caribs would have destroyed the Tainos as the Tainos had destroyed the Ciboneys. Some have written of the ancient Caribbean as if it had been Elysium. But it was an Elysium with savagery in the wings" (Thomas, *Rivers of Gold,* 115).
9. West and Kling, "Reflections," 22–24.
10. Orson Hyde, in *Journal of Discourses,* 6:368.
11. Facts and Statistics, http://www.mormonnewsroom.org/facts-and-statistics/, accessed 17 April 2014. Writing in 2003, historian Hugh Thomas noted that in 1492, "men and women [from Spain] were soon to find themselves in tropical or subtropical America, and there they would establish a new and ingenious society whose time may still be to come" (*Rivers of Gold,* 84).
12. Gordon B. Hinckley, "Santo Domingo Dominican Republic Temple Dedicatory Prayer," http://www.ldschurchtemples.com/santodomingo /prayer/, accessed 20 May 2013.
13. Wilford Woodruff, in *Journal of Discourses,* 19:229. See Appendix 2 for additional details on these ordinances.
14. The four were George Washington, John Wesley, Benjamin Franklin, and Christopher Columbus. See *Teachings of Ezra Taft Benson,* 604.

Appendix 2: Temple Ordinances for Columbus and Crew of the First Voyage

1. Wilford Woodruff, *Journals,* 7:367–69.
2. *Teachings of Ezra Taft Benson,* 603, from an address given at Sandy, Utah, 30 December 1973.

SOURCES

Five authors who were contemporaries of Christopher Columbus wrote in some detail about him and his voyages. Peter Martyr d'Anghiera, an Italian native who served as a chaplain in the court of Ferdinand and Isabella, was present when Columbus attended the court in Barcelona after the First Voyage. A prolific letter writer, Peter Martyr published his letters with some additions beginning in 1511 as the first volume of his work *Decadas de orbe novo.* The complete series was published in 1530, and the first three sections were published in English in 1555. Transcriptions of the original Spanish are found in *Documentos inéditos para la historia de España.* These chatty letters provide a contemporary view of Columbus as Martyr observed events from his position in the court.

Andrés Bernáldez, with whom Columbus lived for a period of time, wrote *Historia de los reyes católicos don Fernando y doña Isabel.* An English translation was published as part of the *Nuova raccolta colombiana* series in 1992.

Gonzalo Fernández de Oviedo supervised gold smelting in Santo Domingo and published portions of his extensive *La historia general de las Indias* in Seville in 1535, although the complete work was not published until 1855. Both Fernando Columbus and Las Casas charge

Oviedo with numerous factual errors, but his work provides a vast amount of information on the early decades of Spanish exploration and colonization in the New World.

Bartolomé de Las Casas, who as a boy saw Columbus in Seville in 1493, sailed with his father to Hispaniola in the Ovando expedition in 1502 and spent many years in the New World, where he knew Columbus and his brothers. He wrote several works, the most extensive of which is his *Historia de las Indias,* written between 1527 and 1561. Not published until 1875, it provides keen and critical insights into the life of Columbus and the first decades of Spanish colonization. Portions of the work were translated into English by Andrée Collard and published in 1971.

Fernando Columbus wrote in Spanish a biography of his father entitled *Historia del almirante,* which was first published in Italian in 1571. A version in Spanish was published in 1749. When *Historia* is quoted in this volume in English, the translation is mine. A useful English translation by Benjamin Keen was published in 1959. While Fernando clearly has a bias in favor of his father, his eyewitness account of the Third Voyage is of particular value.

Christopher Columbus himself left a large body of personal writings. Most of them have been transcribed and published in Consuelo Varela and Juan Gil's *Cristóbal Colón: Textos y documentos completos,* originally published in 1982; a revised edition that includes new material was published in 1992. Although this book is not available in English, many of the individual documents are available in English translations in other publications. A complete Spanish transcription of Columbus's "Book of Prophecies," together with an English translation of them, was published in 1991 (West and Kling). A new transcription and translation, based on better source documents, was published in 1997 (Rusconi and Sullivan). When quoting Columbus, I have generally cited *Textos,* except for quotations from the *Diario* (where I usually cite Dunn and Kelley's bilingual edition) and the "Book of Prophecies" (where I generally cite West and Kling).

Among the numerous biographies of Columbus, Samuel Eliot Morison's *Admiral of the Ocean Sea,* first published in 1942, is a landmark work. Morison was the first historian to make a serious effort to trace Columbus's voyages through the Caribbean and carefully identify landfalls and anchorages. Monumental in scope, Morison's work is not without fault but is unlikely to be superseded by any new work for many years. Subsequent histories shed new light, make some corrections, and add some detail, but more than seventy years after its publication, *Admiral of the Ocean Sea* remains the standard work on the life of the Discoverer. Miles Davidson, in *Columbus Then and Now: A Life Reexamined,* provides documentation to correct some errors or assumptions by Morison; Paolo Taviani, in *Christopher Columbus: The Grand Design,* adds a wealth of documentation for Columbus's early life; and Felipe Fernandez-Armesto's *Columbus* is useful in separating verifiable facts from circumstantial evidence. Carol Delaney's *Columbus and the Quest for Jerusalem* helps put to rest many of the modern distortions around Columbus by carefully documenting and describing the fifteenth-century culture in which Columbus lived, worked, wrote, and thought and, as a result, delivers what I consider to be the most accurate and fair-minded treatment of Columbus in the past quarter century.

Anderson, Vicki Jo. *The Other Eminent Men of Wilford Woodruff.* Salt Lake City: Nelson Book, 2000.

Atlas ilustrado de Cristóbal Colón. Madrid: Susaeta Ediciones, 2014.

Benson, Ezra Taft. *The Teachings of Ezra Taft Benson.* Salt Lake City: Bookcraft, 1988.

Bernáldez, Andres. *Historia de los reyes Católicos.* Vol 1. Seville: José María Geofrin, 1870. Available at http://www.archive.org/details/historiadelosrey 00bern.

Biggar, H. P., ed. and trans. *The Precursors of Jacques Cartier, 1497–1534: A Collection of Documents Relating to the Early History of the Dominion of Canada.* Ottawa: Government Printing Bureau, 1911. Available online at http://www.bris.ac.uk/Depts/History/Maritime/Sources/1498ayala.htm.

Bown, Stephen R. *1494: How a Family Feud in Spain Divided the World in Half.* New York: Thomas Dunne Books, 2012.

Brigham, Kay. *Cristóbal Colón: Libro de las profecias.* Terrassa, Spain: Libros Clie, 1992.

———. *Christopher Columbus: His Life and Discovery in the Light of His Prophecies.* Terrassa, Spain: Libros Clie, 1990.

Bushman, Claudia L. *America Discovers Columbus: How an Italian Explorer Became an American Hero.* Hanover, N.H.: University Press of New England, 1992.

The Original Catholic Encyclopedia: An International Work of Reference on the Constitution, Doctrine, Discipline, and History of the Catholic Church. 16 vols. Edited by Charles G. Herberman et al. New York: Encyclopedia Press, 1907–14. Reprint, Catholic Answers, 2014. Available at http://oce.catholic.com.

Clark, E. Douglas. *The Grand Design: America from Columbus to Zion.* Salt Lake City: Deseret Book, 1992.

Cohen, J. M., ed. and trans. *The Four Voyages of Christopher Columbus.* London: Penguin Group, 1969.

Colón, Fernando. *Historia del almirante.* 1892. Reprint, [Barcelona]: Planeta, 2006.

———. *The Life of the Admiral Christopher Columbus, by His Son Ferdinand.* Translated and annotated by Benjamin Keen. New Brunswick, N.J.: Rutgers University Press, 1959.

Davidson, Miles H. *Columbus Then and Now: A Life Reexamined.* Norman: University of Oklahoma Press, 1997.

Delaney, Carol. *Columbus and the Quest for Jerusalem.* New York: Free Press, 2011.

———. "Columbus's Ultimate Goal: Jerusalem." *Comparative Studies in Society and History* 48, no. 2 (2006): 260–92.

Dunn, Oliver, and James E. Kelley Jr., eds. and trans. *The Diario of Christopher Columbus's First Voyage to America, 1492–1493.* Norman: University of Oklahoma Press, 1991.

Facts and Statistics, http://www.mormonnewsroom.org/facts-and-statistics/.

Farina, Luciano F., and R. Tolf, eds. *Columbus Documents: Summaries of Documents in Genoa.* Detroit: Omnigraphics, 1992.

Fernandez-Armesto, Felipe. *Columbus.* Oxford: Oxford University Press, 1991.

———. *Columbus on Himself.* Indianapolis: Hackett, 2010.

———. *1492: The Year the World Began.* New York: Harper Collins, 2009.

Ford, Paul Leicester, ed. *Writings of Christopher Columbus.* New York: Charles L. Webster, 1892.

Fuson, Robert H. "The Turks and Caicos Islands as Possible Landfall Sites for Columbus." In Gerace, *Columbus and His World,* 173–84.

Garr, Arnold K. *Christopher Columbus: A Latter-day Saint Perspective.* Provo, Utah: BYU Religious Studies Center, 1992.

Gerace, Donald T. "Additional Comments Relating Watlings Island to Columbus' San Salvador." In Gerace, *Columbus and His World,* 229–36.

———, comp. *Columbus and His World: Proceedings of the First San Salvador Conference.* Fort Lauderdale, Fla.: College Center of the Finger Lakes, 1987.

Gil, Juan. *Columbiana: Estudios sobre Cristóbal Colón, 1984–2006.* Santo Domingo, D.R.: Academia dominicana de la historia, 2007.

Gould, Alice Bache. *Nueva lista documentada de los tripulantes de Colón en 1492.* Madrid: Real Academia de la Historia, 1984.

Hoffman, Charles A. "Archaeological Investigations at the Long Bay Site, San Salvador, Bahamas." In Gerace, *Columbus and His World,* 237–46.

Humboldt, Alexander von. *Examen critique de l'histoire de la géographie du nouveau continent et des progrès de l'astronomie nautique aux quinzième et seizième siècles.* Vol. 1. Paris: Librairie de Gide, 1836.

Irving, Washington. *The Life and Voyages of Christopher Columbus.* Boston: Twayne, 1981.

Irizarry, Estelle. *Christopher Columbus: The DNA of His Writings.* San Juan, Puerto Rico: Ediciones Puerto, 2009.

———. "Three Sources of Textual Evidence of Columbus, Crypto Jew." Lecture presented at an international conference on Columbus's origin, Ibiza, Spain, April 2006. Available at http://www.tbspr.org/_kd/Items/actions.cfm?action=Show&item_id=2026.

Jane, Cecil, ed. and trans. *The Four Voyages of Columbus.* New York: Dover, 1988.

Jensen, De Lamar. "Christopher Columbus and the Pinzóns of Palos." *BYU Today,* November 1992, 20–44.

———. "Columbus and the Hand of God." *Ensign,* October 1992, 6–13.

———. "Crew of Columbus's First Voyage, 1492." Unpublished manuscript.

———. "Discovering Columbus's Crew." *Fourth Annual Alice Louise Reynolds Lecture.* Friends of the BYU Library Newsletter 40 (1992).

Johnson, Timothy J. "The Apocalypse in St. Augustine: Christopher Columbus, Religion, and the New World." Paper presented at Culturally La Florida: Spain's New World Legacy, St. Augustine, Fla., 4 May 2012. Available at http://www.culturallylaflorida.org/papers/Johnson.pdf.

Journal of Discourses. London: Latter-day Saints' Book Depot, 1854–86.

Kelley, James E., Jr. "The Navigation of Columbus on His First Voyage to America." In Gerace, *Columbus and His World,* 121–40.

Kenney, Alice P. "America Discovers Columbus: Biography as Epic, Drama, History." *Biography* 4, no. 1 (Winter 1981): 45–65.

Kirkpatrick, Sale. *The Conquest of Paradise: Christopher Columbus and the Colombian Legacy.* New York: Alfred A. Knopf, 1990.

Las Casas, Bartolomé de. *Historia de las Indias.* 3 vols. Madrid: Miguel Ginesta, 1875.

———. *History of the Indies.* Translated by Andrée Collard. New York: Harper and Row, 1971.

López de Gómara, Francisco. *Historia general de las Indias.* 2 vols. Madrid: Calpe, 1922.

Madriaga, Salvador de. *Christopher Columbus.* London: Hollis and Carter, 1949.

Manzano Manzano, Juan. *Colón y su secreto: el predescubrimiento [Christopher Columbus: Seven decisive years of his life, 1485–1492].* 2nd ed. Madrid: Ediciones Cultura Hispánica, 1982.

Martyr d'Anghiera, Peter [Pedro Mártir de Anglería]. *Epistolario de Pedro Mártir de Anglería I, libros I–XIV, epístolas 1–232.* Translated by José Lopez de Toro. *Documentos inéditos para la historia de España* 9. Madrid: Imprenta Góngora, 1953.

———. *Epistolario de Pedro Mártir de Anglería II, libros XV–XXIV, epístolas*

232–472. Translated by José Lopez de Toro. *Documentos inéditos para la historia de España* 10. Madrid: Imprenta Góngora, 1955.

Molander, Arne B. "Egg Island Is the Landfall of Columbus—A Literal Interpretation of His Journal." In Gerace, *Columbus and His World,* 141–72.

Morison, Samuel Eliot. *Admiral of the Ocean Sea.* Boston: Little, Brown, 1942.

———. *The European Discovery of America: The Southern Voyages, 1492–1616.* New York: Oxford University Press, 1972.

———. *Journals and Other Documents on the Life and Voyages of Christopher Columbus.* New York: Heritage, 1963.

Navarette, Martin Fernandez de. *Colección de los viages y descubrimientos que hicieron por mar los Españoles desde fines del siglo XV.* 5 vols. Madrid: Imprenta Real, 1825–37.

Nibley, Hugh. *The Prophetic Book of Mormon.* Edited by John W. Welch. Vol. 8 of *The Collected Works of Hugh Nibley.* Salt Lake City: Deseret Book, 1989.

Obregón, Mauricio. "Columbus' First Landfall: San Salvador." In Gerace, *Columbus and His World,* 185–96.

Oviedo, Gonzalo Fernández. *La historia general y natural de las Indias.* Madrid: Real Academia de la Historia, 1851.

Peck, Douglas T. *Cristoforo Colombo: God's Navigator.* Columbus, Wis.: Columbian, 1993.

———. "The Controversial Skill of Columbus as a Navigator: An Enduring Historical Enigma." *Journal of Navigation* 62 (2009): 417–25.

———. "The Controversial Historical Image of Columbus from the Sixteenth-Century to Modern Times." Available at http://www.newworld explorersinc.org/ColumbusImage.pdf.

———. "The History of Early Dead Reckoning and Celestial Navigation: Empirical Reality Versus Theory." Available at http://www.newworld explorersinc.org/EarlyNavigation.pdf.

———. "The Navigation of Columbus and the Controversy Over His Landfall Island in the New World." Available at http://www.newworld explorersinc.org/ColumbusNav%20&%20Landfall.pdf.

Perez de Tudela y Bueso, Juan. *Mirabilis in altis: Estudio crítico sobre el origen y significado del proyecto descubridor de Cristóbal Colón.* Madrid: Consejo

Superior de Investigaciones Científicas, Instituto Gonzalo Fernández de Oviedo, 1983.

Phillips, Carla Rahn. "Sizes and Configurations of Spanish Ships in the Age of Discovery." In Gerace, *Columbus and His World*, 69–98.

Phillips, William D., Jr. "Book Review: The 'Libro de las profecías' of Christopher Columbus, by Christopher Columbus." *Medieval Academy of America* 69, no. 1 (January 1994): 124–25.

Provost, Foster. "Columbus's Seven Years in Spain Prior to 1492." In Gerace, *Columbus and His World*, 57–68.

Quinn, David B. "John Day and Columbus." *Geographical Journal* 133, no. 2 (June 1967): 205–9.

Raccolta di documenti e studi pubblicati dalla Reale Commissione Colombiana pel quarto centenario dalla scoperta dell'America. 6 vols. in 11 books. Rome: Ministero della Pubblica Istruzione, 1892–96. Many of the key documents contained in this collection are now published in other sources which are more readily available, but the *Raccolta* remains an important source for many documents.

Rubin, Nancy. *Isabella of Castile: The First Renaissance Queen.* New York: St. Martin's, 1992.

Rumeu de Armas, Antonio. *Libro copiador de Cristóbal Colón.* Madrid: Testimonio Compañía Editorial, 1989.

Rusconi, Roberto, ed. *The Book of Prophecies, Edited by Christopher Columbus.* Translated by Blair Sullivan. Vol. 3 of *Repertorium Columbianum.* Berkeley, Calif.: University of California Press, 1997.

Sale, Kirkpatrick. *The Conquest of Paradise: Christopher Columbus and the Columbian Legacy.* New York: Knopf, 1990.

Skinner, Andrew C. "Forerunners and Foundation Stones of the Restoration." In *Prelude to the Restoration: From Apostasy to the Restored Church, the 33rd Annual Sidney B. Sperry Symposium,* 1–23. Salt Lake City: Deseret Book, 2004.

Taviani, Paolo Emilio. *Christopher Columbus: The Grand Design.* London: Orbis, 1985.

———. *Columbus: The Great Adventure.* New York: Orion Books, 1991.

———. "Columbus the Man: A Psychologically Modern Man of the Middle Ages." In Gerace, *Columbus and His World*, 1–12.

————. "Why We Are Favorable for the Watling-San Salvador Landfall." In Gerace, *Columbus and His World*, 197–228.

Thacher, John Boyd. *Christopher Columbus: His Life, His Work, His Remains.* 3 vols. New York: G. P. Putnam's Sons, 1903–1904.

Thomas, Hugh. *Rivers of Gold: The Rise of the Spanish Empire from Columbus to Magellan.* New York: Random House, 2003.

Varela, Consuelo. "Florentine's Friendship and Kinship with Christopher Columbus." In Gerace, *Columbus and His World*, 33–44.

————. *La caída de Cristóbal Colón: El juicio de Bobadilla.* Madrid: Marcial Pons Historia, 2006.

Varela, Consuelo, and Juan Gil, eds. *Cristóbal Colón: Textos y documentos completos.* Madrid: Alianza Editorial, 2003.

Verdera, Nito. "The Connection between Ibiza and Christopher Columbus's enigma." Lecture given at the 41st Annual Meeting of the Society for the History of Discoveries, Library of Congress, Washington D.C., October 14, 2000. Available at http://www.cristobalcolondeibiza.com/eng/eng04.htm.

Vignaud, Henry. *Historie critique de la grande entreprise de Christophe Colomb.* 2 vols. 1476–93. Reprint, Paris: H. Welter, 1911.

Wallis, Helen. "What Columbus Knew." *History Today* 42, no. 5 (May 1992): 17–24.

Watts, Pauline Moffitt. "Prophecy and Discovery: On the Spiritual Origins of Christopher Columbus's 'Enterprise of the Indies.'" *American Historical Review* 90, no. 1 (February 1985): 73–102.

West, Delno C. "Christopher Columbus and His Enterprise to the Indies Scholarship of the Last Quarter Century." *William and Mary Quarterly* 49, no. 2 (April 1992): 254–77.

————. "Wallowing in a Theological Stupor or a Steadfast and Consuming Faith: Scholarly encounters with Columbus' Libro de las Profecias." In Gerace, *Columbus and His World*, 45–56.

West, Delno C., and August Kling. *The Libro de las profecías of Christopher Columbus.* Gainesville: University of Florida Press, 1991.

————. "Reflections on the Coincidences of Christopher Columbus's 'Libro de Las Profecias' and the American Dream." *Encounters,* nos. 5–6. Available at http://libertyparkusafd.org/lp/Columbus/primers.htm.

Woodruff, Wilford. *Journals, 1833–1898.* Edited by Scott G. Kenney. 9 vols. Midvale, Utah: Signature Books, 1983.

Yorgason, Blaine M., Richard A. Schmutz, and Douglas D. Alder. *All That Was Promised: The St. George Temple and the Unfolding of the Restoration.* Salt Lake City: Deseret Book, 2013.

Young, Filson. *Christopher Columbus and the New World of His Discovery: A Narrative.* 2 vols. London: E. Grant Richards, 1906. Available at http://archive.org/details/christophercolum04116gut.

INDEX